Social Choice and Legitimacy
The Possibilities of Impossibility

Governing requires choices and hence trade-offs between conflicting goals or criteria. This book asserts that legitimate governance requires explanations for such trade-offs and then demonstrates that such explanations can always be found, although not for every possible choice. In so doing, John W. Patty and Elizabeth Maggie Penn use the tools of social choice theory to provide a new and discriminating theory of legitimacy. In contrast with both earlier critics and defenders of social choice theory, Patty and Penn argue that the classic impossibility theorems of Arrow, Gibbard, and Satterthwaite are inescapably relevant to, and indeed justify, democratic institutions. Specifically, these institutions exist to do more than simply make policy – through their procedures and proceedings, these institutions make sense of the trade-offs required when controversial policy decisions must be made.

John W. Patty is Associate Professor of Political Science at Washington University in St. Louis. His research focuses on mathematical models of political institutions. His work has been published in various journals, including *American Journal of Political Science, Games & Economic Behavior, Journal of Politics, Journal of Theoretical Politics, Quarterly Journal of Political Science,* and *Social Choice & Welfare.* He also coauthored *Learning While Governing* (2013) with Sean Gailmard, which won the William H. Riker Prize awarded by the Political Economy Section of the American Political Science Association for the best book published on political economy.

Elizabeth Maggie Penn is Associate Professor of Political Science at Washington University in St. Louis. A formal political theorist whose work focuses on social choice theory and political institutions, her work has been published in the *American Journal of Political Science, Journal of Politics, Journal of Theoretical Politics, Mathematical & Computer Modelling, Public Choice, Social Choice & Welfare,* and *Complexity.*

POLITICAL ECONOMY OF INSTITUTIONS AND DECISIONS

Series Editors

Stephen Ansolabehere, Harvard University
Jeffry Frieden, Harvard University

Founding Editors

James E. Alt, Harvard University
Douglass C. North, Washington University of St. Louis

Other Books in the Series

Alberto Alesina and Howard Rosenthal, *Partisan Politics, Divided Government and the Economy*

Lee J. Alston, Thrainn Eggertsson, and Douglass C. North, eds., *Empirical Studies in Institutional Change*

Lee J. Alston and Joseph P. Ferrie, *Southern Paternalism and the Rise of the American Welfare State: Economics, Politics, and Institutions, 1865–1965*

James E. Alt and Kenneth Shepsle, eds., *Perspectives on Positive Political Economy*

Josephine T. Andrews, *When Majorities Fail: The Russian Parliament, 1990–1993*

Jeffrey S. Banks and Eric A. Hanushek, eds., *Modern Political Economy: Old Topics, New Directions*

Yoram Barzel, *Economic Analysis of Property Rights, 2nd edition*

Yoram Barzel, *A Theory of the State: Economic Rights, Legal Rights, and the Scope of the State*

Robert Bates, *Beyond the Miracle of the Market: The Political Economy of Agrarian Development in Kenya*

Jenna Bednar, *The Robust Federation: Principles of Design*

Charles M. Cameron, *Veto Bargaining: Presidents and the Politics of Negative Power*

Kelly H. Chang, *Appointing Central Bankers: The Politics of Monetary Policy in the United States and the European Monetary Union*

Peter Cowhey and Mathew McCubbins, eds., *Structure and Policy in Japan and the United States: An Institutionalist Approach*

Series list continues following the Index.

Social Choice and Legitimacy

The Possibilities of Impossibility

JOHN W. PATTY
Washington University in St. Louis

ELIZABETH MAGGIE PENN
Washington University in St. Louis

CAMBRIDGE
UNIVERSITY PRESS

CAMBRIDGE
UNIVERSITY PRESS

32 Avenue of the Americas, New York, NY 10013-2473, USA

Cambridge University Press is part of the University of Cambridge.

It furthers the University's mission by disseminating knowledge in the pursuit of education, learning, and research at the highest international levels of excellence.

www.cambridge.org
Information on this title: www.cambridge.org/9780521138338

© John W. Patty and Elizabeth Maggie Penn 2014

First published 2014

Printed in the United States of America

A catalog record for this publication is available from the British Library.

Library of Congress Cataloging in Publication Data
Patty, John W.
Social choice and legitimacy : the possibilities of impossibility / John W. Patty, Washington University in St. Louis; Elizabeth Maggie Penn, Washington University in St. Louis.
   pages.   cm. – (Political economy of institutions and decisions)
Includes bibliographical references and index.
ISBN 978-0-521-19101-2 (hardback) – ISBN 978-0-521-13833-8 (paperback)
   1. Social choice – Political aspects.   2. Rational choice theory – Political aspects.   3. Legitimacy of governments.   4. Government accountability.   I. Penn, Elizabeth Maggie, 1977–   II. Title.
HB846.8.P376   2014
320.101–dc23   2013042825

ISBN 978-0-521-19101-2 Hardback
ISBN 978-0-521-13833-8 Paperback

Contents

Acknowledgments   *page* ix

PART I   THE UBIQUITY OF AGGREGATION

1   Goals and Trade-Offs   3
   1.1 *Many Goals, One Choice*   5
   1.2 *Structure of the Book*   7
   1.3 *Theory and Method*   10

2   The Debates Surrounding Social Choice   12
   2.1 *The Arrow and Gibbard-Satterthwaite Theorems*   15
   2.2 *Riker and the Arbitrariness of Democratic Choice* 26
   2.3 *Mackie's Defense of Democracy*   28
   2.4 *Additional Rebuttals by Democratic Theory*   31
   2.5 *Riker and His Critics: Unlikely Allies?*   34

3   Social Choice Defended   36
   3.1 *Inputs to the Aggregation Problem*   39
   3.2 *Unrestricted Domain*   42
   3.3 *Independence of Irrelevant Alternatives*   48
   3.4 *Pareto Efficiency*   64
   3.5 *No Dictator*   66
   3.6 *Transitivity*   67

PART II   A THEORY OF LEGITIMATE CHOICE

4   Legitimacy and Choice   73
   4.1 *Legitimacy of What?*   75
   4.2 *The Bases of Legitimacy*   80

5   Principles and Legitimate Choice   84
    5.1 Characterizing Legitimacy   88
    5.2 Legitimate Decision Sequences   97

6   A Social Choice Theory of Legitimacy   104
    6.1 Existence of Legitimate Procedures   109
    6.2 Characterization of Legitimate Procedures   109
    6.3 Strengthened Notions of Legitimacy   114
    6.4 Comparing Principles   117
    6.5 Conclusion   119

7   Theory and Method   121
    7.1 Disagreeing About Principles   122
    7.2 Defining the Set of Possible Choices   124
    7.3 Actual versus Perceived Decision Sequences   126

PART III   LEGITIMATE POLICY MAKING IN PRACTICE

8   Legislative Legitimacy and Judicial Review   131
    8.1 Legislative Rationality and Judicial Review   133
    8.2 Rational Basis Review and Legitimacy   136
    8.3 Two-Tiered Review   140
    8.4 Strict Scrutiny and Legitimacy   142
    8.5 Linking Judicial Review and Legitimacy   145

9   Structuring Discussion   147
    9.1 Germaneness in the House of Representatives   148
    9.2 Single-Subject Provisions   154

10 Administrative Legitimacy   162
    10.1 Delegation and Legitimacy   165
    10.2 Agency Explanations and Avoiding Nondelegation   175
    10.3 Choosing Principles: Limits on Agency Discretion   179

11 Conclusion   189
    11.1 Legitimacy and the Inadequacy of Structure   190
    11.2 Legitimacy and Making Sense of Aggregation   193

Bibliography   197
Index   207

Acknowledgments

Fittingly, this book represents the aggregation of multiple and extended sequences of conversations, reactions, and decisions. We owe many people for various combinations of helpful advice, thoughtful criticism, sincere skepticism, and general forbearance. Numerous friends and colleagues gave invaluable feedback on various parts of the manuscript or their antecedents, including Jake Bowers, Ethan Bueno de Mesquita, Sean Gailmard, John Gasper, Matthew Graham, Clarissa Hayward, Frank Lovett, Adam Meirowitz, Scott Moser, Bob Pahre, Andrew Rehfeld, Ken Shepsle, Ken Shotts, and Cara Wong. In a similar vein, we acknowledge helpful comments and feedback from seminar audiences at Harvard University, the London School of Economics, Texas A&M University, University of Essex, University of Illinois, UC Berkeley, University of Chicago, and Washington University. We thank our parents, Roy, Stephanie, Dee, and Seldon, who have never hesitated to put their own lives on hold in order to support ours. Our editor Lew Bateman provided essential guidance and encouragement throughout this process. And we particularly want to single out and thank Norman Schofield for his friendship and encouragement through the years and for the suggestion – made late one night in a bar in Barcelona – that we write this book.

Finally, we are grateful to two individuals who we never had the chance to meet but who nonetheless shape us and our thinking in every respect. Our greatest goal is to instill in Hazel Miriam Patty even part of the late Richard McKelvey's curiosity, humility, and generosity. This book is dedicated to them.

PART I

THE UBIQUITY OF AGGREGATION

The simple point which I am concerned to make is that where ultimate values are irreconcilable, clear-cut solutions cannot, in principle, be found.... The need to choose, to sacrifice some ultimate values to others, turns out to be a permanent characteristic of the human predicament.

Isaiah Berlin, *Four Essays on Liberty* p. 1–li (1969)

I

Goals and Trade-Offs

In 1986 the Supreme Court addressed the question of whether political gerrymanders – redistricting plans intended to electorally disadvantage one particular political party – were capable of being, and should be, resolved by the courts. The case in question, *Davis v. Bandemer*,[1] centered on an allegation by Indiana Democrats that Indiana's 1981 reapportionment plan was drawn by Republicans in order to dilute the Democratic vote and thus violated their right to equal protection under the Fourteenth Amendment. The Court ruled that while an equal protection violation could not be conclusively shown by the appellants in the particular redistricting plan under consideration, such political gerrymandering cases were properly justiciable (or capable of being resolved by the courts) under the Equal Protection Clause. A majority of the Court could not, however, agree on any specific standard for assessing future political gerrymandering claims.

In 2004 the Court revisited the question of political gerrymanders in the case *Vieth v. Jubelirer*[2] in which Pennsylvania Democrats argued that a political gerrymander had occurred in redrawing Pennsylvania's legislative districts after the 2000 census. However, in this case, a plurality of the Court reversed itself on the *Bandemer* decision and argued that claims of political gerrymanders were *not* capable of being decided by a court. Interestingly, the court unanimously agreed that severe political gerrymanders are incompatible with democratic principles.[3] However, Justice Scalia, writing for the plurality, argued that no constitutionally discernible standards for evaluating a political gerrymandering claim can exist. Thus, the issue under consideration was "not whether severe partisan gerrymanders violate the Constitution, but whether it is for the courts

[1] 478 U.S. 109 (1986).
[2] 541 U.S. 267 (2004).
[3] 541 U.S. 267, 292 (2004) (plurality opinion).

to say when a violation has occurred, and to design a remedy."[4] Absent a principle of "fair districting" that could be applied to all such cases, the Court held that the Pennsylvania redistricting plan could not be declared unconstitutional.

Underlying both the *Vieth* and *Bandemer* decisions were a multitude of opinions held by the various justices and appellants concerning the principles that should underlie a fair districting plan. In four dissenting opinions filed in *Vieth*, three different standards of fairness were proposed; each was different from the two conflicting standards proposed in *Bandemer*, and all differed from the standard proposed by the appellants in *Vieth*. The nine Supreme Court justices who signed the five various opinions in *Bandemer* and *Vieth* setting forth these standards all believed that the Fourteenth Amendment granted judges both the power and the duty to control the practice of gerrymandering. At the same time, in neither case could a majority of the justices reach agreement on how exactly to ascertain whether a partisan gerrymander violates the law. The following six standards provide a sense of the complexity of the problem faced by the two courts. Each was proposed as a yardstick by which the constitutionality of a districting plan could be measured.

1. The existence of a political boundary without a neutral justification[5]
2. A proven intent to discriminate against an identifiable political group and a proven discriminatory effect on that group[6]
3. A disregard for contiguity, compactness, respect for political subdivisions, and conformity with geographic features[7]
4. The inability of a majority of votes to be translatable into a majority of seats[8]
5. The inability of a majority of votes to be translatable into a majority of seats in two successive elections, with the failure not being attributable to the existence of multiple parties or other neutral principles[9]
6. Numerous factors, although none being dispositive on its own, including district shape, established political boundaries, and the nature of legislative procedure and history in the drawing of lines[10].

In expressing frustration with the task of choosing among these multiple standards for adjudicating political gerrymandering claims, the plurality in *Vieth* argued that every reasonable principle of fairness under consideration could easily be incompatible with another and that no proposed standard for drawing legislative districts could be deemed best. Lacking such a standard, the plurality effectively declared that there is no judicial solution to claims

---

[4] 541 U.S. 267, 292 (2004) (plurality opinion).
[5] 541 U.S. 267, 326 (2004) (Stevens, J., dissenting).
[6] *Davis v. Bandemer*, 478 U.S. 109, 127 (1986) (plurality opinion).
[7] 541 U.S. 267, 347–48 (2004) (Souter & Ginsburg, JJ., dissenting).
[8] Page 20 of appellant's brief, *Vieth v. Jubelirer*, cited at 541 U.S. 267, 297 (2004).
[9] 541 U.S. 267, 366 (2004) (Breyer, J., dissenting).
[10] *Davis v. Bandemer*, 478 U.S. 109, 173 (1986) (Powell & Stevens, JJ., concurring).

of political gerrymandering. Responding directly to Justice Powell's opinion in *Bandemer* that gerrymandering claims should be assessed on the basis of multiple factors relevant to the fairness of a redistricting plan, Scalia wrote:

> "Fairness" does not seem to us a judicially manageable standard. Fairness is compatible with noncontiguous districts, it is compatible with districts that straddle political subdivisions, and it is compatible with a party's not winning the number of seats that mirrors the proportion of its vote. Some criterion more solid and more demonstrably met than that seems to us necessary to enable the state legislatures to discern the limits of their districting discretion, to meaningfully constrain the discretion of the courts, and to win public acceptance for the courts' intervention into a process that is the very foundation of democratic decision making.[11]

1.1 MANY GOALS, ONE CHOICE

The existence of multiple conflicting goals characterizes many, if not most, meaningful political decisions. Indeed, we conceive of "politics" as shorthand for the processes by which groups reconcile these goals with each other. A redistricting plan that most strongly respects existing political subdivisions may also be the plan that produces the least compactly shaped collection of districts. A plan that produces a compact collection of districts may simultaneously be the least politically neutral. In short, political problems are generally complex, and numerous factors play into the resolution of these problems. If several goals conflict with each other then there may exist no unambiguously "best" way of resolving a political problem short of declaring one criterion unequivocally more important than another. It may, for example, be impossible to design a district that is simultaneously compact and politically neutral.

This book is about decision making when goals come into conflict with one another. More specifically, we describe and characterize a notion of legitimacy for political decisions when the defining features of those decisions – the societal goals that the decisions are meant to further – are inconsistent with one another. We begin with the premise that collective decisions involve trade-offs in the sense of comparing and combining multiple goals so as to produce a policy choice. A different, prominent conception of the combining of multiple goals to form a final choice is provided by the notion of government as a system of *preference aggregation*. In classical social choice theory, a preference aggregation rule represents a method of translating the (individual) preferences of a group's members into a collective, or group, ranking of all the possible choices. Much of the mathematical study of voting systems adopts this approach and is motivated by the fact that any group seeking to make a collective decision must choose some method of translating the diverse preferences of the group members into a societal outcome.

---

[11] 541 U.S. 267, 292 (2004) (plurality opinion).

While preference aggregation is merely one example of a setting in which the arguments we make in this book will have purchase, the study of preference aggregation within the field of social choice has yielded insights that are directly applicable to the issues and debates with which we are concerned. Accordingly, we discuss the results from this literature and their connections with our own theory at the outset of this book. In Part I we describe and detail several well-known results that are termed *impossibility theorems*. These results mathematically prove that in many situations, it is impossible to design a system of aggregation – be it aggregation of preferences or goals – that satisfies certain properties of sensibility and fairness. In these instances, any reasonable method of aggregating conflicting goals may be ill-behaved in that it may be incapable of deeming one alternative (or one collection of alternatives) "best." An immediate corollary of this is that there may be no optimal way of resolving a political issue. How, then, can we judge the success of a political decision when there may be no unambiguously good solution to a particular problem?

We address this question by developing a theory of collective decision making that focuses on the decision-making process – the sequence of arguments leading up to any final decision. Given that it is often impossible to make a political decision that can be declared better than any other decision that could have been made,[12] one of the biggest tasks facing a democratically elected government is convincing its citizens that the decision made in such circumstances is nonetheless legitimate. That is, why should the citizens respect and obey a potentially suboptimal decision involving a nontrivial trade-off between competing goals?[13] The government needs to provide a rationale for why it made the trade-offs and choices as it did. The legitimacy of a political decision in such cases rests on a *justification*.

The theory of decision making that we offer encompasses two fundamental features of governance. First, we posit that many political decisions are based on principles that have combined multiple and possibly contradictory goals. By describing a political decision as being "based on" such principles, we mean that more than one factor is relevant to the decision. These "factors" could be the preferences of various individuals, communities, or groups. Or they could be a collection of objective characteristics that a society may wish to consider when crafting a policy (e.g., the variation in populations, the contiguities, compactnesses, and political neutrality of a set of legislative districts). Our point is simply that democratic institutions must come to terms with the fact that there may exist multiple reasonable ways of considering the collection

---

[12] Or, in terms of representation, it is often impossible to make a decision that does not disenfranchise some person or group of people.

[13] We deliberately use the word "should" here, as opposed to a more empirical term such as "will." As we discuss in more detail in Chapter 4, there are important differences between notions of legitimacy based on theoretical obligation and those based on observed obedience. These differences are of secondary importance to our goals in this book. Thus, where relevant, we generally speak of legitimacy as a theoretical concept of obligation.

of choices available to a group, and they must be responsive to these various considerations.

Second, a political decision should be rationalizable, or defensible, in terms of the principle on which it is based. Put another way, the knowledge that a decision was indeed motivated by the appropriate goal or goals is not sufficient for legitimacy. Rather, the final choice should be consistent with the underlying goal or goals. This second feature of governance is most relevant when there is some conflict between the underlying goals.[14] Thus, our theory is most interesting in the wide variety of situations in which there are multiple decisions that are reasonable in the sense that, for each of these decisions, there is some goal or combination of goals justifying it. Ultimately, our theory argues that democratic institutions govern not only the types of policies chosen, but also, perhaps more important, the ways in which necessarily imperfect political decisions can be rationalized and defended.

1.2 STRUCTURE OF THE BOOK

Chapter 2 focuses on the debates surrounding the field of social choice theory and its application to the study of politics. In that chapter we present several social choice–theoretic results – the impossibility theorems – both technically and descriptively. We then detail William Riker's interpretation of these impossibility theorems and the various criticisms that have been leveled at Riker and his followers. Our position is that both Riker, who famously argued that the results of social choice represent a fundamental and ultimately fatal challenge to the legitimacy of populist democracy, and his critics, who variously argued that Riker misapplied the results or that the results themselves were inappropriate, misinterpret both the foundations and conclusions of social choice theory. Specifically, social choice theory informs us about the possibilities and impossibilities of aggregation. Furthermore, and tellingly, aggregation is simply that: putting various things together to produce an output. Thus, social choice theory is as applicable to judicial review and administrative policymaking – each of which uses various criteria in rendering rankings of, and choices from, sets of feasible policies – as it is to its traditional domain, electoral systems. When viewed in this way, it is clear that Riker's criticisms of social choice place an undue burden on the product of aggregation: his view denies that there is anything special (i.e. "legitimate") about the choices produced through democratic procedures. Similarly, many of the critics of Riker's argument miss the mark when they attempt to refute his conclusions by inaccurately denying the relevance of social choice theory. Somewhat ironically, as we illustrate, Riker's conclusions are most effectively set aside by the very results he cites in support of his argument.

---

[14] In other words, when the decision is motivated by a unitary and well-defined goal, then consistency between the choice and the goal is (at least in theory) easily verifiable.

In Chapter 3 we then turn to an extended presentation and discussion of the relevant foundations of social choice theory. In addition to clarifying the structure and logic of the impossibility theorems, a principal goal is to clarify a proper (and more general) interpretation of the impossibility theorems. Rather than taking the theorems as negatives, to be either ignored or worked around, we argue that these results motivate the entire study of politics. The potential irreconcilability of multiple societal and individual goals is exactly the raison d'être of government. In making our argument in favor of the real-world relevance of the theorems, we address both Riker and his critics in detail, arguing that both sides have been misguided in their interpretation of these results.

In Part II of the book we present our own theory of how collective choices can be legitimized in the face of irreconcilable goals. Chapter 4 presents a general discussion of various notions of legitimacy and how we interpret the term in this book. Choices have to be made with such a large and inevitably contested concept as "legitimacy," and our goals are specific insofar as our arguments are grounded in the traditions of social choice theory. While any useful theoretical framework is admittedly restrictive in certain ways, we argue that the constraints imposed by our use of social choice theory have important benefits. Specifically, social choice theory provides a unique combination of both analytical clarity and abstract generality that affords a clear view of our arguments while simultaneously sidestepping and acknowledging the importance of contextual factors. Many, if not most, of the restrictions apparently induced by the use of [a] social choice–theoretic framework are illusory: what one might term the "thinness," or "context-freeness," of social choice theory is exactly what allows the framework to capture any variety of contexts.

Chapters 5 and 6 then present our theory of legitimacy. In Chapter 5 we first present an informal and extended description of the theory's foundations and central conclusions. Our theory is axiomatic: we define a specific notion of legitimacy and then characterize the policies and procedures that satisfy these axioms. The principal goals of this chapter are first to explain how our theory captures procedural details, such as deliberation, reason giving, and sequence, and then to justify our axiomatic definition of legitimacy. This is an inherently verbal exercise precisely because it focuses on the questions of both how we represent real-world collective choice situations and why we choose to represent them in the ways that we do.

Chapter 6 then formally presents our theory. This is the most technical chapter of the book and includes both formal proofs and expository discussion of the theory's conclusions. One could arguably write a version of this book that omits Chapter 6 (or, perhaps, relegates the chapter's central arguments to an appendix). However, we believe that taking such an approach would be a mistake for a variety of reasons, including the fact that some of the results have not been published elsewhere. Most important among the various reasons is the constructive and illustrative nature of the formal proofs of many of the results. In other words, reading the proofs themselves will demonstrate not only why each of the various results is true but also illustrate and clarify the requisite analogies between the "moving parts" of the theoretical framework and real-world instantiations of collective choice, a question that we turn to in the final chapters of the book, contained in Part III. Chapter 7 concludes Part II with a discussion of several relevant gaps between our theoretical framework and real-world instances of collective decision making, with attention paid to clarifying the context of the empirical chapters that follow.

The three chapters in Part III discuss, in turn, examples of collective choice procedures in the judicial, legislative, and executive branches of the U.S. federal government. The primary goal in each of these chapters is to illustrate the similarity of each institution with the theoretical framework presented and discussed in Part II. In Chapter 8 we illustrate the analogy between our notion of legitimacy and the structure of judicial review in the U.S. federal judiciary. Specifically, Chapter 8 considers judicial review in the context of cases involving equal protection claims. The doctrine of equal protection is a classic example of aggregation, potentially requiring the comparison of individual and collective rights. We discuss several standards of review used by the U.S. Supreme Court when considering whether a statute violates the Fourteenth Amendment's basic guarantee to the citizens of the "equal protection of the laws." We argue that the analogy between the standards of review and our notion of legitimacy is strongest for the most demanding standard, known as *strict scrutiny*.

Chapter 9 discusses the consideration of legislation within the U.S. Congress. We discuss the use of scope limitations during legislative deliberations (specifically, germaneness requirements and single-subject provisions) and link the utilization of these such constraints with our theoretical framework and the axiomatic foundations of our notion of legitimacy.

Chapter 10 then turns to the executive branch and discusses the most commonly used institutional form of executive policymaking, "informal" (or "notice and comment") rulemaking by executive agencies. The structure of this policymaking institution has evolved over the past sixty-five years. We present and discuss this structure, as well as the origins of the institution itself and how its use has been interpreted and shaped by the federal judiciary. We illustrate the analogy between the various requirements of the process and the axiomatic foundations of our notion of legitimacy. We argue that this analogy is an important consideration for those who question how one can consider legitimate the very real policy decisions made on a daily basis by unelected officials throughout the federal government. Finally, Chapter 11 concludes with a summary of the book's argument and a sketch of its broader and deeper implications for both the rarefied air of democratic theory and the frequently fetid fumes of democratic governance.

1.3 THEORY AND METHOD

Before proceeding further, we think it helpful to briefly frame what our theory is intended to "do." To put it simply, our theory is not intended to be predictive. Much of modern social science research centers on an idealized version of the scientific method in which a model is built on first principles, predictions are derived from this model, and these predictions are then subjected to empirical verification. The driving force in this approach is falsification: while a theory can rarely if ever be shown to be true, sufficient empirical data can conclusively reveal if the theory is false.

Our approach in this book is arguably orthogonal to the classical one. In particular, our theory offers a characterization of legitimate choice that most assuredly need not be satisfied by actual political choices. Our theory of legitimacy is descriptive, and we do not believe that all (or even most) decisions are legitimate. A useful referent in this regard is the concept of Nash equilibrium from game theory.[15] In a nutshell, a Nash equilibrium describes a situation in which each individual in a strategic situation (i.e., "game") is acting in such a way as to maximize his or her well-being, given the behaviors of every other individual. Nash famously proved that such a situation always exists in a wide array of strategic situations. This result is purely abstract and accordingly valid regardless of whether individuals actually behave in a manner consistent with it. Nash's Theorem and the impossibility theorems we detail in the following chapters represent flip sides of the same theoretical coin: the impossibility theorems establish that certain aggregation methods simply do not exist, and Nash's Theorem establishes that certain configurations of individual behaviors *do*.

While the impossibility theorems serve as the principal theoretical motivation for our theory, our main results have more in common with Nash's theorem than these results. We establish that a notion of legitimate choice is theoretically nonvacuous and characterize the types of decisions that satisfy it. Furthermore, just as the Nash equilibria of a game are entirely determined by the individuals' preferences, the choices that satisfy our notion of legitimacy are completely dependent on the principle by which choice is supposed to be structured. Neither Nash equilibrium nor our theory of legitimacy provides any guidance about either what the primitives (preferences or principles, respectively) tend to be from an empirical perspective or even about how these primitives "should" be configured.

Nash's existence theorem is important regardless of whether it is descriptive of real-world behavior precisely because it establishes that one *could* achieve a stable configuration of individual behaviors in a wide variety of games. Our results are of the same flavor in the sense that our notion of legitimacy is theoretically relevant regardless of whether any observed behavior is "consistent"

[15] Nash, Jr. (1950).

with it. This is because we are not positing any theory of the relationship between legitimacy and individual behavior. Specifically, and as discussed in more detail in Section 4.1, the theory we present in Part II is independent of notions such as individuals, agency, preferences, behavior, etc. Rather, as we discuss in the following chapters, social choice theory provides sufficient structure to discuss aggregation and choice – and thus, we argue, legitimacy – without reference to individuals or groups.

Accordingly, even if one finds that individuals and groups seem to establish and support illegitimate policies and enshrine the selection of such policies in the rules and processes used by collective choice institutions, this would in our view be evidence only of a disconnect between behavior and legitimacy. Such a finding would not, in our minds at least, reduce the theoretical relevance of the theory. Indeed, one could argue that our theory is more relevant for discussion, refutation, and extension to the degree that one finds it is not emulated in observed behavior. Just as many people write, buy, and use cookbooks because they "cannot cook," one can view our theory as prescriptive: it guides choice in the range of situations in which a "mere" aggregation of goals falls short in terms providing unambiguous guidance.

This line of logic is central to our approach in the final part of this book: rather than attempting to determine how often our notion of legitimacy describes any particular decision, we instead argue by drawing analogies between our theoretical framework and the processes and structures of various political institutions that are at least partially justified in terms of their legitimating influence. The primary goal of this exercise is to put some meat on the bones of an abstract theory: while we do not believe that many decisions are perfectly legitimate as we have defined it, we do believe that the foundations of our theory are descriptive of mechanisms and processes by which groups have chosen to vet and validate contentious policy choices.

2

The Debates Surrounding Social Choice

The question of how multiple, competing, goals can be reconciled is the foundation of a branch of political science termed "social choice theory" or "collective choice theory," the study of which can be traced to the writings of a collection of French mathematicians and philosophers of the late eighteenth century, most notably Jean-Charles de Borda and the Marquis de Condorcet. Condorcet in particular was focused on the search for truth in public discourse, and his most well-known thoughts on politics are found in his *Essai sur l'application de l'analyse a la probabilite des decisions rendues a la pluralite des voix* ("Essay on the Application of Mathematics to the Theory of Decision-Making"). In this work he proved his famous jury theorem, which says that if a group is choosing between two alternatives (e.g., *acquit* or *convict*) and if each individual member of the group is more likely than not to reach a correct decision, then the probability that a majority of the members of the group reach the correct decision is higher than the probability that any individual reaches the correct decision and increases as the size of the group increases. This is a positive result, as it shows that a simple majority vote does well at producing a correct outcome when there are two alternatives and many voters.[1]

However, Condorcet also realized that group choices frequently involve more than two alternatives, and he sought a similar result for these cases. In playing with possible distributions of voter preferences, Condorcet, in his essay, identified what is now a well-known conundrum.[2] *Condorcet's paradox,* or more simply, *the paradox of voting* famously illustrates a problem stemming

[1] Condorcet was also deeply committed to liberal causes, including universal suffrage and universal public education for both men and women (along with subsidies to agricultural families whose children attended public schools and could no longer provide farm labor). See Block (1998), pp. 1015–1018.

[2] Block (1998), pp. 1004–1006.

from majority rule in which pairwise voting over three or more alternatives can lead to intransitive (or cyclic) outcomes. The paradox goes as follows: suppose there are three individuals (Persons 1, 2, and 3), and suppose there are three alternatives to be voted upon (*A*, *B*, and *C*). Finally, suppose that Persons 1, 2, and 3 have the following preferences over the alternatives:

Person	Preferences
1	$A \succ_1 B \succ_1 C$
2	$B \succ_2 C \succ_2 A$
3	$C \succ_3 A \succ_3 B$

As we discuss in more detail later in the chapter, the notation $A \succ_1 B$ means that Person 1 prefers *A* to *B*. With this in hand, now suppose that the above individuals are asked to cast pairwise votes over the three alternatives. Then, by the votes of Persons 1 and 3, a majority vote between *A* and *B* would yield *A* as the winner, the votes of Persons 1 and 2 would give *B* a majority over *C*, and the votes of Persons 2 and 3 would yield *C* as the winner between *A* and *C*. Thus, majority voting in this case produces a *cycle* by deeming alternative *A* superior to alternative *B*, alternative *B* superior to alternative *C*, and alternative *C* superior to alternative *A*. Put another way, no alternative can be deemed "best" in terms of satisfying a majority of voters.[3] Situations like this in which the majority preference relation is cyclic on a set of three alternatives is often referred to as a *Condorcet cycle*. Conversely, an alternative that is majority preferred to every other alternative is referred to as a *Condorcet winner*.

Condorcet's work on voting procedures had little influence on his contemporaries but was later rediscovered by Duncan Black in a series of essays written in the 1940s and culminating in his book *Theory of Committees and Elections*.[4] This work is considered to be the beginning of modern social choice theory.[5] In the 1950s economist Kenneth Arrow independently rediscovered the ideas of Condorcet while working on his text *Social Choice and Individual Values*. This book, published in 1951 and for which Arrow received the Nobel Memorial Prize in Economic Sciences in 1972, presents Arrow's seminal "impossibility theorem." Put succinctly, Arrows impossibility theorem demonstrates that when voters have three or more options to choose from, then any voting system that meets certain minimal conditions of fairness and sensibility *will* fail to produce "rational" outcomes in some situations. More specifically, if the system satisfies the fairness conditions, it must necessarily succumb to instances in which it deems an alternative *A* weakly superior to an alternative *B*, that

---

[3] More strongly, the three alternatives are essentially indistinguishable from each other: they are identical in every way except for identities of the voters that support them. This example arguably represents the foundation of social choice because of its special combination of simplicity and intractability.

[4] Riker (1982), p. 2. Note that some people, including Charles Dodgson, rediscovered the work in the nineteenth century.

[5] Block (1998), p. 984; Black (1958) and Riker (1982), footnote 13, pp. 1–2.

alternative B weakly superior to another alternative C, and that alternative C strictly superior to A. In other words, many minimally democratic systems will in some situation produce an intransitive ordering of the alternatives similar to the cyclic outcomes that Condorcet identified nearly 200 years earlier.

Social choice–theoretic concepts such as the paradox of voting and results such as Arrow's theorem have had a tremendous impact on the study of politics. Perhaps the most influential and controversial interpretation of these results can be found in the late William Riker's famous book, *Liberalism Against Populism*, in which he used the paradox of voting and Arrow's Theorem to argue that any notion of a "popular will" is meaningless, that political decisions are in a continual state of disequilibrium, and that perhaps the only benefit of democracy is that it enables voters to throw bad politicians out of office. This argument in favor of what some have termed "democratic irrationalism,"[6] or the idea that the preferences of individuals cannot be amalgamated in any meaningful way because of the possibility of majority voting cycles, has had a broad impact, influencing both academics and policymakers. For example, in the 1989 Supreme Court foreword to the Harvard Law Review, Erwin Chemerinsky uses Arrow's Theorem as the cornerstone of his argument that democratic legislatures cannot "reflect the views of a majority in society."[7]

In defending the idea that democratic choices do (or at least can) reflect a nonvacuous popular will against attacks like Riker's, a strain of literature has arisen that attempts to evade the consequences of Arrow's Theorem. This literature argues that Riker and his followers are misguided because the social choice results themselves are of limited relevance. These results, it is argued, are either empirically irrelevant, based on incorrect underlying assumptions, or both. Gerry Mackie's nearly 500-page tome *Democracy Defended* focuses exclusively on discrediting Riker's arguments by attempting to demonstrate that virtually every published empirical claim of a paradox arising from Arrow's Theorem has been made in error, and moreover, that the conditions of Arrow's Theorem have "no descriptive or normative force of their own."[8]

Despite the lively intellectual debate described above, over the past quarter century social choice theory as a descriptive tool has fallen out of fashion with academics. Even its allies have characterized the social choice impossibility results as intellectual dead ends, and much of social science theorizing now uses a game-theoretic approach, wherein equilibrium existence is much easier to obtain.[9] More challengingly, the field has been criticized as being nonfalsifiable and useless as an empirical tool.[10] Arrow's result has been described as "an

---

[6] Gerry Mackie's term.

[7] Chemerinsky (1989), p. 79, quoted in Pildes and Anderson (1990), p. 2124.

[8] Mackie (2003), p. 156.

[9] However, one should note the subtle and cogent points raised by David Austen-Smith and Jeffrey Banks about the relationship between these types of approaches (Austen-Smith and Banks (1999), pp. 187–194).

[10] Green and Shapiro (1994).

abstract limit case" that "does not describe the real world,"[11] and some have gone so far as to claim that

> [o]riginating in profound misconceptions about the structure of public values, the nature of democratic politics, and the concept of rationality itself, social choice theory only muddies efforts to think clearly about democracy.[12]

Taken as a whole, while few authors dispute that results such as Arrow's Theorem provide *some* insight into what voting systems are (and are not) capable of accomplishing, the real-world relevance of these results is less well understood and accordingly more contested. The remainder of this chapter presents a brief and semitechnical introduction to two of the most well-known impossibility theorems: Arrow's theorem and the Gibbard-Satterthwaite Theorem. We then describe Riker's view of the impossibility theorems, as his interpretation is regarded by many to motivate the role of these theorems in mainstream political science. Finally, the chapter concludes with a discussion of the various criticisms that have been leveled at Riker's arguments and at the impossibility results themselves. We set up these debates as a prelude to the chapters that follow, in which we hope to convince the reader that *both* Riker and his critics are wrong. Specifically, we will demonstrate that the social choice results are of real-world relevance and that the aggregation problem – the dilemma of comparing and reconciling competing interests and goals – is simultaneously the defining problem of political science and the logical foundation for democratic governance.

2.1 THE ARROW AND GIBBARD-SATTERTHWAITE THEOREMS

Arrow's Theorem and the Gibbard-Satterthwaite Theorem are two impossibility results that are commonly interpreted as applying to systems of voting (or, slightly more generally, methods of preference aggregation). We will argue later that such an interpretation is narrower than necessary, but this interpretation suffices for the purposes of describing the results. Adopting this interpretation for the time being also facilitates our discussion of existing debates about the results and their relevance to democratic politics.

The Arrow and Gibbard-Satterthwaite Theorems each take a minimal set of normatively appealing criteria and then formally demonstrate that these criteria are internally inconsistent. That is, each of the results implies that it is impossible for *any* voting system to simultaneously satisfy the given set of criteria. Despite this commonality, the theorems otherwise appear at first to be quite different. For example, Arrow's Theorem concerns the ability of a voting

---

[11] Mackie (2003), p. 156.
[12] Pildes and Anderson (1990), p. 2213.

procedure to produce outcomes that are collectively "rational," where collective rationality is described in terms of a procedure satisfying various common sense-type properties. The Gibbard-Satterthwaite Theorem, on the other hand, concerns the ability of a procedure to be immune from strategic manipulation by voters or to not reward insincere voting behavior. Despite their differences, the two results are mathematically similar, and it has been demonstrated that the two results can be derived from a more general "metatheorem" on social aggregators, which we discuss in more detail in the following chapter.[13]

To present these results, some simple notation is needed. First, we will assume that there are two or more individuals seeking to make a collective choice. Second, we will assume that there is a finite set of alternatives, or policies, under consideration by the group. We will denote this set by X, and will assume (to begin with) that X contains at least three different alternatives. Third, we will assume that each person has his or her own preference ordering of the alternatives under consideration. This *preference relation* is denoted $\succ_i$ for person i. Thus, if person i likes alternative x more than alternative y, it is denoted $x \succ_i y$. People are presumed to be *rational* in the sense that their preference relation is transitive: if $x \succ_i y$ and $y \succ_i z$, then $x \succ_i z$. Finally, we will use the term ρ to describe the entire collection of individual preferences, a set of preference relations for each person in the group under consideration. Thus, if there are n people in our group, then $\rho = (\succ_1, \succ_2, \ldots, \succ_n)$.[14]

To make this concrete, suppose that we have two people in our group and that we have three alternatives under consideration, so that $X = \{x, y, z\}$. Suppose that Person 1 strictly prefers x to y and z and strictly prefers y to z (i.e., $x \succ_1 y \succ_1 z$) and Person 2 strictly prefers y to z and x and z to x (i.e., $y \succ_2 z \succ_2 x$). Then the preference profile ρ characterizes our group and the preferences of its members as follows:

$$\rho = \begin{pmatrix} x \succ_1 y \succ_1 z \\ y \succ_2 z \succ_2 x \end{pmatrix} \tag{2.1}$$

Now that we have described the collection of alternatives, people, and their preferences over the alternatives, we can begin to consider various ways of conceptualizing collective choice. We will consider two different types of mechanisms for generating a group choice. The first is termed a *preference aggregation rule*, and the second is a *choice function*. Arrow's Theorem concerns preference aggregation rules; the Gibbard-Satterthwaite Theorem concerns choice functions. We now briefly discuss each of these two representations of collective decision making in turn.

---

[13] Reny (2001) and Eliaz (2004).

[14] Throughout this part of the book we presume that individual preferences are strict, so that if $x \succ_i y$, then it must be the case that *not* $y \succ_i x$. This is solely for ease of exposition. Collective preference, as generated through a to-be-defined preference aggregation rule, need not be strict, so that it may be the case that both $x \succ y$ and $y \succ x$.

PREFERENCE AGGREGATION RULES. A preference aggregation rule takes a preference profile ρ as an input and generates a collective preference relation, $\succ$, over all alternatives. An arbitrary preference aggregation rule is denoted by f, so that $f(\rho) => \succ$ describes the "group's preferences" over the alternatives when the individual preferences are as described by ρ.

While we use the term "collective preference" to refer to $\succ$, it is important to note that $\succ$ need not be transitive. As mentioned earlier in our discussion of Condorcet's seminal contributions, the paradox of voting is based on a preference aggregation method (pairwise majority voting) that can generate cyclic collective preferences. A preference aggregation rule that always returns a transitive collective preference relation is commonly referred to as a *social welfare function*. An example of a preference aggregation rule f that is also a social welfare function is the method of Borda count.

The Borda count method, which we will denote by f_B, or $\succ_B$, works as follows. For each individual preference relation $\succ_i$, *each alternative x receives the number of points equal to the number of alternatives ranked below x* in $\succ_i$. The collective preference is then given by the ordering of the alternatives in terms of these points: an alternative x is weakly collectively preferred to another alternative y given a profile ρ if and only if x receives at least as many points as y does at ρ.

For example, consider the preference profile ρ described in Equation 2.1. As there are three alternatives under consideration, Borda count works as follows: an alternative that a voter ranks first receives two points, an alternative he ranks second receives one point, and an alternative he ranks third receives zero points. The social ranking is then the sum of these scores across individuals. Thus, given the ρ in Equation 2.1, x receives two total points (two from Voter 1 and zero from Voter 2), y receives three total points (one from Voter 1 and two from Voter 2), and z receives one total point (from Voter 2). It follows that Borda count ranks the alternatives $y \succ_B x \succ_B z$.

Preference aggregation rules are appealing because what they produce – a collective preference relation – allows a collective comparison of any pair of alternatives. This is useful if one believes that preference aggregation involves contingencies; in some cases the group may be forced to rank alternatives before knowing which of the alternatives will actually be feasible. Put another way, the notion of collective preference facilitates an analogy between individual and collective choice and, accordingly, collective and individual rationality. From a practical standpoint, however, true preference aggregation is often unnecessary or inefficient. That is, while there are strong theoretical arguments in favor of representing group decision making as a preference aggregation rule, it is rare that preference aggregation rules are needed or applied. Rather, many collective decision-making procedures return simply a final choice. Choice rules bear a greater verisimilitude to such institutions, and we now turn to these.

CHOICE FUNCTIONS. While a preference aggregation rule f takes a preference profile ρ and produces a collective preference ordering over the entire

collection of alternatives under consideration, a *choice function* takes a preference profile and returns a single alternative as the final collective choice. Thus,
while preference aggregation rules are admittedly a scholarly abstraction, a
choice function is similar to an electoral rule: individuals submit their preferences and the choice function identifies the winner. We denote an arbitrary
choice function by F, so that the final choice when the preference profile is
given by ρ is denoted by $F(\rho) \in X$. We can also think of Borda count as a
choice function, denoted by F_B. In this case, our function would return the
alternative with the highest Borda score, breaking a tie by some arbitrary rule
if need be.[15] Referring again to the profile ρ described in Equation 2.1, the
Borda count as a choice function would simply select alternative y:

$$F_B(\rho) = y.$$

Of course, choice functions and preference aggregation rules are distinguished
only by what they produce. Because choice rules return a single alternative and
the individuals are presumed to have preferences over the set of alternatives,
choice functions have been used extensively to consider the effect of collective
choice mechanisms on individual incentives when voting and otherwise sig-
naling their preferences. We return to this question later when we discuss the
Gibbard-Satterthwaite Theorem, but it is important to consider for a moment
the linkage between choice functions and preference aggregation rules. A choice
function produces a single winner, while an aggregation rule produces a comparison between each pair of alternatives, represented by $\succ$. If it is the case that
the aggregation rule is such that there exists some $y \in X$ such that $y \succ x$ for
all $x \in X \setminus \{y\}$ and for all such x it is also not the case that $x \succ y$, then y is the
uniquely top-ranked element of $f(\rho)$ and a natural "collective choice" given
that aggregation rule. However, if $f(\rho)$ is such that two or more alternatives
are tied as best, or if $f(\rho)$ is cyclic and there *is no best*, then the aggregation
rule cannot produce a collective choice without more structure being placed on
the collective decision-making process.

The theory we present in Chapters 5 and 6 provides an answer to the question of how to appropriately (or "legitimately") translate a cyclic collective
preference relation into a single collective choice. As we will discuss throughout the next few chapters, this situation characterizes the heart of the debate
about the political relevance of Arrow's Theorem in particular and the theory
of social choice in general. Cyclic collective preference is potentially insufficient
to unambiguously discern a collective choice and to construct a coherent representation of a "collective will." By bridging this divide between the output
of "pure aggregation" (of preferences or other criteria) and the selection of a

---

[15] How one breaks ties in choice functions can have very important consequences for both individual and collective behavior. However, these issues, and tie breaking in general, are not relevant
to our purposes in this book.

final choice, our theory provides a reconciliation of the inputs of the aggregation problem and the instrumental requirement that one policy ultimately be chosen.

Given the centrality of the problem of cyclic collective preferences, a natural next question is why one would adopt a preference aggregation rule that might ever produce such a thing. That is, are there reasons that one might choose an aggregation method that might not yield an unambiguous "best" outcome? Arrow's Theorem provides an affirmative answer to this question. In a nutshell, any minimally democratic aggregation procedure must encounter some situations in which it fails to produce a coherent (or, perhaps, "well-ordered") collective preference. In the following section, we turn to a more precise definition and discussion of how the theorems of Arrow and Gibbard-Satterthwaite characterize minimally democratic preference aggregation rules and choice functions, respectively. Before this, however, we briefly discuss the question of what preference aggregation rules and choice functions must take as "inputs." In social choice terms, this issue is described as the *domain* of the aggregation rule or choice function.

Preference Domains

Recall that preference aggregation rules and choice functions are each presumed to take preference profiles as their inputs. The only distinction between the two concepts is what they produce upon receiving a preference profile.[16] The set of preference profiles for which a preference aggregation rule or choice function (or more simply, a "rule") is defined is referred to as the rule's *domain*.

A rule that is capable of considering (i.e., defined for) all possible preference profiles is said to satisfy *unrestricted domain*. In other words, as long as a choice function always returns a choice (or, respectively, a preference aggregation rule always returns a collective preference relation), it satisfies unrestricted domain. Of course, requiring that a rule satisfy unrestricted domain does not imply that every preference profile is possible. Accordingly, unrestricted domain is in reality simply a technical condition that is satisfied by any well-defined rule.

Some scholars have argued in both substantive and normative terms that unrestricted domain concerns whether the rule can (or should) restrict the preferences that individuals may have.[17] These arguments, it should be noted, are completely beside the point. Preference aggregation rules and choice functions are necessarily abstract constructions and to assert that a real-world instantiation of such a rule does not satisfy unrestricted domain is either inaccurate

---

[16] It is important to note again at this point that we are using the term "preference" here simply for the purposes of illustration. One of our main points is that the social choice results we discuss apply to any aggregation problem, regardless of the substantive nature or context of the inputs.

[17] Or, perhaps, whether a rule can or should restrict the preferences that individual may claim to have. We return to this point, and the previous arguments we allude to here, in Section 3.2.

or an assertion that there is some situation in which the rule "does nothing." Deferring discussion of the possible inaccuracy of this statement for the moment, it is important to consider how nonsensical "doing nothing" is in this context. It is impossible for the output of a real-world rule to "not be defined." There is always something that happens after a real-world rule is given a set of inputs (e.g., a preference profile). Generally, the phrase "do nothing" is used to describe what happens when the rule makes no change to the prevailing policy. Regardless, some policy will indeed prevail after the rule receives its inputs. Whatever this policy is *defines the rule*. In short, unrestricted domain is truly a regularity condition for the purposes of analysis.

An inaccuracy that offers an explanation for the debates about unrestricted domain concerns a traditional divide between theory and empirics. As mentioned earlier, in no way should the assumption of unrestricted domain be taken to imply anything about the presumed frequency or possibility of the rule in question *observing* every preference profile as an input. However, this is an empirical question first and foremost. As we discuss in more detail in Section 3.2, there are misunderstandings about exactly how much purchase one gets from restricting the set of preference profiles that can be observed. Even more important, these arguments have almost always ignored the fact that aggregation in political institutions frequently involves inputs other than preferences. Ultimately, though, the question at hand in such empirical debates is not about whether a rule satisfies unrestricted domain. Rather, these debates should be interpreted in terms of the degree to which one should be concerned about satisfaction of the other democratic criteria, to which we now turn.

Arrow's Theorem

Arrow lays out four simple axioms that he argues any reasonable aggregation rule should satisfy. He then proves that these axioms are incompatible with each other, that no rule can simultaneously satisfy all four.[18] In so doing, his result implies that *any* aggregation rule – regardless of what is being aggregated or for what purpose – must violate at least one of these axioms. Put another and more specific way, every democratic institution, be it electoral, legislative, administrative, or judicial in character, violates at least one of these axioms. We now define each of these four axioms – Pareto efficiency, independence of irrelevant alternatives, transitivity, and no dictator – in turn.

Pareto Efficiency
We begin with the observation that perhaps one of the least demanding requirements a group would seek to impose on its voting system is that a group decision

---

[18] It should be noted that Arrow's original theorem (Arrow, 1951) used the axioms of *monotonicity* and *non-imposition* instead of the Pareto condition described below. The more common version of the theorem presented here (Arrow, 1963) replaces those axioms with Pareto efficiency and is a stronger result, because it uses weaker conditions.

be minimally responsive to the preferences of the members of that group. Arrow captures the notion of minimal responsiveness with the condition of *Pareto efficiency*. An aggregation rule f is *Pareto efficient* if whenever *every* individual i strictly prefers x to y, then our aggregation rule f generates a collective ranking of the alternatives that ranks x strictly higher than y. This condition rules out aggregation rules that, for example, always rank $x \succ y$, regardless of the group members' x, y preferences.

Independence of Irrelevant Alternatives

The second condition Arrow required of an aggregation method is that it should not consider "irrelevant" alternatives when generating a ranking between two other alternatives. Specifically, the group members' preferences between alternatives c and d should not affect how the group decides between two different alternatives, a and b. This property is captured by Arrow's second condition, which is termed *independence of irrelevant alternatives*.

An aggregation rule f is *independent of irrelevant alternatives* (IIA) if for any two *different* profiles, ρ and ρ' in which each individual's x, y ranking under ρ agrees with their x, y ranking under ρ',[19] then the collective ranking of x and y ranking generated by $f(\rho)$ should agree with the collective ranking of x and y ranking generated by $f(\rho')$. In other words, if something alters people's preferences only about alternatives other than x and y, the collective ranking of x and y should remain the same.

As we discuss in more detail in Section 3.3, IIA is the most conceptually difficult of Arrow's conditions. This difficulty largely stems from the fact that it is a condition that applies *across* different preference profiles. For example, Pareto efficiency and transitivity are intraprofile conditions; it is possible to determine a violation of either of these axioms by considering a single preference profile. This is not the case with IIA-to determine that an aggregation rule violates IIA requires that one compare the output of the rule for at least two different preference profiles.[20]

While IIA is an abstract condition, an equivalent formulation is this: if any one individual's ranking of a particular alternative under consideration (call it z) changes, then this change alone should not affect how the *group* decides between two other alternatives, x and y. It is important to pause for a moment and consider this reformulation. If an aggregation method f violates IIA, then there is a pair of preference profiles, ρ and ρ' that (1) differ only with respect to the preferences of *one* individual, (2) do not differ at all with respect to *any* person's ranking of two alternatives x and y, and (3) at these two profiles f generates different collective rankings for x and y. Thus, it should be clear that violating IIA opens up the possibility for strategic manipulation

---

[19] That is, for each individual i, $x \succ_i y$ if and only if $x \succ'_i y$.

[20] This interprofile characteristic is shared by the no dictator axiom discussed later. However, no dictator is quite transparent in both its implications and, relatedly, which aggregation rules violate it.

of the aggregation process: a single individual may in some cases have the opportunity to alter the ranking of two alternatives simply by misrepresenting his or her preferences about some other alternative. This possibility is at the heart of the Gibbard-Satterthwaite Theorem, which we discuss later in this section. For now, though, consider the following example to make the concept behind IIA more concrete. In so doing, we will also illustrate how and why the Borda count procedure violates IIA.

Consider the following two profiles, ρ and ρ':

$$\rho = \begin{pmatrix} x \succ_1 y \succ_1 z \\ y \succ_2 z \succ_2 x \end{pmatrix} \qquad \rho' = \begin{pmatrix} x \succ_1 z \succ_1 y \\ y \succ_2 x \succ_2 z \end{pmatrix} \qquad (2.2)$$

As discussed earlier, Borda count (denoted again by f_B, or $\succ_B$), when applied to profile ρ, collectively ranks y above both x and z and ranks x above z:

$$y \succ_B x \succ_B z.$$

Meanwhile, at ρ', Borda count ranks x above y and z and ranks y above z:

$$x \succ'_B y \succ'_B z,$$

because at this profile x receives three combined points, y receives two, and z receives one. Note now that if we look solely at the two individuals' rankings of x and y, these two profiles look identical: voter 1 prefers x to y ($x \succ_1 y$) under both ρ and ρ', and Voter 2 prefers y to x ($y \succ_2 x$) under both ρ and ρ'. However, $f_B(\rho)$ generates $y \succ_B x$, and $f_B(\rho')$ generates $x \succ'_B y$. Accordingly, Borda count violates IIA.[21]

The fact that Borda count violates IIA is in a sense the basis of some of the more sustained critiques of the axiom as a desideratum of aggregation methods, and we discuss this debate in much greater detail in Section 3.3. Now, however, we turn to the third axiom, transitivity.

Transitivity

Arrow's third condition, *transitivity*, focuses on the ability of a preference aggregation rule to generate an unambiguous winner, or collection of winners, if there is a tie. As discussed earlier when comparing preference aggregation rules and choice functions, an aggregation rule that generates the social ranking $x \succ y$, $y \succ z$, and $z \succ x$ is not particularly useful to a group seeking to collectively choose one alternative from among x, y, and z. An aggregation method that does return such a cyclic relationship is said to *cycle*. In particular, an aggregation method that cycles may not provide an unambiguously "best" alternative when it returns a cyclic relationship between some or all of the alternatives.

An aggregation rule f is *transitive* if it always produces a transitive ordering of the alternatives. Thus, if f produces an ordering in which $x \succ y$ and

---

[21] Indeed, IIA is the only one of Arrow's four axioms that the Borda method violates.

$y \succ z$, then it must also be the case that $x \succ z$. This condition guarantees that the social ordering generated by f satisfies the same rationality condition as the individual preference orderings it was constructed from and that it cannot cycle. Moreover, it ensures the existence of an alternative (or collection of alternatives) that are not ranked strictly lower than anything else. As we discuss in more detail in Section 3.6, one can defend the desirability of this axiom from a number of perspectives, most notably the degree to which aggregated "social" preferences can be thought of as equivalent to individual preferences. In this light, Arrow's Theorem indicates important normative and logical concerns with anthropomorphizing groups when discussing group decision making. Deferring this discussion, however, we now discuss the fourth and final of Arrow's axioms, no dictator.

No Dictator

Arrow's final axiom, *no dictator*, concerns the responsiveness of the preference aggregation rule to the preferences of more than one person. An aggregation rule is *dictatorial* if there is one particular voter whose individual preferences always determine the social preference ordering, irrespective of the preferences of the other voters. Formally, this condition says that there exists one voter i, so that every time $x \succ_i y$, the aggregation rule f produces a strict ranking $x \succ y$. An aggregation rule f satisfies *no dictator* if it is not dictatorial. We discuss defenses of the no dictator condition in more detail in Section 3.5, but it is useful at this point only to note how weak this axiom is. In particular, a dictatorial aggregation rule is *completely independent* of all of the inputs to the aggregation problem except one.[22] If there is even one preference profile and one pair of alternatives at which the aggregation does not exactly match a given voter's preference ordering, then that voter is not a dictator under the rule.[23]

With unrestricted domain and the four axioms of Pareto efficiency, IIA, transitivity, and no dictator defined and described, we are now ready to state Arrow's Theorem.

Theorem 1 *(Arrow, 1950, 1963). With three or more alternatives, any aggregation rule satisfying unrestricted domain, Pareto efficiency, IIA and transitivity is dictatorial.*

---

[22] This claim relies on individuals having strict preferences. If a dictator has weak preferences (in which some alternatives are tied in his estimation), then the output of the dictatorial aggregation rule is not defined by the dictator and may (or may not) be generated by considering other individuals' preferences.

[23] More specifically, an aggregation rule can satisfy no dictator and nonetheless always return one given voter's most preferred alternative as the collectively most preferred alternative. This point is important both when contrasted with the definition of a dictatorial choice function below and, more generally, when considering the previously discussed linkages between aggregation rules and choice functions.

Arrow's Theorem then tells us that if a group wishes to design a preference aggregation rule that is Pareto efficient, transitive and independent of irrelevant alternatives, and if we place no restrictions on the preferences that individuals may have, then the rule must grant all decision-making authority to a single individual. Thus, any aggregation rule that is not dictatorial *must* violate transitivity, Pareto efficiency, or IIA. And practically speaking, it will violate either transitivity or IIA because the only nondictatorial aggregation rules that are ruled out by the addition of Pareto efficiency are those rules that are either null (generate a tie over all alternatives) or inverse dictatorships.[24] This extension of Arrow's Theorem to non-Pareto efficient rules was proved by Wilson (1972) and is known as Wilson's Impossibility Theorem.

The Gibbard-Satterthwaite Theorem

Our second impossibility theorem, proved independently by Gibbard (1973) and Satterthwaite (1975), differs from Arrow's Theorem in several important ways. First, it concerns choice functions rather than preference aggregation rules (i.e., rules that produce a single winner, as opposed to a social ordering of the alternatives). Second, the Gibbard-Satterthwaite Theorem does not assume that the rule is given a "true" preference profile as an input. Rather, it considers rules (e.g., voting systems) that take reported preferences, (e.g., individuals' ballots) as an input. The focus, in this case, is then on whether there are choice functions that can be relied upon to elicit truthful inputs (e.g., "sincere" ballots). In slightly different terms, the Gibbard-Satterthwaite Theorem considers whether and how a choice function might be implemented so as to make collective decisions when the preference profile must be elicited from individuals with an interest in the collective decision itself.

Formally, Gibbard and Satterthwaite consider what is referred to as the *strategy-proofness* of a choice function. A strategy-proof choice function entirely negates any gains from insincere behavior by any single voter. Consider two preference profiles, ρ and $(\succ_i', \rho_{-i})$, that are as follows:

$$\rho = (\succ_1, \ldots, \succ_i, \ldots, \succ_n)$$

is a "true," or "sincere," preference profile, and

$$(\succ_i', \rho_{-i}) = (\succ_1, \ldots, \succ_i', \ldots, \succ_n)$$

is a profile that differs from ρ only in that Voter i reports the "insincere" or "incorrect" preferences $\succ_i'$, as opposed to his true preferences $\succ_i$. A choice function F is *strategy-proof* if, in every situation, ρ, F never chooses an alternative at $(\succ_i', \rho_{-i})$ that Voter i strictly prefers to the outcome it selects

---

[24] Wilson's Theorem additionally requires the very weak axiom of non-imposition.

at ρ. Formally, for a strategy-proof F, it is the case that for every ρ and every $i \in N$:

$$F(\rho) \neq F(\succ_i', \rho_{-i}) \Rightarrow F(\rho) \succ_i F(\succ_i', \rho_{-i}).$$

In other words, F being strategy-proof implies that no voter can ever strictly benefit by claiming to have preferences that are different than what they actually are (or more specifically, by claiming preferences $\succ_i'$ when his true preferences are $\succ_i$). Put less formally, honesty is always a "good policy" when voting or otherwise submitting information to a strategy-proof choice function.

Note that there is a class of very simple choice functions that are strategy proof. One could simply choose a single voter and choose whatever that voter reports as his or her most preferred alternative. That voter can never strictly gain from misreporting his or her preferences. Similarly, none of the other voters can affect the chosen alternative by what they report, so they too have no incentive to report something other than their true preferences. Such choice functions are referred to as *dictatorial*. Note that the definition of "dictator" used in this theorem is modified slightly from our previous definition to accommodate the fact that we are considering choice functions: here, a choice function F is dictatorial if it always generates a collective choice that is the dictator's top-ranked alternative. Gibbard and Satterthwaite demonstrate that, if at least three different voting outcomes are possible, these choice functions are the *only* ones that are strategy proof. In other words, there is no nondictatorial procedure that is strategy proof.

Theorem 2 *(Gibbard, 1973; Satterthwaite, 1975) With unrestricted domain and the possibility of three or more voting outcomes, any strategy-proof choice function is dictatorial.*

From the perspective of choice functions as representing voting systems, the Gibbard-Satterthwaite Theorem proves that the possibility of strategic voting, or voting against one's true preferences, is endemic to *every* nontrivial voting system. While the scope of this result is surprising (in that it tells us that there is *no* nondictatorial voting system that is nonmanipulable), it should not be surprising that individuals frequently have incentives to cast insincere ballots in elections. In the plurality system frequently used in elections in the Unites States, for example, supporters of third-party candidates often have a perceptible incentive to vote for their favorite major party candidate because a vote for a third party may be considered a "wasted vote."

The profundity of the Gibbard-Satterthwaite Theorem is more easily seen when one adopts a more general interpretation of choice functions than as mere voting systems. In particular, when one abstracts from individual preferences and conceives of the "preference profile" as a profile of objective information about different criteria that the choice function is designed to use when selecting a final outcome, strategy proofness can be more easily reinterpreted as requiring the choice function to respond to the criteria in a way that is, for lack of a better word, faithful to each of them. In other words, nothing in the Gibbard-Satterthwaite Theorem restricts its applicability to voting or electoral systems.

Implications of the Theorems

Having described both Arrow's Theorem and the Gibbard-Satterthwaite Theorem, it is natural to ask: What do these theorems tell us about democratic processes? After all, the results themselves are purely mathematical statements and, indeed, from a technical standpoint, each is a relatively simple and straightforward application of formal logic. Nonetheless, the stark clarity provided by this abstraction imbues the conclusions with the rarefied quality of truth. Simply put, the theorems are indisputably *correct*. Accordingly, it follows that one's perception of the value, or lack thereof, of these results depends entirely on how one chooses to interpret them.

For the remainder of this chapter we discuss several strands of literature that argue that despite the optimistic name Arrow gave to his theorem – the "General Possibility Theorem" – the social choice enterprise as pioneered by Arrow is a fundamentally hopeless endeavor.[25] Although these literatures are at odds with each other, and indeed one arose as a refutation of the other, we argue that they both take a similar conception of successful democratic choice. One strand argues that democracy, conceived of as the amalgamation of the preferences of members of society, is impossible because of the social choice results; another argues that democracy is possible because these results are not likely to be of real-world relevance. We argue that both approaches are wrong – that democracy is meaningful precisely *because of* the far-reaching relevance of the impossibility theorems.

2.2 RIKER AND THE ARBITRARINESS OF DEMOCRATIC CHOICE

Early on in *Liberalism Against Populism* in a chapter titled "Different Choices from Identical Values," William Riker discusses various voting systems used throughout the world and observes that, for many profiles of preferences, different voting systems will yield different outcomes. Each of the systems is a sensible one (otherwise we might not expect it to be widely used), and the fact that these systems yield different outcomes is not entirely surprising (otherwise we might expect that a nation's choice of electoral system is not a particularly important or meaningful choice). At the same time, the fact that different fair and sensible procedures can produce different outcomes when applied to the same set of voters troubles Riker because it implies that real-world voting outcomes cannot be regarded as true and accurate amalgamations of voters' preferences.

---

[25] Sen (2012), p. 263.

Taking this fact as a starting point, Riker goes on to make the stronger claim that even if an unambiguously "best" voting system was agreed upon, the aforementioned impossibility theorems prove that we still cannot take its output as any meaningful reflection of the popular will. As discussed earlier in Section 2.1, Arrow's Theorem implies that if the (nondictatorial) rule satisfies the "fairness conditions" of Pareto efficiency and independence of irrelevant alternatives, then it must produce intransitive outcomes; essentially, it must cycle.[26] Riker argues that this conclusion implies that any outcome produced by a "fair" electoral system is meaningless.

Second, the Gibbard-Satterthwaite Theorem implies that this agreed-upon system faces a potentially even bigger hurdle than the possibility of cyclic outcomes: it would not be able to elicit the truthful preferences of voters and would always be susceptible to situations in which voters faced a strategic incentive to misrepresent their preferences by casting "insincere" ballots. Thus, real-world voting outcomes cannot be regarded as accurate amalgamations of voters' preferences because the voting systems themselves have no way of eliciting what those preferences actually are. Riker argues that because social amalgamations of individuals' preferences are meaningless, a populist conception of democracy in which voters' preferences are translated into social outcomes, such as through a direct vote, is "absurd."[27] Rather, the best we can hope for is what Riker terms a liberal democracy, in which voters may not see their wishes translated into outcomes by their leaders but are free to vote their leaders out of office.

This is clearly a provocative argument, and it is an argument that has pervaded the study of social choice theory to such an extent that many scholars equate Riker's counterdemocratic interpretation of the impossibility theorems with the field of social choice itself.[28] In this sense, social choice theory as a field has come under fire as undermining the normative appeal of democracy itself. It is not surprising, then, that Riker's work has spurred a widespread effort by democratic theorists to defend democratic ideals in the face of this attack. If one takes Riker's argument seriously and takes his interpretation of the social choice results to be correct, then an obvious line of defense is to discredit the impossibility theorems themselves. This is an avenue that many of these critics have taken, and we discuss these critics in the sections that follow.

Another line of criticism has come from the positive political theory community, the establishment and development of which Riker himself played an

---

[26] It should be noted (and Riker notes) that transitivity is a sufficient condition to ensure that an aggregation rule does not cycle, but it is not a necessary condition. A necessary and sufficient condition is that the rule be *acyclic*. When Arrow's Theorem is extended to include this broader class of rules, his dictator condition is weakened to the existence of an individual who can veto certain decisions.

[27] Riker (1982), pp. 238–239.

[28] See Shepsle and Bonchek (1997), Mackie (2006)'s "Reception of Social Choice Theory by Democratic Theory," and the citations therein.

instrumental role in while at the University of Rochester in the latter half of the
20th century.[29] These critics argue that Riker's argument contains several logical inconsistencies. Coleman and Ferejohn (1986) summarize these criticisms
succinctly, noting that two crucial parts of Riker's argument are, first, that all
(populist) democratic procedures produce *arbitrary* outcomes, and second, that
constitutional limitations on the power of elected officials produce *less* arbitrary outcomes. The problem with the former claim is that it is not true; many
authors have shown that certain institutional constraints can shrink the set of
feasible policy outcomes considerably.[30] The problem with the second claim is
that Riker provides no theoretical ground for the argument that liberal institutions produce outcomes that are less arbitrary than do populist institutions.[31]
While we agree wholeheartedly with these critiques of Riker's argument, we
omit a further discussion because our own criticism of Riker's argument takes a
different tack. That is, while we agree that Riker's interpretation of the impossibility results misses his intended target for various reasons, we believe that
a different interpretation of the social choice results provides a more effective
refutation of Riker's conclusions.[32]

2.3 MACKIE'S DEFENSE OF DEMOCRACY

In *Democracy Defended*, Gerry Mackie argues that by rejecting populist
notions of democracy, Riker rejects democracy itself because "[w]hat almost
everyone means by democracy is what Riker calls populist democracy."[33] In
defending democracy against Riker's particular school of thought, Mackie aims
to accomplish a single task: to demonstrate "the possibility of the accurate and
fair amalgamation of opinions and wants."[34] And because Riker's argument
hinges in large part on the impossibility theorems of Arrow and Gibbard and
Satterthwaite, this task is largely undertaken by an exhaustive denouncement
of nearly every claim made by those authors. Thus, if these results are shown
to have little or no normative force of their own, Mackie argues, then fair
preference amalgamation is possible, and then Riker is wrong. How one moves
from the *possibility* of fair amalgamation to the *implementation* of fair amalgamation is a different question but one that we will see is not particularly
difficult to resolve given Mackie's argument.

---

[29] Amadae (2003), p. 169.
[30] See Shepsle (1979), Banks (1985), Miller (1977), Miller (1980), and McGann (2006), among
others.
[31] Coleman and Ferejohn (1986), p. 8.
[32] In colloquial terms, one can describe many of the prior positive political theory critiques of
Riker's arguments as "yeah, but..." objections, whereas we believe our critique to be of a more
assertive "no" variety.
[33] *Ibid.*
[34] *Ibid.*

In an attempt to negate (or, perhaps, neuter) the impossibility theorems Mackie, point by point, argues that each criterion of fairness or sensibility used in the theorems is in some way misguided as a desideratum of preference amalgamation. Arrow's Theorem tells us that with an unrestricted preference domain, every aggregation rule that is Pareto efficient, independent of irrelevant alternatives, and transitive is a dictatorship. Mackie argues that there is no reason to think of unrestricted domain, Pareto efficiency, independence of irrelevant alternatives, or transitivity as necessarily desirable properties of voting rules. Therefore, there may be many sensible and good procedures that violate one or more of these conditions and that are nondictatorial.

More specifically, what is wrong with the axioms? While Mackie focuses in large part on independence of irrelevant alternatives and unrestricted domain, Mackie's critique of unrestricted domain is arguably the heart of his argument. More than half of the book's nearly 500 pages is dedicated to the notion of the Condorcet cycle (i.e., the "paradox of voting" discussed earlier). Specifically, Mackie attempts to debunk every empirical claim of a real-world preference cycle, many of which were originally forwarded by Riker. The possibility of cycles forms the basis of Riker's argument that democratic politics is meaningless, as a majority preference cycle occurs only if pairwise majority voting generates an intransitive outcome. If cycles do not occur in practice, then pairwise majority voting is capable of yielding an unambiguously best outcome consistent with the majority will. Accordingly, Mackie argues, the absence of majority rule cycles implies that a coherent and meaningfully populist conception of democracy is possible. Mackie's principal "defense" of democracy, then, involves demonstrating that majority preference cycles do not occur in practice.

Establishing that majority rule cycles do not occur in practice requires that one demonstrate that the realized distributions of individuals' preferences in society are (or at least tend to be) "restricted" and possess a common structure so as to yield a Condorcet winner. Put another way, one must show that, in a specific sense, there is never too much preference heterogeneity or diversity. Put another way, preferences must be similar enough to guarantee that there is a "best" outcome in the sense that it is preferred to every other alternative by a majority of voters. A standard restriction that implies the existence of such an alternative is that preferences satisfy a *single-peakedness condition*. We return to this condition later, but for now it can be described as requiring that the collection of alternatives essentially differ from each other along one identifiable dimension (e.g., policies can be ordered along a liberal-conservative axis, each individual has a favorite spot (or "ideal point") on this axis, and each individual dislikes policies that are increasingly liberal or conservative, moving away from the individual's ideal point). Mackie (and others, to be discussed later) argue that there are many reasons to think that peoples' preferences are restricted in one of these ways. Essentially, these reasons come down to the fact that people "live in the same world and have similar interests in that world;

for example most prefer prosperity to torture of kittens to suicidal nuclear war."[35] If preferences are sufficiently homogenous, then Condorcet cycles may not exist, and the practical import of Arrow's condition of unrestricted domain is negated. This is important because Arrow's Theorem implies only that an aggregation rule satisfying Pareto efficiency, IIA, and no dictator will violate transitivity at *some* configuration of preferences. If a rule produces undesirable outcomes only in situations that will never occur in practice (i.e., preference profiles that do not occur empirically), then, at least in practical terms, it is arguable that such a violation should not be viewed as a criticism of the rule.

As noted earlier, the proofs of the theorems of Arrow and Gibbard and Satterthwaite are closely related. For example, the proof of the Gibbard-Satterthwaite Theorem also leverages the presumption of unrestricted domain to show that any nondictatorial voting rule offers individuals an incentive to strategically misrepresent their preferences. As with Arrow's theorem, the conclusion is that this incentive exists "at some preference profile." If one posits that some preference profiles do not occur in practice, then the Gibbard-Satterthwaite Theorem's conclusion may be irrelevant from an empirical standpoint. In particular, there are nondictatorial choice functions that induce no incentive for strategic misrepresentation if (stated and) revealed preferences can be restricted so as to not admit a cyclic majority preference relation.

Taken as a whole, refuting the relevance of unrestricted domain can lead to the conclusion that not only does a majority will exist but also that there also exists a voting system that can elicit it: majority voting over all pairs of alternatives. Mackie's interpretation of the Arrow and Gibbard-Satterthwaite Theorems can thus be summarized as follows. Attempts to directly and meaningfully translate individuals' preferences into a collective choice will not necessarily fail because, in general, majority preference cycles do not exist. In general, there exists an outcome that reflects the "majority will," and moreover, when such an outcome exists, many voting systems will be able to discover it.

Of course, the assertion that majority preference cycles will *never* occur empirically is ridiculous. Mackie acknowledges this but asserts that they are either rare or inconsequential. More important, perhaps, Mackie suggests that when a cycle does exist, a "cyclebusting" voting rule such as the Borda count or plurality rule can always be used.[36] While such a rule does not remedy the fact that any alternative chosen by the group will be viewed by a majority of voters as being inferior to some other alternative, Mackie argues that the rule will provide a measure of stability to the political process and will, hopefully, produce an outcome with a broad degree of support.[37]

---

[35] *Ibid.*

[36] *Ibid.*

[37] While our goal here is not to refute Mackie's arguments per se, it is important to note that Mackie's suggestion here is unsatisfactory for several reasons. Most important, as described earlier, the objections of Riker were partially founded on the fact that the choice of rule will

2.4 ADDITIONAL REBUTTALS BY DEMOCRATIC THEORY

Although Mackie provides what may be the most comprehensive critique of the countermajoritarian interpretation of social choice, other democratic theorists have tackled Riker's objections from different angles.

Deliberation and Structuring Preferences

One strain of democratic theory, exemplified in work by Habermas (1987), Miller (1992), and Dryzek and List (2003),[38] argues that the process of *deliberation* provides a route around the dilemmas raised by the impossibility theorems. Similar to Mackie, these authors take aim at Arrow's condition of unrestricted domain. However, unlike Mackie, who argues that the condition is *prima facie* incorrect in most situations, these authors argue that the deliberative process works to alter individuals' preferences in such a way so as to induce "preference structuration," or change. That is, as opposed to positing that preferences are initially restricted so as to yield an unambiguous "collective preference," this line of thought suggests that deliberation generates (or, "structures") individual preferences so as produce such a collective preference.

Dryzek and List (2003) provide one particularly clear account of the process of structuration, whereby deliberation produces consensus at least on a single, underlying, and shared dimension of conflict, if not on which alternative should be chosen. When this type of structuration occurs, the resulting preferences can satisfy the single-peakedness condition described earlier, and pairwise majority voting will not be susceptible to cycling. Thus, these authors argue, the impossibility results can be reconciled with "populist style" democratic voting when democratic procedures have a deliberative aspect.

Rejectionist Critiques

Another group of scholars, whom Mackie terms the "rejectionist democrats,"[39] argues that social choice theory as an intellectual endeavor is meaningless on its own merits and, more provocatively, that both the substance and ensuing interpretations of the impossibility theorems pose a threat to democracy itself.

---

in effect be a choice of the outcome in such situations (e.g., when there is a cyclic majority preference relation), there is no guarantee that any two "cyclebusting" rules such as Borda count or plurality rule will return the same choice. Accordingly, to argue that one should use a cyclebusting rule to deal with majority preference cycles, one is forced to suggest which rule should be used or at least the rule that should be used by the group to choose which rule should be used to select which policy should be chosen.

[38] *Ibid.*
[39] *Ibid.*

Pildes and Anderson (1990) offer a critique in this vein, beginning their attack on social choice theory by asking: "...does the formal logic of social choice theory truly compel us to abandon the search for collective decision-making processes that are both fair and rational; must we relinquish the effort to find meaning in our collective actions?"[40] To prove their assertion that the answers to both questions are "no," they critique what they claim are the underpinnings of social choice theory: in particular, the notion that individual preferences, the inputs to the Arrovian aggregation rule, are "consistent" in the sense of being transitive. This is because to suppose that individuals have transitive orderings of the alternatives under consideration is, in Pildes and Anderson's words, to suppose that individuals seek "the maximization of some single value..."[41] And this cannot be the case; individuals seek to maximize multiple, potentially competing, values, and "as individuals actually experience these values, they do not rest on a single scale and cannot be reduced to comparisons along a single, shared dimension."[42] Without transitive inputs there is no reason to expect collective choices to be transitive, and thus, they argue, Arrow's Theorem is seriously misguided to the point of being totally meaningless.

While the logic of Pildes and Anderson's argument is fatally flawed,[43] we are nonetheless in complete agreement with many of their claims. Similar to them, we believe that the incommensurability of values may lead to irresolvable conflicts and that these conflicts pose particular challenges to democratic governance.[44] In the face of these challenges, we similarly see the role of democratic politics as being, in part, "to involve not just choices but the reasons behind those choices..."[45] However, unlike Pildes and Anderson, we argue that it is *precisely* the impossibility theorems that give import to these claims. After all, Arrow's Theorem tells us that, in the face of these irresolvable conflicts, democratic procedures must do more than simply select a best outcome, as such an outcome will often not exist. In such cases, it follows, democratic procedures must legitimate their choices on a basis other than being the unambiguous product of popular will.

To claim, as Pildes and Anderson do, that the impossibility theorems are irrelevant to our understanding of democratic politics because a richer theory of choice is needed is to ignore an important selection effect. In particular, arguing that the impossibility theorems are irrelevant because "...social norms and institutional rules and practices are critical to enable democratic outcomes to be

---

[40] Pildes and Anderson (1990), p. 2127.
[41] *Ibid*, p. 2214.
[42] *Ibid*.
[43] *Ibid*.
[44] *Ibid*, p. 2166.
[45] Pildes and Anderson (1990), p. 2166, and quoted in Mackie (2003), p. 35.

meaningful or coherent..."[46] misses the most crucial point: these results precisely and elegantly indicate *why* such norms, rules, and practices are required to produce meaningful and coherent democratic outcomes. In other words, if the impossibility theorems were indeed irrelevant and an unambiguous "best" social choice always existed, then a richer theory of institutions and collective choice would not be needed. The theory we present in Chapters 5 and 6 acknowledges and leverages this logical step as it presents an explicit social choice–theoretic notion of legitimacy.

Similarly, counter to the views of Pildes and Anderson, we argue that social choice theory is particularly well suited to studying value pluralism and incommensurability.[47] Value pluralism is, after all, captured by the assumption and utilization of the presumption of unrestricted domain. Particularly, when one notices that the impossibility theorems are about aggregation in the abstract and does not rely in any fashion on a linkage with individual or social "preferences," the imposition of IIA is *exactly* an acknowledgement of incommensurability.[48] In other words, Arrow's framework *embraces* the premise that the criteria to be aggregated are incommensurable, regardless of the nature of the criteria themselves.

In sum, Pildes and Anderson's arguments mirror those discussed earlier in focusing too narrowly on one particular interpretation of the impossibility results. Furthermore, arguments about the impossibility theorems that rely on the presumption that inputs to the aggregation problem need be individual preferences are fatally flawed. Of course, such a presumption is not inconsistent with the results, but it is logically incorrect to ascribe or deny substantive importance to the results themselves on the basis of such an interpretation.

On the other hand, our interpretation – which we develop in the following chapter – is wholly consistent with many of the arguments forwarded by Pildes and Anderson. Indeed, we believe that our approach productively formalizes and enhances many of their arguments. Similar to the match between our arguments and those of Riker, our approach comports with that of Pildes and Anderson in structure and starting points but yields entirely opposing conclusions. As noted earlier, we will argue in the following chapter that Arrow's independence of irrelevant alternatives condition captures precisely the kind of value incommensurability with which Pildes and Anderson are preoccupied. Moreover, the theory of legitimate choice we present in the second half of the book focuses exclusively on the linkage between collective choices and the reasons supporting those choices and does so within a purely social choice–theoretic framework.

---

[46] Pildes and Anderson (1990), p. 2200.
[47] *Ibid*, pp. 2143–2166.
[48] We return to this point in more detail in Section 3.3.

2.5 RIKER AND HIS CRITICS: UNLIKELY ALLIES?

In the end, we believe that Riker and many of his critics ask very little – indeed, too little – of democracy. To Riker, democracy is a "second-best" system in which collective choices do not necessarily reflect anything meaningful about the values of the societies they govern. Democratic procedures simply let people throw the *really* bad politicians out of office. While democratic institutions and procedures may enable collective decision making, they can confer no legitimacy to the resulting decisions themselves. To Mackie, democratic procedures are, in a very real sense, irrelevant. Because the preferences of individuals in society are structured so similarly in terms of either what people explicitly want or at least in terms of how individuals perceive the issues under consideration, there always exists a best outcome, and all we ask of democracy is to find it. Mackie argues that many reasonable systems are capable of finding such an outcome – in which case, problem solved; democracy is easy. The deliberative democrats argue in a similar vein that the process of deliberation induces preference structuration and thus returns us to Mackie's world in which there is a best outcome.

We take a very different view than Mackie, Riker, and the deliberative democrats by arguing that it is the possibility of cycles that makes democracy *meaningful.* The fact that there may be no best decision, that any choice we make can always be deemed inferior to other possible choices on the basis of criteria that society collectively deems relevant and important, is precisely what makes democratic decision making challenging and significant. Our argument bears some similarity to Anthony McGann's argument that Riker's critics yield too much, that all of these individuals presuppose that the widespread existence of cycling undermines democracy.[49] However, McGann argues that cycling *strengthens* democracy because the existence of cyclic preferences coincides with the existence of multiple alternative majorities that can each win and lose on different issue dimensions; deliberation and compromise will ensue as winners acknowledge that they must compensate losers sufficiently so as not to be quickly undermined themselves.[50] McGann argues that institutions limiting cycling, and majority rule cycling in particular should be viewed as suspect because they necessarily advantage certain individuals and alternatives over others. Majority rule, as a principle, is the unique decision process that is procedurally fair. The downside of majority rule, McGann acknowledges, is that it fails to produce a unique outcome.

While we find McGann's argument reasonable and persuasive in many respects, one question remains: How can an outcome – one that was selected via majority rule for example – be justified as a legitimate social choice when other outcomes clearly dominate it via the same majority principle? Here McGann is

---

[49] McGann (2006), p. 74.
[50] Miller (1983) and cited in Mackie (2006), p. 9.

less specific and says that the set of outcomes attainable via majority rule can be narrowed to the uncovered set, and that particular choices "... will result in part from bargaining."[51] While we agree that the impossibility theorems tell us that one should not hold out hope of a single, best social choice, our response to this is more in line with that of Pildes and Anderson: the possibility of cycles necessitates an approach to collective decision making in which reasons, or explanations, play a central role. Intransitivities arise when for any decision *A*, there is some other decision *B* that dominates it. Accordingly, justifying (or legitimating) the selection of *A* requires the provision of a rationale not only for the selection of *A* but also for the failure to choose *B*. In Part II of this book, we present a theory in which reasons or explanations along these lines are treated as a fundamental aspect of legitimate democratic governance.

To our knowledge, *Democracy Defended* represents the most comprehensive critique of the "Rikerian" interpretation of social choice and provides, along the way, particularly damning indictments of each of Arrow's axioms. These indictments synthesize decades' worth of arguments made by numerous scholars against the real-world relevance of the social choice enterprise. By nature of its scope and the tone and the pointedness of its attacks, we feel that the ball is now in our court, and we dedicate the following chapters to our aim of defending Arrow's axioms against the charges leveled at them and to show, counter to Riker's claim, that the impossibility results are wholly consistent with a meaningful conception of democratic choice. We do this through the best means we know how: through the use of social choice–theoretic concepts, tools, and arguments. Ultimately, our interpretation of the impossibility theorems is intended to motivate our own theory of democratic decision making that follows in the second part of the book.

---

[51] McGann (2006), p. 210.

3

Social Choice Defended

The previous chapter details a long-standing debate concerning the field of social choice theory. On one side stands Riker's *Liberalism Against Populism*, in which the impossibility results are interpreted as proof of the arbitrariness and meaninglessness of populist methods of democratic choice, methods intended to embody a "will of the people" in the actions taken by elected representatives on their behalf.[1] On the other side is a large literature intending to counter these claims by arguing that the impossibility theorems themselves are of little relevance, and perhaps even counterproductive, to the study of democracy. The problem with the theorems, these authors argue, is first that the axioms are unfounded as desiderata of good collective choice procedures, and second, that even if the axioms were well founded, the "impossibility" Arrow predicts is empirically so unlikely to be observed that the theorems themselves are irrelevant.

In this chapter we take up the debate in a more detailed, "claim-by-claim" fashion. In so doing, we argue that the conditions underlying the theorems are in fact both normatively desirable and applicable to many real-world settings. We describe how many of the arguments of scholars who attack social choice theory are based on gross misinterpretations of the meaning of the impossibility results. We begin by reiterating a point we made in the introduction to this book: *virtually every meaningful decision involves trade-offs between potentially conflicting goals.*

In politics, these trade-offs are made at every level of government and color every aspect of political life. At the individual level, a voter may face a trade-off between casting a vote in favor of a candidate who mirrors his own views on taxation versus another who mirrors his views on war; a politician may trade-off appeasing his constituents versus voting his conscience. More generally,

---

[1] Riker (1982), p. 11.

every democratically elected government must choose policies when the goals of its citizens conflict with one another. For example, as Pildes and Anderson point out, the Founders described their purpose in drawing up what became the Constitution of the United States of America as "to form a more perfect Union, establish justice, insure domestic tranquility, provide for the common defense, promote the general welfare, and secure the blessings of liberty to ourselves and our posterity."[2] Of course, it is easy to think of situations in which providing for the common defense have conflicted with securing the blessings of liberty. Even more important, of course, concepts such as general welfare and justice are essentially contested precisely because any sensible definition implies nontrivial trade-offs between the rights and interests of various individuals and groups.

Considering the actual practice of policymaking, examples of such conflicts are ubiquitous. The redistricting cases discussed earlier are a specific instance in which courts are faced with the task of reconciling national laws or constitutional provisions with the decisions of state and local authorities. Central banks have the potentially conflicting goals of high employment and low inflation. Legislatures are expected to provide high-quality public services at the lowest possible cost. Government officials at various levels ("bureaucrats") are often explicitly directed by statutes, executive orders, and court directives to consider multiple substantive and technical criteria when making public policy determinations. More than simple check boxes that government officials must fill in before promulgating their decisions, these criteria are often presented explicitly as requiring that the official make trade-offs when the criteria disagree with one another.[3] For example, the Federal Aviation Administration describes its "continuing mission" as "to provide the safest, most efficient aerospace system in the world."[4] As described by statute, the Federal Communications Commission's mission is to "make available, so far as possible, to all the people of the United States, without discrimination on the basis of race, color, religion, national, origin, or sex, rapid, efficient, Nation-wide and world-wide wire and radio communication service with adequate facilities at reasonable charges."[5] Similarly, the Department of Homeland Security describes its mission in terms of multiple goals:

> We will lead the unified national effort to secure America. We will prevent and deter terrorist attacks and protect against and respond to threats and hazards to the Nation. We will secure our national borders while welcoming lawful immigrants, visitors, and trade.[6]

These examples are intended to make a couple of important points. First, practical policy decisions are often explicitly based on aggregation of various

---

[2] Preamble, United States Constitution. Quoted in Pildes and Anderson (1990), pp. 2145–2146.
[3] Consider, for example, Cass, Diver, and Beermann (2002), pp. 333–502.
[4] http://www.faa.gov/about/mission. Accessed on January 4, 2013.
[5] 47 U.S.C. §151.
[6] Department of Homeland Security 2008 Strategic Plan, p. 3.

criteria, both objective and subjective.[7] When confronted with the task of furthering various criteria, each of the decision-making bodies discussed could likely make a number of reasonable decisions. No given decision, however, can be deemed "perfect" because each decision will involve a compromise with respect to one or more goals. Moreover, if the goals of government are not hierarchically ranked – if the goals are deemed to be of equal importance or even incommensurable – then the task of defending a decision that has traded off one such goal for another becomes politically difficult. Accordingly, the impossibility theorems are relevant beyond voting or other "preference aggregation" settings. This point clarifies the importance of a broader interpretation of both the axioms undergirding and the conclusions flowing from the theorems. In other words, as we engage more directly later in the book, the primitives of social choice theory are helpful for formalizing and theorizing about general policymaking institutions. Indeed, given the complexities of the interactions between voters and their elected representatives,[8] these tools are arguably even more useful in the analysis of policymaking institutions that are *not* directly accountable to voters. Courts and bureaucratic agencies, as classes of political institutions, are excellent examples of policymaking apparatuses that are (or perhaps should be) capable of being described as either aggregation rules or choice functions.

Second, the examples remind us that, in many contexts, the choice of factors to be considered by government officials in making their decisions is a fundamentally political decision.[9] This point is particularly important when considering debates about the empirical relevance of the unrestricted domain assumption. In other words, the political design of policymaking institutions by, for example, representative bodies such as legislatures can be thought of as a problem that includes the specification of the goals of the institution in choosing policies and, more precisely, the criteria that should be used to measure or gauge the institution's performance. As the redistricting example makes clear,

---

[7] Note that we have not touched upon the difficulty of gauging or measuring the criteria to be aggregated. Furthermore, we *will not* touch upon this important and interesting issue in this book. Including this additional complexity does nothing to simplify the aggregation problems that motivate our analysis. More provocatively, the choice of how to measure a criterion is itself an aggregation problem (e.g., choosing and combining summary statistics, aggregating expert opinions, constructing and analyzing survey instruments). Accordingly, we acknowledge this empirically relevant dimension of complexity and move along.

[8] Specifically, representative democracy is a particularly vexing principal-agent problem in the sense that even if there is a collective will, there may be serious difficulties in ensuring that an elected representative will discern and then faithfully implement it.

[9] With respect to administrative policymaking, see Cushman (1941), pp. 417–478; 666–698 for a discussion of this before the passage of the Administrative Procedure Act (APA) (1946). McCubbins, Noll, and Weingast (1987, 1989) provide a canonical treatment of the political implications of institutional design in the post-APA era.

there is most assuredly no reason to suppose that the set of possible criteria is structured or restricted in some a priori fashion.[10]

3.1 INPUTS TO THE AGGREGATION PROBLEM

We now return to the redistricting example presented in our introductory discussion of *Veith* v. *Juberlier*. In this case, the Supreme Court sought a "fairness" standard for assessing the constitutionality of the State of Pennsylvania's congressional districting plan. The Court's specific concerns in that case were whether a political gerrymander had occurred and, if so, whether it was appropriate for the Court to review its particulars (i.e., whether such a gerrymander was "justiciable"). While the Court ultimately maintained that political gerrymanders are justiciable, the justices could not agree on a constitutionally discernible standard for evaluating such claims. In essence, the Court sought a formula for aggregating a diverse set of fairness criteria into a single manageable standard; they failed in their attempt. In colloquial terms, a majority of the justices agreed that the Court could find a formula to judge and potentially repair districting plans drawn for political purposes, but no majority agreed on what that formula should be.

Redistricting as Aggregation

Conceiving of redistricting as an aggregation problem is straightforward. In this section, we lay out an explicit conceptualization of redistricting as the aggregation of various criteria, each of which ranks various redistricting plans. There are countless other ways one can think of redistricting as an aggregation problem: for example, while we focus on properties of the districts themselves, one could consider the effect of districts on various political outcomes. Fortunately, our purposes here are more modest than offering "the" conclusive

---

[10] A subtle point remains here. In particular, one could argue that, while the set of criteria should be construed as satisfying unrestricted domain, perhaps individual preferences over the choice of such criteria might inherit the restricted structure that, for example, Mackie asserts describes much of politics. There are three responses to this objection. First, this argument is dispositive only with respect to environments in which the structure holds. In other words, even if preferences are relatively constrained (e.g., single peaked) with respect to some policies, it is unclear that this is true for all policy realms. Relatedly, such a conclusion then prompts the question of why a legislature representing such constituents would grant discretion to unelected agents as opposed to simply statutorily enshrining the "correct" policy and delegating "mere" implementation to unelected officials. Second, the argument requires that this form of structure exists in a stable form through time and, furthermore, that this stability is perceived and believed by political actors through time. The final point is practical: it is unclear at best whether legislators and voters universally reveal preferences over the criteria in a sophisticated fashion that accords with what their latent political preferences should rationally "induce" in terms of revealed instrumental preferences over the choice of criteria.

representation of redistricting. Rather, we are interested only in clarifying that representing redistricting as an aggregation problem is feasible and sensible.

To these purposes, we note first that the seven goals listed below have been recognized by the judiciary as neutral "traditional districting principles," above and beyond the prioritized goal of equal population. While federal law does not explicitly identify these goals, they are generally acknowledged as being reasonable and neutral principles of fairness in districting.[11]

1. Compactness[12]
2. Contiguity[13]
3. Preservation of counties and other political subdivisions[14]
4. Preservation of communities of interest[15]
5. Preservation of cores of prior districts[16]
6. Protection of incumbents[17]
7. Compliance with Section 2 of the Voting Rights Act[18].

Of these seven principles, compliance with the three more objective principles of compactness, contiguity, and the preservation of counties and political subdivisions has been regarded by the courts as being fundamental to a successful districting plan.[19] Furthermore, the statutes and constitutions of many states mandate that redistricting plans be drawn so as to maximize one or more of the above criteria.[20] For example, West Virginia explicitly requires that congressional districting procedures maximize compactness, respect contiguity, and preserve counties:

> For the election of representatives to Congress, the state shall be divided into districts, corresponding in number with the representatives to which it may be entitled; which districts shall be formed of contiguous counties, and be compact. Each district shall contain, as nearly as may be, an equal number of population, to be determined according to the rule prescribed in the constitution of the United States.[21]

---

[11] "Racial Gerrymandering," in *Redistricting Law 2000*, National Conference of State Legislatures: Denver, CO, 1999.

[12] *Shaw v. Reno*, 509 U.S. 630, 647 (1993); *Bush v. Vera*, 517 U.S. 952, 959 (1996); *DeWitt v. Wilson*, 856 F. Supp 1409, 1414 (E.D. Cal 1994), summarily affirmed, 515 U.S.1170 (1995).

[13] *Shaw v. Reno*, 509 U.S. 630, 647 (1993).

[14] *Shaw v. Reno*, 509 U.S. 630, 647 (1993); *Abrams v. Johnson*, 521 U.S. 74(1997).

[15] *Shaw v. Reno*, 509 U.S. 630, 647 (1993); *Abrams v. Johnson*, 521 U.S. 74(1997).

[16] *Abrams v. Johnson*, 521 U.S. 74 (1997).

[17] *Abrams v. Johnson*, 521 U.S. 74 (1997).

[18] *Shaw v. Hunt*, 517 U.S. 899, 915 (1996).

[19] "Racial Gerrymandering," in *Redistricting Law 2000*, a publication of the National Conference of State Legislatures.

[20] Details of each state's set of criteria are summarized and discussed in Levitt (2010).

[21] Constitution of West Virginia, Article I, Section 4.

Although each state effectively ascertains on its own what it means to "meet" any of the goals implied by these principles, our point stands on the fact that these goals can and do conflict with one another under any sensible measurement scheme.

Thus, the process of redistricting involves aggregating various criteria such as contiguity, compactness, and preservation of political communities into a single choice. Regardless of whether one is considering an election, the construction and passage of a statute by a legislature, the formulation and implementation of a policy by an administrative agency, or the evaluation and adjudication of a redistricting plan by a court or independent commission, the goal is to *aggregate multiple criteria into a single choice*. Furthermore, in nearly every interesting case, the process is intended to do so in a way that renders *no single criterion dispositive*. Referring to the redistricting example, district plans are not ranked solely based on, say, the compactness of the districts.[22]

This point is made clearer in a social choice framework, so we now revisit Equation 2.1, in which we described the preferences of two individuals, Persons 1 and 2, over three alternatives x, y, and z as follows:

$$\rho = \begin{array}{l} x \succ_1 y \succ_1 z \\ y \succ_2 z \succ_2 x \end{array}$$

While the above profile was originally used to describe two individuals' preferences (Person 1 prefers x to y to z, and Person 2 prefers y to z to x), the same profile could just as easily describe three districting plans, x, y, and z, as follows. In particular, $\succ_1$ could represent "Principle 1" (say, compactness) and $\succ_2$ could represent "Principle 2" (say, equal population). In this interpretation, districting plan x is more compact than plan y, which is more compact than plan z. The districts under plan y have "more equal" populations than plan z, the districts of which have "more equal" populations than plan x.[23]

The simple point we are making here before turning to a more detailed discussion of Arrow's axioms is that one can conceive of the inputs to the collective choice problem as being factors that we deem relevant to the decision-making process – in other words, the inputs to the aggregation problem are simply criteria that should be (or, perhaps, simply are) considered in order to make the decision. Each relevant factor orders the alternatives under consideration, and these orderings may or may not conflict with one another. With this more general interpretation of the aggregation problem made clear, we now consider each of Arrow's axioms in turn. Our purpose is to describe and defend each of the axioms in this more general interpretation.

---

[22] There are several extant measures of compactness. Good reviews of these measures are provided by Young (1988); Niemi, Grofman, Carlucci, and Hofeller (1990); Altman (1998); and Chambers and Miller (2008).

[23] As mentioned earlier, numerous measures of compactness could be used in practice to generate an ordering analogous to $\succ_1$. With respect to equal population, there are similarly numerous measures that one could use to generate an ordering analogous to $\succ_2$.

3.2 UNRESTRICTED DOMAIN

As discussed earlier, the condition of unrestricted domain requires that the aggregation process can return an ordering of the alternatives under consideration for any given profile of inputs. The requirement has been criticized by numerous authors as being empirically unrealistic. However, these authors universally focus attention on the problem of aggregating individual preferences over alternatives and then argue that, in reality, individual preferences are structured similarly in most decision-making contexts. This can mean either of two things: first, it could be the case that, when a group of people sets about making a collective choice, their preferences will likely agree on what is the best choice. Alternatively, it could mean, even if there is significant disagreement within the group about what the best choice is, the members will at least agree that the potential choices can be arrayed along a single "dimension" of disagreement. These two cases are substantively different and deserve separate treatment, to which we now turn.

In the first case, the absence of significant disagreement about the best outcome may stem from the fact that most individuals prefer outcomes that are universalistic in nature as opposed to those that are more closely associated with narrow self-interest. Indeed, Mackie makes a vocal argument for the empirical likelihood of such preferences, citing examples such as a ruling by the Los Angeles County Board of Supervisors to divide federal funds equally among its five districts and experimental evidence showing that committees asked to divide a sum of money frequently settled on equal distributions.[24] In the case that all or most individuals have universalistic preferences favoring "the common good," then it is empirically unlikely, Mackie argues, to ever observe preference distributions that could generate a cycle. In this case, there is a best alternative, and it is clearly the alternative that maximizes the common good.

Of course, general support for universalistic (or, more generally, "group-oriented") outcomes is a common characteristic of individual behavior and individual preferences in collective decision-making environments. However, there is absolutely no reason to presume that the inputs to an aggregation problem – whether they are preferences or goals – are structured so as to support the contention that unrestricted domain is empirically irrelevant. For example, we do not disagree that groups frequently choose universalistic outcomes in environments in which people are asked to divide a sum of money among themselves. However, these cases represent a "best case" for observing the selection of universalistic outcomes. This is because the notion of universalism that Mackie leans on is entirely unambiguous in such cases: each individual's allocation of the pie is transparent and unambiguous in the sense of being

---

[24] Mackie (2003), pp. 102–103.

easily comparable across individuals. In more complex environments – as are commonly observed in real-world political decision making – the proper notion of "the common good" will often not be so clear.

For example, what is a universalistic outcome when people have dramatically different conceptions of the good life? Some individuals may prefer spending on common green spaces, others on environmental cleanup efforts, and still others on improving public schools. Is a universalistic outcome determined by the amount of these goods provided or the amount of resources devoted to each? How does one account for how many people prefer, all things considered, an extra dollar of education spending to an extra dollar spent on cleanup efforts? How does one properly figure in factors such as the effects of the decision on health outcomes or personal liberties? In short, the definition and characterization of a universalistic outcome is itself an aggregation problem. Accordingly, *objections to the applicability of the impossibility theorems based on the claim that individual preferences tend to favor group-oriented outcomes are ironically overturned by the impossibility theorems themselves.*

Turning to the second case in which preferences disagree, majority rule cycles might not emerge because a single dimension of disagreement exists. As discussed earlier, such a critique is based on a presumption that individuals have single-peaked preferences over the set of feasible alternatives. Such claims are rarely based on a belief that innate individual preferences over the alternatives themselves do indeed satisfy the strong restrictions implied by single-peakedness. Rather, individuals might recognize that compromise need occur along one well-defined aspect of the problem at hand.

For example, a group of citizens may face a choice between various tax policies. If they all agree that the only thing differentiating these policies is the tax rate (if it is a flat tax, for example), then compromise might be possible along this well-ordered dimension and there will exist a "best" policy in the sense of one policy being majority-preferred to every other policy (i.e., a Condorcet winner) with respect to what we might call the individuals' "structured" preferences. Along these lines, Dryzek and List specifically argue that the process of deliberation can serve to reduce complex disagreements into such a single dimension of conflict. The reduction of conflict occurs through the structuring of individual preferences so as to vary only with respect to that single dimension. Dryzek and List describe the emergence of such individual preferences as *agreement at a meta-level*, which occurs when participants agree "on a common dimension in terms of which the alternatives are to be conceptualized."[25] Thus, even if citizens did not *initially* agree that only tax rates mattered, deliberation might produce agreement on all of the criteria other than the tax rate and thus reduce the problem to a single dimension. Claims that structuration

---

[25] Dryzek and List (2003), p. 14.

may be produced through deliberation have been forwarded by many scholars, and some empirical evidence supports this claim.[26]

We definitely agree that, as an empirical matter, a deliberative process might alter preferences so as to effectively produce agreement about what the question is "really about" and that this agreement might result in structured preferences that satisfy single-peakedness. Furthermore, if deliberation does produce such structure, then a majority vote can subsequently reveal a "best" choice in the sense of one alternative that is majority preferred to every other alternative. However, this possibility is at best only a possibility: the claim that deliberation *always* produces a Condorcet winner is simply not true. More powerfully, even if individuals only suspect that structuration *may* not emerge after deliberation, this contingency combined with strategic individual incentives can undermine the deliberative processes by which structuration might be produced.

This point is made in more detail by Penn, Patty, and Gailmard (2011), who also demonstrate that single-peakedness is not a panacea to the impossibility theorems that plague social choice. Dryzek and List, for example, argue that when preferences are single-peaked, then strategic voting cannot occur, and the Gibbard-Satterthwaite problem is solved: there exist collective decision mechanisms that are guaranteed to induce all individuals to sincerely reveal their true preferences. This argument is used to bolster their claim that deliberation is beneficial because it alters preferences so as to induce single-peakedness, and in many respects, their arguments provide hope for deliberative democrats despite the generally negative conclusions about the coexistence of collective rationality and democratic collective choice. A key claim in Dryzek and List's argument is that preference structuration can eliminate the incentive for a deliberator to misrepresent his or her preferences at the point at which the collective is faced with making a final decision. Citing this work, Mackie goes so far as to state

> We do know for sure that if the distribution of preference orders is such that they are single-peaked, the Gibbard-Satterthwaite Theorem does not apply, there is no chance for strategic voting to succeed.[27]

Despite the evident certainty with which Mackie forwards this claim, it is plainly and tellingly incorrect. As Penn, Patty, and Gailmard (2011) point out, this is not true even for simple, textbook examples of sequential voting over an amendment agenda. In particular, even if preferences are known by the voters to be single-peaked strategic (or "sophisticated") voting strategies will often dictate voting for choices other than one's sincere preference. The existence of such differences is exactly the implication of the Gibbard-Satterthwaite theorem.

---

[26] Theories discussing the production of structuration through deliberation include Mansbridge (1983), Goodin (1986), and Miller (1992). Empirical studies of the emergence of structuration have been offered by Radcliff (1993) and Farrar, Fishkin, Green, List, Luskin, and Paluck (2010).

[27] Mackie (2003), p. 161.

TABLE 3.1. *Manipulation of the "Dimension of Conflict"*

	ρ_1	ρ_2	ρ_3	Cycle
Person 1	$x \succ z \succ y$	$x \succ y \succ z$	$x \succ y \succ z$	$x \succ y \succ z$
Person 2	$y \succ z \succ x$	$y \succ x \succ z$	$y \succ z \succ x$	$y \succ z \succ x$
Person 3	$z \succ x \succ y$	$z \succ x \succ y$	$z \succ y \succ x$	$z \succ x \succ y$
Outcome	Median = z	Median = x	Median = y	x: 1 manipulates ρ_1 y: 2 manipulates ρ_2 z: 3 manipulates ρ_3

Furthermore, these differences are caused exactly by the "chance" that strategic voting might "succeed."

More generally, the preceding table illustrates why individuals with single-peaked preferences may not want the true "dimension of conflict" revealed. This simple example depicts three different preference profiles that are each single-peaked. Because each profile is single-peaked and there are three individuals, Black's Median Voter Theorem informs us that each profile yields a unique Condorcet winner.[28] Accordingly, suppose that policy is ultimately chosen by a choice function that selects the Condorcet winner whenever one exists (after all, one benefit of preference structuration is the existence of such a policy). Thus, for ρ_1 it yields z as the outcome, and so on.

What does this choice function yield when it receives a collection of ballots that does not admit a Condorcet winner? Table 3.1 shows that regardless of which outcome the choice function chooses, the function is always manipulable by someone at a single-peaked profile of preferences. For example, if the choice function chooses x as the outcome when it receives a cyclic profile of ballots, then the function is manipulable by Person 1 at the (sincere) profile ρ_1. In particular, Person 1 has an incentive to report that his preferences are $x \succ y \succ z$, when they are truly $x \succ z \succ y$. By misrepresenting his preferences this way, he switches the outcome from z (the median voter's ideal point) to x (his own ideal point).

In each case, profitable manipulation by any individual requires that he or she submit a ballot that is itself not single-peaked with respect to the true ordering of alternatives. In this sense, if individuals are not constrained to choose only from the set of ballots that are themselves single-peaked with respect to the ordering of the alternatives that the deliberative process was intended to uncover, we cannot guarantee that some group of individuals (or perhaps an individual on his or her own) will have no incentive to lie about

---

[28] Black (1958). Specifically, the Condorcet winner is the alternative that is the median of the voters' individually most-preferred policies according to any ordering of the alternatives with respect to which the preferences of the individuals are single-peaked (i.e., any ordering consistent with the "dimension of conflict").

the true dimension of conflict. When this incentive manifests itself, the ballots will appear to imply that the policy space is multidimensional in the sense that "there is no single dimension of conflict" or, in other words, that the problem at hand is more complex than a simple "left-right" or "more-less" choice. In other words, even if we begin with a situation in which preferences are already structured in a desirable way, we cannot design an institution that is guaranteed to truthfully elicit those preferences.

In general, one must impose much more restrictive conditions on the preferences produced by the structuration process than simply requiring that they "satisfy single-peakedness" to guarantee that it offers no benefit from misrepresentation.[29] Indeed, the conditions are far more restrictive than has been claimed elsewhere.[30] Specifically, a nondictatorial decisionmaking institution can be ensured to offer no benefit from misrepresentation by a person or coalition only if the details of the structure of the individuals' preferences are written into the rules of the institution itself (i.e., the institution knows and can use the underlying ordering of alternatives). This is akin to saying that designing a deliberative institution that will eliminate the incentive to participate insincerely in a process of collective preference structuration requires that the institution must use a priori knowledge of the true structure of preferences. In other words, eliminating the possibility of profitable manipulation requires institutional knowledge and utilization of the left-right ordering of the alternative space that will emerge from deliberation *before* the deliberative process begins. Clearly, supposing that the collective choice mechanism itself embodies such knowledge makes the deliberative process unnecessary.

Penn, Patty, and Gailmard's results imply that one should be careful in interpreting the outcome of group choice as representing a social "best" in any real-world collective choice setting *even when preferences are presumed to be single-peaked*. This point is highly relevant for scholars who insist that majority rule cycles are infrequent or untroubling. Our results directly imply that – even if preferences are known to be single-peaked and accordingly admit no cycles – *any* nondictatorial institution will be vulnerable to instances in which one or more groups of individuals may profit by *claiming* that preferences are cyclic. Single-peakedness does not eliminate the possibility of gains through strategic manipulation within real-world institutions because few (if any) policymaking institutions are dictatorial, and few (if any) policymaking institutions limit the preferences that individuals and groups can *claim* to have.

Similarly, it turns out that single-peakedness itself does not solve the problems raised by Arrow's Theorem in the real world. In particular, Gailmard, Patty, and Penn (2008) prove, even if preferences are known to be

---

[29] Penn, Patty, and Gailmard (2011).

[30] In addition to Dryzek and List (2003), the results in Penn, Patty, and Gailmard (2011) appear to be at odds with some of the relevant claims of Grofman and Feld (1988), Miller (1992), and Mackie (2003), among others.

single-peaked, any preference aggregation rule that is Pareto efficient, independent of irrelevant alternatives and transitive must be *neutral*; it must treat each alternative under consideration in precisely the same way, regardless of label. Single-peakedness thus enables us to weaken Arrow's dictator to a neutrality condition.[31] While this is a less disturbing conclusion than provided by Arrow's Theorem, it is nonetheless problematic from an empirical perspective: few real-world institutions satisfy this requirement in the sense that the prevailing (i.e., status quo) policy is typically privileged due to provisions for supermajority requirements, multicameral consideration, or veto players. Thus, any non-neutral decision-making procedure – i.e., most real-world procedures as used in practice – will under some circumstances generate an incentive for individual or collective strategic misrepresentation even when preferences are known to be single-peaked.

In conclusion, we have argued that the condition of unrestricted domain is reasonable and that violations and relaxations of it (e.g., preferences for universalism or preference structuration such as single-peakedness) do not negate the issues raised by the impossibility theorems. Furthermore, while there may be certain settings in which individual preferences are structured through norms of universalism or through deliberation, there is certainly no reason to believe that there should be a common latent structure to which the criteria subject to aggregation will conform. Even when a common structure seems plausible, such settings are necessarily highly stylized and do not represent the vast majority of complex aggregation problems that successful democratic institutions are tasked with solving. Finally, we have illustrated that such a structure is not the panacea that previous authors have suggested. Even if one constrains attention to preference aggregation and supposes that these inputs to the aggregation problem are single-peaked with respect to some common ordering of the alternatives, no real-world political institution is capable of ensuring that elicited preferences will conform to that ordering unless that ordering is known a priori. Accordingly, contra to both Riker and his critics, *we have no assurance that the policy selected by a majoritarian institution reflects the majority will, even in settings in which this notion is well-defined and returns an unambiguously majoritarian choice from the set of alternatives.* This elicitation difficulty is intimately related to the independence of irrelevant alternatives axiom, to which we now turn.

---

[31] It is important to note that the single-peaked domain considered by Gailmard, Patty, and Penn (2008) and Penn, Patty, and Gailmard (2011) includes *all* possible single-peaked profiles and thus profiles that are single-peaked with respect to different underlying orderings of the alternative space. This differentiates them from nearly all prior work on single-peaked domains, which tended to assume that the ordering of the alternatives was known and then required that both preferences and ballots (in the case of the Gibbard-Satterthwaite theorem) be single-peaked with respect to that ordering. By relaxing this assumption, Penn, Patty, and Gailmard (2011) consider scenarios in which many unidimensional orderings are possible and individuals must, for example, deliberate over the final ordering.

3.3 INDEPENDENCE OF IRRELEVANT ALTERNATIVES

We now set about the task of defending the most opaque and least well-understood of Arrow's axioms, that of independence of irrelevant alternatives (IIA). Specifically, we address the three most well-known criticisms of the condition. Our defense centers on presenting and discussing theoretical truths that do not appear to be widely known among democratic theorists.[32] Before moving on to detailed treatments of each of the three criticisms, we offer a brief overview of them.

The first criticism we address concerns the interpretation of IIA as requiring the aggregation rule to use only information about binary, "pairwise" comparisons of alternatives.[33] Some have claimed that this implication of the IIA condition asks too much and that IIA is thus simply about pairwise choices and not about the role of "irrelevant" alternatives at all. We call this the "binary choice critique" and counter this claim with an argument, proved by Blau, that IIA can be replaced with a far weaker condition that is not expressly defined in terms of pairs and that is inarguably about the effect of "irrelevant alternatives" on social choices.[34]

The second criticism we address concerns past confusion surrounding the IIA principle; indeed, Arrow himself at one point in *Social Choice and Individual Values* verbally defends IIA with an argument that does not logically follow from the definition of IIA and later admitted to the error.[35] The concern is that IIA "... cannot be defended as intuitively obvious if sophisticated commentators have trouble grasping even its content." We do not claim that IIA is intuitively obvious, and, of course, the merit of a decision rule should not necessarily depend on its intuitive obviousness. At the same time, we acknowledge that it is difficult to argue for the importance of a condition that is hard to conceptualize. To clarify the appeal of the axiom, we detail and discuss deep and well-known connections between IIA and other more intuitive social choice–theoretic axioms such as strategy-proofness and monotonicity. Specifically, we note and discuss a recently published "meta-theorem" that encompasses both the Arrow and Gibbard-Satterthwaite Theorems and that provides a conceptual linkage between IIA and many of the concepts heretofore described. This result succinctly and clearly establishes that these concepts can be unified and conceptualized in a straightforward way and that they are important considerations for the aggregation problem.

---

[32] At least, we have not seen these facts cited in that literature. Of course, the relevance of our points does not depend on whether notice has been taken of them in other quarters.

[33] Indeed, the condition of IIA is commonly and interchangeably referred to as *binary independence*.

[34] Blau (1971).

[35] See Arrow (1951), p. 27 and Mackie (2003), p. 127. The confusion in question concerns whether the "irrelevant" alternatives are in the choice set or not.

The last criticism we address concerns not only the condition of IIA but also the general notion of an aggregation rule (or choice function). The definition of an aggregation rule takes a profile of ordinal preferences as an input. In other words, in the classic formulations of the aggregation problem, the collective preference (or collective choice) does not respond to numerical scores (e.g., individual utilities) beyond the degree to which these scores order the alternatives. In terms of preference aggregation, this formulation implies that if some measure of an individual's utility from the alternatives in question changes without an accompanying change in the individual's *rankings* over the alternatives, then the social ranking produced by the aggregation rule must remain unchanged.[36] For example, the collective preference (or collective choice) will not change if some individual who initially assigned a score of 10 to alternative *A*, a score of 9 to alternative *B*, and a score of 4 to alternative *C* unilaterally changed his or her scores so that alternative *A* is assigned a score of 100, alternative *B* is assigned a scores of 5, and alternative *C* is assigned a score of 0. In response to these concerns, we present and discuss an observation made by Sen that the requirement of ordinality does not much affect Arrow's result. Arrow's Theorem can be extended to accommodate aggregation rules that take cardinal profiles as an input, provided that the rules do not make interpersonal comparisons of utility.

Before proceeding to our detailed responses to each of these criticisms, it is important to clarify that our goal here is not to argue that IIA should be considered a kind of normative rubicon for the design of successful decision-making procedures. To the contrary, many reasonable procedures that violate this condition are used in practice, including the straightforward and canonical method of plurality rule. Indeed, the use of procedures that violate IIA is itself consistent with Arrow's Theorem to the degree that one thinks that IIA is seen as "less desirable" than the conditions of transitivity, unrestricted domain, Pareto efficiency, and no dictator.

Rather, our goal here is simply to show that violations of IIA do indeed constitute a perversity. Furthermore, the perversity is particularly troubling in contexts in which many alternatives are considered simultaneously, there is good information about the quality of each alternative with respect to each criterion being aggregated, decisions can be scrutinized and revisited, or the correlation between how the various criteria rank alternatives is low. In other words, we believe the normative appeal of IIA is maximized for aggregation problems that occur frequently and involve objective and varying criteria (e.g., routine administrative and judicial decisions). Accordingly and importantly, a mass election is precisely a decision-making scenario that satisfies *none* of these conditions; often the field of candidates is small, there is no specific information about how each voter evaluates each of the candidates, electoral outcomes are not revisited unless there is a claim of fraud, and there is frequently strong

---

[36] Sen (1970*a*), p. 89.

"ideological" correlation between how a slate of candidates is ranked by one voter versus another. In this sense, our "defense" of IIA can be described even more accurately as an explanation of the axiom that both defends its reasonableness and offers guidance regarding its use in the sense of clarifying the implications of its violation.

The Binary Choice Critique

The definition of independence of irrelevant alternatives provided in *Social Choice and Individual Values* states that for any subset of alternatives $S \subseteq X$, the social ranking of alternatives in S should depend only on the individuals' rankings of the elements of S. Since this condition must hold for every subset of alternatives, it must hold in particular for all pairs; consequently, Arrow writes, "[k]nowing the social choices made in pairwise comparisons in turn determines the entire social ordering and therewith the social choice function $C(S)$ for all possible environments." This fact has led some to refer to IIA as binary independence, a term that arguably magnifies the restrictiveness of the IIA axiom.

However, it was speculated, and later proved by Blau, that the requirement that independence hold for all subsets of X could be weakened considerably to only requiring that independence hold on subsets of a certain size.[37] To explain, suppose that the set X contains k alternatives. An aggregation rule f satisfies "m-ary independence" for any integer $m \leq k$ if, for any two profiles ρ_1 and ρ_2 where ρ_1 and ρ_2 are identical on an m-element subset of X, the aggregation rule f yields the same ordering on the m-element subset when applied to each profile.

To make this more concrete, suppose that $X = \{a, b, c, d\}$ and thus contains four elements. First note that, by definition, any aggregation rule will satisfy quaternary (or four-ary) independence on this set. That is, any aggregation rule will satisfy "k-aryness," as this requires that the aggregation rule return the same collective preference when individual preferences over all outcomes are held constant; this means that the aggregation rule returns the same collective preference when given an identical preference profile or, formally, for each preference profile ρ, $f(\rho) = f(\rho)$.

In other words and returning to the case of $X = \{a, b, c, d\}$, any two profiles that are identical on a four-element subset of X are actually the same profile. Now suppose that we require ternary (three-ary) independence but not binary independence. To see exactly how and why ternary independence is weaker than binary independence, consider the following two four-person profiles, ρ_1 and ρ_2, and suppose that we know the social ranking produced at ρ_2 is $b \succ c \succ d \succ a$, as displayed in Table 3.2.

---

[37] Murakami (1968) speculated; Blau (1971) proved.

TABLE 3.2. *Two Preference Profiles*

	ρ_1	ρ_2
Person 1	$a \succ b \succ c \succ d$	$d \succ c \succ a \succ b$
Person 2	$c \succ b \succ a \succ d$	$b \succ c \succ d \succ a$
Person 3	$b \succ a \succ d \succ c$	$b \succ c \succ d \succ a$
Person 4	$a \succ c \succ d \succ b$	$d \succ c \succ a \succ b$
Social Ranking	?	$b \succ c \succ d \succ a$

Note that ternary independence is consistent with *any* collective preference ordering at ρ_1. In other words, knowing that our aggregation rule satisfies ternary independence provides us with no immediate leverage in terms of knowing what the rule produces at ρ_1. This is because there is no triple (i.e., no subset of $\{a, b, c, d\}$ containing three elements) on which ρ_1 and ρ_2 are identical. On the other hand, if we required the aggregation rule to satisfy binary independence, then we would know that at ρ_1, the aggregation rule would have to produce a collective preference satisfying $b \succ a$ because ρ_1 and ρ_2 are identical when restricted to the two-element subset $\{a, b\}$. However, this need not hold if one requires only that the aggregation rule satisfy ternary independence.

It is relatively straightforward to see that any aggregation rule satisfying binary independence necessarily satisfies ternary independence.[38] What Blau proved was that the converse holds as well whenever there are at least four alternatives. That is, even though ternary independence appears to be a weaker condition than binary independence, it in fact implies binary independence. More generally, requiring an aggregation rule to satisfy m−ary independence, with at least $m + 1$ total alternatives, will imply that the rule also satisfies $(m - 1)$-ary independence. By an inductive argument, m−ary independence then implies binary independence, which in turn leads to Arrow's result. The intuition for Blau's result is simple and is illustrated in Table 3.3. Suppose that f satisfies ternary independence and reconsider the two profiles discussed above, ρ_1 and ρ_2. These profiles have identical individual rankings on subset $\{a, b\}$ but not on any triple. However, we can construct a new profile, ρ_3, that is identical to ρ_1 on triple $\{a, b, c\}$ and is identical to ρ_2 on triple $\{a, b, d\}$. By ternary independence, f yields the same social ranking for ρ_1 and ρ_3 on $\{a, b, c\}$ and for ρ_2 and ρ_3 on $\{a, b, d\}$. Thus, f produces the same $\{a, b\}$ ranking for ρ_1 and ρ_2 and consequently satisfies binary independence. Table 3.3 illustrates this logic and shows that knowing the social ordering produced at ρ_2 can provide us with (partial) knowledge of the orderings produced at ρ_1 and ρ_3 with simply the assumption of ternary independence.

---

[38] More generally, if $j \leq k$, satisfaction of j-ary independence by an aggregation rule f implies satisfaction of k-ary independence.

TABLE 3.3. *An Example of Ternary Independence*

	ρ_1	ρ_2	ρ_3
Person 1	$a \succ b \succ c \succ d$	$d \succ c \succ a \succ b$	$d \succ a \succ b \succ c$
Person 2	$c \succ b \succ a \succ d$	$b \succ c \succ d \succ a$	$c \succ b \succ d \succ a$
Person 3	$b \succ a \succ d \succ c$	$b \succ c \succ d \succ a$	$b \succ d \succ a \succ c$
Person 4	$a \succ c \succ d \succ b$	$d \succ c \succ a \succ b$	$d \succ a \succ c \succ b$
Social Ranking	$b \succ a$	$b \succ c \succ d \succ a$	$b \succ d \succ a$

Mackie states a common interpretation of IIA when he notes that "[t]he IIA [condition] would better be named the pairwise comparison condition, as it requires that choices among several alternatives be carried out only with information about choices between pairs."[39] The point we have made here is that there is nothing explicitly about *pairs* that drives Arrow's result. Instead, the relevant condition is that we require that choices among k alternatives be carried out only with information about $(k-1)$-tuples so that moving a single alternative up or down in our individuals' rankings should not flip or otherwise alter the group's ranking of the remaining $k-1$ alternatives. In fact, one can go further. To do so, we define a very minimal regularity condition that is a relaxation of m-ary independence. Letting n denote the number of individuals, a pair of profiles $\rho^1 = (\succ_1^1, \ldots, \succ_n^1)$ and $\rho^2 = (\succ_1^2, \ldots, \succ_n^2)$ is said to represent a *unilateral single-alternative deviation by individual i with respect to alternatives x and y* if there is exactly one individual i such that

1. the profiles ρ^1 and ρ^2 are identical for all individuals j other than i (i.e., $\succ_j^1 = \succ_j^2$ for all $j \neq i$) and
2. individual i "flips" the ranking of x and y in the two profiles (i.e., $y \succ_i^1 x$ and $x \succ_i^2 y$), but $\succ_i^1$ and $\succ_i^2$ are otherwise identical.

Thus, a unilateral single-alternative deviation by individual i with respect to alternatives x and y involves individual i changing only his or her relative ranking of a single pair of alternatives, x and y.

A preference aggregation rule f satisfies *unilateral flip independence* if, for any individual i, any pair of alternatives x and y, and any pair of profiles ρ_1 and ρ_2 such that ρ_1 and ρ_2 are a unilateral single-alternative deviation by individual i with respect to alternatives x and y, $f(\rho_1)$ and $f(\rho_2)$ differ at most in the collective ranking of x and y: for every w distinct from x and y and every $z \in X$, it must be the case that $w f(\rho^1) z \Leftrightarrow w f(\rho^2) z$ and that $z f(\rho^1) w \Leftrightarrow z f(\rho^2) w$. The following result states that satisfaction of unilateral flip independence is both necessary and sufficient for IIA to hold.

---

[39] Mackie (2003), p. 139.

Theorem 3 *If X contains at least three alternatives, an aggregation rule f satisfies unilateral flip independence if and only if f satisfies IIA.*

Proof: That satisfaction of IIA implies satisfaction of unilateral flip independence is straightforward. Accordingly, we demonstrate only that satisfaction of unilateral flip independence implies satisfaction of IIA.[40]

Let X be any finite set of alternatives containing $m \geq 3$ alternatives and let f be a preference aggregation rule. Suppose, by way of obtaining a contradiction, that f violates IIA but satisfies unilateral flip independence. The IIA violation implies that there are two profiles, ρ^1 and ρ^2, and a pair of alternatives, x and y, such that $x \succ_i^1 y \Leftrightarrow x \succ_i^2 y$ for all i, and $xf(\rho^1)y$ but not $xf(\rho^2)y$.

We start with the first person i for whom $\succ_i^1 \neq \succ_i^2$. Then, alternative by alternative, we transform $\succ_i^1$ into $\succ_i^2$. To do this we first find the highest ranked alternative for $\succ_i^2$ whose ranking differs from the ranking provided by $\succ_i^1$. Call this alternative a_1. We move a_1 one place up in $\succ_i^1$ to create a new preference relation for Person i, called $\succ_i^{1'}$. If this move alters the social ranking of x and y, we are done. Otherwise, we move a_1 up one more step in Person i's ranking. We proceed until we have either altered the social ranking of x and y or until a_1 reaches the ranking it is given at $\succ_i^2$. When this occurs, say after a_1 has moved up k steps in Person i's ordering, we move to the second highest ranked alternative at $\succ_i^2$ whose ranking differs from the ranking given by our (newly altered) profile for Person i, now $\succ_i^{1^k}$.

We proceed alternative by alternative and person by person to transform ρ^1 into ρ^2 in this way. We know that at some point, moving some alternative z up one step in one person's ranking (call him Person p for "pivotal"), or phrased differently, flipping z and w for Person p, will change the social ordering of x and y. Furthermore, we know that the movement of z up one step for Person p will not change p's personal ordering of x and y. This is because Person p ranks x and y the same relative to each other at ρ^1 and ρ^2, and we begin the transformation of p's preferences by moving up in the $\succ_p^1$ ranking p's highest ranked alternative in $\succ_p^2$ whose ranking differs from the ranking at $\succ_p^1$. If x is above y at $\succ_p^2$, it is also above y at $\succ_p^1$, so the alternatives cannot flip across the two orderings.

We can now state that a violation of IIA implies that there exists a preference profile at which a unilateral flip of w and z for some person p switches the social ranking of x and y produced by f. Moreover, we know that $\{w, z\} \neq \{x, y\}$. It follows that f violates unilateral flip independence, a contradiction. Thus, it must be the case that unilateral flip independence implies IIA, and thus, that the two conditions are logically equivalent. ∎

Theorem 3 demonstrates a fundamental basis of the normative appeal of IIA as a choice axiom. Specifically, the full strength of the axiom can be obtained by

---

[40] The proof closely mirrors that of Geanakoplos's famous proof of Arrow's Theorem using pivotal voters. See Geanakoplos (2005).

requiring only that no single individual be able to change the relative ranking of a third alternative by switching his or her pairwise ranking of two other alternatives. Moreover, the statement can be strengthened further by requiring that the "switch" in rankings only occur for a pair, x and y, that are adjacent to each other in the individual's overall preference ordering.[41] In this way, one can see the (partial) connection between IIA and manipulability. Specifically, IIA rules out the possibility that switching one individual's ranking of a single alternative might alter the relative rankings of the other alternatives. Regardless of whether one thinks that such switches are the result of strategic behavior or some other process (e.g., mismeasurement, incorrectly filled out ballots, or other mistakes), IIA is actually implied by a quite modest condition intended to preserve the fidelity of the produced collective ordering in the face of such perturbations.

The Binary Choice Critique in Terms of Redistricting
Returning briefly to our redistricting example, suppose that ten feasible redistricting plans are to be ranked by a committee. The committee undertakes its task and produces a ranking. Now suppose that one plan was incorrectly measured and that it actually deserves a higher "compactness" score, thus jumping over one or more other plans in its compactness ranking. Then this new information should not alter the committee's relative rankings of the other nine plans, and this is all that is required by Blau's weak independence condition ("nine-ary independence," in this case).

Requiring that the ranking of a single alternative not affect the overall ranking of the other $m - 1$ alternatives is, to us, indisputably a condition concerning the robustness of a social ranking to irrelevant alternatives. The term "irrelevant" should not be interpreted as describing whether or not that one alternative is a feasible or infeasible social choice. Rather, it simply concerns the sensitivity of the social ranking of a subset of alternatives to *information* unrelated (or irrelevant) to that subset, as described earlier. Thus, in the redistricting example, the relevant consideration is whether the mismeasurement of one districting plan with respect to one criterion should affect the judgment of the degree to which the *other* districting plans satisfy a variety of fairness criteria. The implication of the results discussed in this section is that even a mild restriction on the sensitivity of an overall aggregator in terms of such mismeasurement is equivalent to the IIA axiom. Accordingly, while IIA itself might appear strong, the applicability of Arrow's Theorem is not in reality affected by this apparent strength.

We return to the issue of measurement later in this chapter, when we discuss cardinal inputs to the aggregation problem. For now, we accept at face value arguments that the IIA axiom *appears* strong, but the full strength of the axiom

---

[41] We omit this strengthening from our definition of unilateral flip independence, but it is apparent from the proof that the definition could be strengthened in such a way.

can be obtained logically from much less restrictive consistency conditions. Now we turn to the second class of critique, in which IIA is attacked because it is opaque and counterintuitive.

The Counterintuitive Critique

A second, widely voiced criticism of the IIA condition is that it is not transparent, that it cannot be defended as being intuitively obvious, and that the formality with which it is presented in the social choice literature serves to obscure the fact that justifications for the condition are thin. This criticism is not only leveled at IIA but at the field of social choice itself. Mackie writes that it is his "reluctant duty to report a problem with public-choice style of explanation. This style of explanation is often not immediately intuitive yet is gilded with an abstract formalism that suggests that something important and believable is being said."[42] More cheekily, he quotes from Barry and Hardin (1982) to write that "Barry and Hardin . . . agree that Arrow's IIA is a powerful condition. 'Part of its power is that one cannot easily intuit what it means or why it matters. . . . Perhaps because of its subtlety, condition [IIA] is apparently the condition that is most readily taken for granted in the proof of Arrow's and related theorems.'"[43]

The IIA condition *is* subtle, in part because, unlike Pareto efficiency, it is an interprofile condition. As it requires consistency in outcomes across two or more profiles, it requires the reader to conceptualize the idea of a counterfactual preference profile, a collection of different preferences for the same set of individuals that can be compared with their current set of preferences. Moreover, it requires this to be done in what is likely an unnatural way to most readers. The unnaturalness stems from the fact that IIA is a condition on social rankings over *subsets* of alternatives, while aggregation rules, by definition, produce a ranking over *all* alternatives.

At the same time, as we have discussed earlier, there are strong connections between Arrow's Theorem and other impossibility results such as the Gibbard-Satterthwaite Theorem, which do not explicitly use an independence axiom.[44] Reny (2001) derives two side-by-side proofs, one for Arrow's Theorem and one for the Gibbard-Satterthwaite Theorem, showing that both results can be proved with the same constructive method.[45] Most other work exploring these linkages has similarly relied on two proofs for the two theorems, as Arrow's Theorem concerns aggregation rules (generating social rankings) while the Gibbard-Satterthwaite Theorem concerns choice functions (generating social

---

[42] Mackie (2003), p. 246.

[43] Mackie (2003), p. 123, quoting from Barry and Hardin (1982), pp. 217–218.

[44] Other examples include "single-profile" versions of Arrow, Ubeda (2003), and Muller and Satterthwaite (1977).

[45] In addition to Reny (2001), see Geanakoplos (2005).

choices). A notable exception is a recent paper by Kfir Eliaz that has developed a unified and illuminating approach to proving both theorems simultaneously.[46]

Eliaz's meta-theorem concerns objects that he terms "social aggregators." Like an aggregation rule or choice function, a social aggregator, F, takes a profile of preferences or other criteria as an input. However, instead of always producing a social ranking or social choice, an aggregator is required to produce only a binary relation. We discuss and use binary relations in much greater detail later in the book.[47] However, to describe Eliaz's result, it is useful to define and briefly describe binary relations at this point.

Binary Relations

As the term indicates, a binary relation is a list of pairwise (binary) comparisons of the various pairs of alternatives. So far in this book, we have been using the notation $\succ$ to represent "social preferences" (or ranking) and $\succ_i$ to represent individual preferences (or criteria). These are special types of binary relations; for a pair of alternatives, x and y, the notation $x \succ y$ means x is socially preferred to (or socially ranked higher than) y. If both $x \succ y$ and $y \succ x$, then this represents indifference in the sense that each alternative is ranked at least as high as the other. If $x \succ y$ holds and it is not the case that $y \succ x$, then we can say that x is ranked "strictly" higher than y by $\succ$. Finally, if neither $x \succ y$ nor $y \succ x$ holds, then x and y are incomparable under $\succ$ in the sense that neither alternative is ranked at least as high as the other.

A binary relation $\succ$ is *complete* if for every pair of alternative, x and y, it is the case that either $x \succ y$ or $y \succ x$ or both. That is, a complete binary relation can compare each pair of alternatives (although it might rank some pairs equally in the sense of indifference described above). By definition, an aggregation rule produces a complete binary relation, which we have termed a social preference relation. What differentiates a social aggregator as used by Eliaz from the aggregation rules as discussed to this point is that the binary relation produced by a social aggregator F need not be complete. That is, it can be the case that for a pair of alternatives, x and y, a social aggregator might return a binary relation $\succ$ for which neither $x \succ y$ nor $y \succ x$ holds. Eliaz terms the binary relation produced by a social aggregator a "social relation."

Both aggregation rules and choice functions are special types of social aggregators. An aggregation rule is a social aggregator that is complete and a choice function is a social aggregator that is incomplete in the following way: there exists one alternative that is strictly socially preferred to every other alternative, and no other alternative is socially preferred to any other alternative. The one top alternative of this binary relation is revealed as the "choice" of the choice function, but a choice function will not return any information about the relative rankings of unchosen alternatives.

[46] Eliaz (2004).
[47] Chapter 6.

Since a social relation may be incomplete, Eliaz uses the following two properties to characterize the ability of **F** to produce well-defined choices. The first is *acyclicality*, a weakening of transitivity to incomplete binary relations. This property says that if $x \succ y$ and not $z \succ y$, then not $z \succ x$. The second is *existence of a best alternative*, which requires $\succ$ to produce an alternative x such that $x \succ y$ for all $y \neq x$. Note that if $\succ$ is transitive, then it also satisfies acyclicality and existence of a best alternative. Also note that, by definition, every choice function produces a binary relation (as described earlier) that satisfies acyclicality and existence of a best alternative. We omit definitions of dictator and Pareto efficiency for social aggregators, but the definitions are straightforward and reduce to those of the Arrow and Gibbard-Satterthwaite Theorems in the event that the social aggregator is an aggregation rule or choice function.

Given this framework (which admittedly has taken us some time to describe), Eliaz then defines a straightforward condition on social aggregators termed *preference reversal*, and in his impossibility theorem this condition subsumes both IIA and strategy-proofness. The definition of preference reversal is as follows: a social aggregator **F** satisfies preference reversal if for every pair of alternatives, x and y, and any two profiles ρ and ρ', if $x \succ y$ at ρ and not $y \succ x$ at ρ, and if $y \succ' x$ at ρ', then there must exist a person i who has $x \succ_i y$ but $y \succ'_i x$. In words, this condition states that if at some profile of preferences x is deemed strictly better than y by aggregator **F**, and if at another profile of preferences y is deemed weakly better than x by **F**, then there must be at least one person who strictly preferred x to y at the first profile but y to x at the second. In other words, at least one person must have reversed his or her ordering of x and y for the social ranking of these alternatives to have changed. Given this definition of the preference reversal axiom, Eliaz proves the following theorem.

Theorem 4 (Eliaz (2004)) *Let* **F** *be a social aggregator that maps preference profiles into the set of binary relations satisfying acyclicality and existence of a best alternative. If* **F** *satisfies Pareto efficiency and preference reversal, then* **F** *is a dictator.*

Eliaz also proves that for transitive aggregation rules Pareto efficiency and IIA imply preference reversal, and for choice functions, strategy-proofness implies preference reversal.[48] Thus, the Arrow and Gibbard-Satterthwaite Theorems can both be proved by invoking Theorem 4.

We have gone to some lengths to set up this theorem because we think that preference reversal is an intuitive concept, and in combination with Pareto efficiency, it can be appealed to instead of IIA to obtain Arrow's Theorem. Additionally, in line with the discussion of the binary choice critique, this

---

[48] This latter claim is proved indirectly through a monotonicity argument appealing to Muller and Satterthwaite (1977).

condition illuminates the connection between IIA and strategy-proofness, providing a general impossibility result that subsumes the theorems of Arrow and Gibbard-Satterthwaite.

The Counterintuitive Critique in Terms of Redistricting

Suppose again that ten feasible redistricting plans have been ranked by a committee on the basis of general principles of fairness such as compactness, contiguity, and so forth. In the example, our committee's decision-making process is the social aggregator, F. Suppose Plan A is ranked as strictly superior to Plan B. Now suppose new information concerning the fairness measures comes to light, and the committee re-ranks the plans. Under the new ranking, Plan A is ranked as *weakly inferior* to Plan B by the committee. If the committee's decision-making process satisfies preference reversal, then it must have been the case that there is some fairness measure with respect to which Plan A was originally ranked higher than Plan B but that now ranks Plan A as lower than Plan B.

One might ask, "But what if the new information provided to the committee shows Plan B getting *much* better on those measures on which it was already better than Plan A on, and Plan A not improving at all on those measures that it was better than Plan B on? Wouldn't this be a reasonable scenario for the committee to decide to flip the A-B rankings, even though such a flip would violate preference reversal, as A has not dropped below B on any particular fairness measure?"

Our answer to this question is "possibly." Preference reversal, like IIA, is not an immutable axiom that every good decision-making procedure must necessarily satisfy. If cardinal data exist for the fairness measures considered by the committee and if these data are comparable across measures (discussed later), then one could argue that the committee *should* violate preference reversal in order to accommodate the fact that compactness scores of 10 and 9 for Plans A and B, respectively, should be considered to be different than scores of 10 and 0, even though both sets of scores place Plan A above Plan B. At the same time, relying on cardinal measures in this way presents different challenges to the aggregation problem, and it is to these challenges that we now turn.

The Ordinality Critique

In a lengthy passage in *Democracy Defended*, Mackie describes a scenario in which the rushed organizer of a reception seeks to gauge attendees' preferences between beer and coffee by asking them to submit a ranking of beer, coffee, tea, water, milk, and pop (although four of the six options are unavailable, the organizer uses a previous year's form). There are two types of individuals attending the reception, businesspeople and theologians. The businesspeople marginally prefer beer to coffee, ranking the options first and second, respectively. The theologians are teetotalers, however, and rank coffee first and beer last. There are more businesspeople than theologians, and thus merely looking at the coffee-beer comparison yields beer as a winner. Mackie presents this story as an example of the silliness of the IIA condition. He writes:

> [T]he [IIA] condition enforces the ban on information other than individual orderings. What if there had been a discussion about the beverage to be served at the reception? Assume that the theologians have the same mere ordering of preferences. Before the decision, they explain that they are teetotalers, and would rather have anything but beer. Alternatively, suppose that they are prohibited from drinking beer as a matter of their religion, and that they have a right to be served a beverage at the reception that doesn't offend their beliefs. The political scientist, our hapless believer in the [IIA] condition, would have to reject this information and enact the social choice of beer. "Only orderings can be observed," he would reply to the theologians, "and the only ordering that matters is between coffee and beer. That you would rather have any beverage but beer is irrelevant."[49]

There are several problems with this example. First and foremost, the dilemma presented by Mackie is not about IIA at all. Noting that the question at hand is whether one should choose beer or coffee, consider for a moment what would have happened if the organizer had presented the attendees with the relevant decision: a binary choice between beer or coffee. Let us not belabor the argument too much and simply suppose that the organizer used majority rule to determine which to serve. In this hypothetical scenario, beer would be selected. Mackie's objection in this scenario implies that one should not use majority rule. The "hapless believer" in IIA is in actuality a hapless believer in majoritarianism. As with IIA, majoritarianism is, of course, vulnerable to objections. But we find it strange to reject majoritarianism when "defending democracy," as Mackie is attempting to do when presenting this example.

A second problem with this example follows from Mackie's allusion to rights. First, including rights implies that the decision to serve coffee is correct as long as there are *any* theologians attending the reception. Viewed in this way, Mackie's objection leads to a classic conundrum: who, in the end, is to choose what types of views and tastes are to be respected when aggregating preferences? The example is arguably cherry-picked by virtue of its supposition that the theologians are the only ones with some exogenous "right" that should trump majority will. Perhaps the businesspeople all work for a beer company and are not allowed by their employer to drink any beverage other than beer at public events.[50]

A third problem with the example is that the businesspeople are not privy to the discussion between the organizer and the theologians and are not made aware of it even after the beverage decision is rendered. If they were, it is likely

---

[49] Mackie (2003), p. 134.
[50] This point might appear silly, but similar rules are part of some real-world contracts, as we learned from a close friend employed by a large brewery in St. Louis.

that their own preference orderings would change in order to accommodate the theologians; coffee would be chosen, and no *ex post* IIA violation would have occurred. This is in keeping with the preference structuration argument proposed by Dryzek and List (2003). If preferences cannot be structured so as to produce consensus – if, for example, every businessperson has a caffeine allergy – then we are back to square one in terms of the aggregation problem.

The fourth and final problem with the example is the claim that IIA "enforces the ban" on cardinal information about preferences. We view this is as a potentially important objection. In many of the contexts we are concerned with – general settings in which we wish to aggregate multiple criteria, each relevant to an ultimate decision – allowing for cardinality without intercomparability can be particularly natural. In our redistricting example, for instance, the non-comparability requirement states that a 10 score on a scale measuring a plan's adherence to the principle of compactness is not comparable to an 8 on a scale measuring the plan's adherence to contiguity. Thus, while only intracriterion scores are comparable, cardinality allows the aggregation rule to treat the comparison of two plans receiving a 10 and 8, respectively, on a scale of compactness as different than a comparison of those same plans had they received a 10 and 3 on the same scale.

Fortunately for our purposes, claims that IIA "enforces the ban" on cardinal information about preferences are untrue. In particular, Sen (1970a) and others have noted that Arrow's theorem can be readily extended to allow for cardinal inputs; the problem arises when we allow these measures to be comparable across individuals [or criteria] – by normalization, for example. We briefly illustrate Sen's points in as nontechnical a way as we are able.[51]

Ordinality and Cardinality: Sen's Response

Suppose that, as before, X is our collection of alternatives. Now, instead of assuming that each individual simply ranks these alternatives, we allow every individual to assign a number to each alternative. This approach allows the aggregation rule to respond to the cardinality, or strength, of individuals' preferences over the alternatives.

In classic choice theory terms, the aggregation rule can be described in this setting as responding to the individuals' *utilities* for each alternative. That is, for each individual i, the submitted numbers can be thought of as being generated by a *utility function*, denoted by U_i, that assigns a number, $U_i(x)$, to each alternative $x \in X$. Thus, $U_i(x)$ is person i's utility measure for alternative x, so that if $U_i(x) = 10$ then i "gets 10 units of utility" from alternative x. If there are n people in our group, then a utility profile U is a listing of the

---

[51] Our general framework comes from Chapter 8 of Sen (1970a). Kalai and Schmeidler (1977) prove a similar result for cardinal social preference relations, although their result requires a continuity property on the (cardinal) aggregation rule. Related results have been proved by others.

utility functions for each person, or $U = (U_1, \ldots, U_n)$. An *aggregation functional*, f, is then simply a function that assigns a social preference relation, $\succ$, to each utility profile U. Thus, an aggregation functional is just a generalization of aggregation rules as discussed earlier that takes cardinal preferences as an input rather than ordinal preferences, or rankings. Suppose Person i has utility measures $5, 4, 7, 10$ for alternatives w, x, y, z, respectively. While an aggregation rule would be invariant to this person instead having utility measures $0, -10, 5, 100$ for these alternatives, as both collections of numbers rank the alternatives similarly,[52] an aggregation functional can treat these two different utility functions for Person i differently.

Clearly, there are no natural "units" describing individuals' utilities. If we make the standard assumption that individuals have preferences that are representable as von Neumann-Morgenstern expected utilities, then any U_i is only unique up to a positive linear transformation of the form $U_i = a + bU_i'$, where a and b are real numbers and $b > 0$. Thus, representing a person's utility over three alternatives with the numbers $1, 3,$ and 2 is equivalent to representing the person's utility with the numbers $2, 4,$ and 3 (adding 1); the numbers $2, 6,$ and 4 (multiplying by 2); or the numbers $3, 7,$ and 5 (multiplying by 2 and then adding 1).

The assumption that utilities are unique only up to these types of transformations implies that any given individual's utility measures are entirely personal in the sense that the magnitude of one person's utility (i.e., the size of differences in his or her utility between any pair of alternatives) is not comparable to another's. We may try to normalize these numbers to compare numbers across individuals, but such normalizations lead to new problems, which we will discuss in a moment. Maintaining the assumption that utility measures are noncomparable across individuals implies that if any person's utility function is transformed in such a way, the aggregation functional should produce the same social preference relation. This is because a linearly transformed utility function represents the same preferences for that individual. The central point for our argument, then, is that cardinality without comparability does not enable us to get around the problems posed by IIA.

Cardinality without Interpersonal Comparability

We are now in a position to describe a cardinal version of IIA for aggregation functionals. Suppose that for some pair of alternatives x and y and two different utility profiles U and U', we have $U_i(x) = U_i'(x)$ and $U_i(y) = U_i'(y)$ for each individual i. An aggregation functional f satisfies *cardinal IIA* only if it produces the same social ranking of x and y when applied to U and U'. To illustrate why this cardinal version of IIA is no advance over the standard definition of IIA when utilities are not comparable across individuals, consider the following

---

[52] To be clear, an alternative x is ranked higher than an alternative y by individual i (i.e., $x \succ_i y$) if x is assigned a higher utility than is y (i.e., $U_i(x) > U_i(y)$).

five-person example. The table below depicts two utility profiles, U and U', restricted to two alternatives, x and y:

Person i	$U_i(x)$	$U_i(y)$	$U_i'(x)$	$U_i'(y)$
Person 1	10	1	50	1
Person 2	5000	−50	3	2
Person 3	3	17	0	100
Person 4	40	40	5	5
Person 5	0	1	−10	10

At profile U, for example, Person 1 receives 10 units of utility from alternative x and 1 unit from y. For each person, U and U' assign different units of utility to the alternatives. However, individuals order x and y the same way across the two profiles; at both U and U', Persons 1 and 2 rank x above y, Persons 3 and 5 rank y above x, and Person 4 is indifferent between the two alternatives.

Now consider a new profile, U'', shown in the table below, that linearly transforms U' person by person. Since utilities are only unique up to a positive linear transformation, f yields the same social preference relation at both U' and U''; $f(U') = f(U'')$. However, we can see from the table below that U and U'' are identical when restricted to the alternatives x and y. Supposing that f satisfies cardinal IIA, it must be the case that f produces the same social ranking of x and y when applied to both U and U''. And since f also produces the same social ranking when applied to U'' and U', it must be the case that $f(U)$ and $f(U')$ yield the same x, y ranking, even though each utility profile assigns different cardinal scores to the alternatives. While this example is not a formal proof of the fact that cardinal IIA implies IIA, it is intended to illustrate the point that that cardinality without comparability across individuals returns us to the standard (ordinal) definition of IIA.

Person i	Transformation U''	$U_i'(x)$	$U_i'(y)$	$U_i''(x)$	$U_i''(y)$
Person 1	$U_1'' = \frac{40}{49} + \frac{9}{49}U_1'$	50	1	10	1
Person 2	$U_2'' = -1050 + 5050U_2'$	3	2	5000	−50
Person 3	$U_3'' = 3 + \frac{7}{50}U_3'$	0	100	3	17
Person 4	$U_4'' = 8U_4'$	5	5	40	40
Person 5	$U_5'' = \frac{1}{2} + \frac{1}{20}U_5'$	−10	10	0	1

Cardinality Allowing for Interpersonal Comparability

We have shown that cardinality without comparability does not help us, so what if we instead bound utility functions, so as to induce comparability of utilities across individuals?[53] When the units of utility are so scaled, they are arguably comparable across individuals. In particular, it may be sensible to

---

[53] Sen (1970a), pp. 91–98 is particularly useful with respect to this argument and makes similar points about the specific scaling methods we discuss.

simply take a sum of each alternative's score across individuals (or criteria) and rank the alternatives according to the resulting totals.[54]

This utilitarian approach might seem particularly reasonable in the context of our redistricting example. Suppose that the "utility profiles" we seek to aggregate are instead measures of our fairness standards across several redistricting plans. In particular, suppose that "compactness," "contiguity," and "neutrality" scores are generated for three plans, *A*, *B* and *C*, as follows:

Fairness principle	Plan *A* score	Plan *B* score	Plan *C* score
Compactness	3	2	1
Contiguity	2	7	4
Neutrality	14	9	18

To make these three different fairness measures comparable, suppose that we scale each measure so that the lowest ranked plan receives a "0" and the highest ranked plan receives a "1." The rescaled scores would look as follows:

Fairness principle	Plan *A* score	Plan *B* score	Plan *C* score
Compactness	1	0.5	0
Contiguity	0	1	0.4
Neutrality	0.55	0	1
Total	1.55	1.5	1.4

Then, supposing that each principle of fairness is valued equally (which may or may not be the case but is not necessary for our point), we could sum each plan's score. Plan *A* wins, with a total score of 1.55. However, the problem with this example is that the outcome is wholly dependent on the method of scaling that we used. We could just as easily scale the measures so that the lowest ranked plan receives a "0" and the rest of the scores sum to 1. This would lead to the following rescaled scores:

Fairness principle	Plan *A* score	Plan *B* score	Plan *C* score
Compactness	0.66	0.33	0
Contiguity	0	0.71	0.29
Neutrality	0.36	0	64
Total	1.02	1.04	0.93

In this case, Plan *B* wins, with a total score of 1.04. Our point with this example is not that the comparability of cardinal units should be avoided in every

---

[54] Of course, one can do much more than a simple sum, including weighted sums and more esoteric formulations. For our purposes, though, a straightforward sum suffices to demonstrate the potential difficulties with assuming comparability. These difficulties are inherent to presuming comparability as opposed to the functional form one uses to take advantage of it.

decision-making context but that using such data requires a firm belief in the meaningfulness of the measures. In this particular example, it is not immediately apparent how a $(3, 2, 1)$ scoring of the plans on the basis of compactness relates to a $(14, 9, 18)$ scoring on neutrality. Reasonable attempts to render these scores comparable lead to different outcomes that may be more dependent on the scaling method used than any inherent qualities of the plans themselves.

Summarizing the Critiques

Without a doubt, IIA is the most controversial of Arrow's axioms. At the same time, many of the charges that have been leveled against it are unfair. The condition can be weakened considerably with respect to each of the major criticisms it has faced. We can redefine IIA to no longer concern choice over pairs but to concern choice over fixed-sized subsets of the policy space; the impossibility result still holds. We can replace IIA with more intuitive axioms (here we focused on *unilateral flip independence* and *preference reversal*); the impossibility result still holds. We can allow an aggregation rule to consider cardinal preference profiles and thus gauge the intensity of alternatives' rankings relative to each other in order to produce a collective choice; the impossibility result still holds.

In a nutshell, the only reasonable "escape route" for circumventing IIA requires presuming that the inputs to the aggregation problem are cardinal and comparable (be they preferences or other criteria). We do not argue that such an approach is always (or even frequently) unwarranted. However, presuming comparability is not a panacea. From a theoretical point of view, leveraging interpersonal (or intercriterion) comparability to circumvent the conclusions of Arrow's Theorem places a heavy burden on the measurement of the criteria themselves. Measures must be devised that both accurately capture the relevant features of the criteria at hand and that ensure that the scales of the various criteria are inherently comparable. This is a matter of both strategic and practical concern and is an aggregation problem in and of itself. In various ways, the legitimacy of outcomes (in a colloquial sense) that are produced by such a cardinal approach will in general depend much more on the fidelity of the reported and used inputs than outcomes produced by an ordinal approach. Accordingly, to the degree that the inputs themselves represent contestable notions (e.g., ethnicity, efficiency, compactness, neutrality), merely "solving" the aggregation problem may be insufficient to bestow legitimacy upon the selected outcome. With these points made, we now move to a discussion of the Pareto efficiency axiom.

3.4 PARETO EFFICIENCY

Pareto efficiency is arguably the least contested of Arrow's axioms. Returning to the ordinal framework, the axiom can be justified in two ways. The first is technical: without this axiom, there is a "solution" to the resulting aggregation problem. In particular, any preference aggregation rule that always returns some given and fixed social welfare function satisfies unrestricted domain, IIA, no dictator, and transitivity. However, such a rule is an unsatisfying solution to the problem, one that is completely insensitive to the inputs and, accordingly, is an "aggregation" rule in name only.

Moving beyond technical concerns, a second defense of Pareto efficiency is more substantive and closely linked with the concerns of Riker, Mackie, and others. Taking a broader view for a moment and asking why aggregation is interesting, it is apparent that there must (or should) be some normative claim for the collective ranking to be formed from the included criteria. This is also partially implied by the no dictator axiom: a baseline presumption for embarking upon the design of an aggregation rule is that there is some reason to aggregate (at least some of) the criteria in question. With these points in hand, it is nonsensical to suggest that an alternative that is uniformly considered less appealing by every available criterion to some other given alternative should be collectively ranked above that alternative.

However, this point itself raises another important and somewhat subtle point. In particular, the normative appeal of Pareto efficiency is at least partially founded upon the presumption that the inputs are themselves properly coded ("higher" is "better") and, even more important, "well-ordered" in the sense that the inputs are themselves transitive.[55] One could interpret this issue as suggesting that the assumption that the criteria are transitive is unduly restrictive. This is a point argued at length by Pildes and Anderson (1990), for example. However, this objection has no merit in the context of Arrow's Theorem. Rather, as we discuss in Chapters 5 and 6, our theory of legitimacy addresses the difficulty of cyclic inputs, which we believe is better treated as resulting *from* the aggregation problem rather than as a difficulty *for* the result.

Instead of questioning whether criteria "should" be presumed to be transitive – an empirical matter, to be sure – we note that the Pareto efficiency axiom illustrates exactly how the framing of the aggregation problem by Arrow makes the impossibility theorem even more surprising. That is, the impossibility conclusion holds *even with the presumption that one has perfectly well-ordered inputs*. A point that Pildes and Anderson miss in this context is that allowing for cyclic and otherwise "messy" inputs merely amplifies the importance and applicability of the impossibility theorem's conclusions.

In terms of the redistricting example, this discussion illustrates the importance of Pareto efficiency in general aggregation problems. In particular, violating Pareto efficiency is inconsistent with the notion that the criteria considered by (say) the Court were actually treated "as advertised." In other words, a

<hr/>

[55] As mentioned earlier, one could enlarge the scope of discussion and require only acyclicity, but focusing on transitive criteria is in line with most of our discussion and sufficient for our purposes here.

violation of Pareto efficiency would involve the Court deeming a plan that is uniformly inferior on all criteria to another plan as superior to that plan. It is important to note in this regard that the Pareto efficiency condition is operational only if the two plans are *strictly* ranked by *all* of the criteria. Thus, Pareto efficiency is silent about how "ties" are "broken." In this way, the Pareto efficiency axiom is truly minimal.

In sum, Pareto efficiency is not a terribly controversial axiom for the aggregation problem. Nonetheless, consideration of it and, in a sense, why it is uncontroversial is illustrative of the structure of the aggregation problem itself. This is useful to keep in mind as we turn now to the no dictator axiom.

3.5 NO DICTATOR

As with Pareto efficiency, Arrow's no dictator axiom has attracted little controversy. In addition to the (perhaps unnecessarily) pejorative connotations of relaxing the axiom, the no dictator axiom is similar to Pareto efficiency in that it essentially rules out a "trivial solution" to the aggregation problem. As discussed earlier, the inputs are presumed to be transitive. Accordingly, one way to guarantee that the aggregation rule returns a Pareto efficient transitive ordering is to simply pick one criterion (or person, in the case of preference aggregation) and use that ordering as the collective ordering in all situations, regardless of how the alternatives are ranked by the other criteria.

It should be noted that although this solution is trivial in an abstract theoretical sense, it represents an important baseline. This general solution to the aggregation problem is simultaneously normatively appealing (in the sense that it satisfies Pareto efficiency and IIA) and practical (in the sense that it is simple to implement and reliable insofar as it requires eliciting very little information). Furthermore, it is used in a wide variety of situations. In terms of collective choice, it is common that an individual be appointed to "represent" the group. Such arrangements, when implemented in an ex ante fashion (i.e., before the particulars of the decision[s] the dictator will confront are known), represent an instantiation of a dictatorial aggregation rule. At a more general level, any heuristic that focuses on a single criterion – cost minimization, for example – is a dictatorial aggregation rule.

The question, then, is why one might want to rule out dictatorial solutions. As with the IIA axiom, our view is that a dictatorial rule is not necessarily bad. For our redistricting example, it may be the case that the criteria for ranking various plans can be hierarchically ranked, so that first a strict equal population test is used to rank the plans and then all plans tied at the top of this ranking are further differentiated on the basis of political neutrality, and then on compactness, and so on. Such a rule could be characterized as an "ordered dictator": the criteria are ordered C_1 through C_n, and a social ranking is made on the basis of C_1's ranking with remaining ties broken by successive criteria until either no ties remain or no criteria remain. The problem, of course, with such a rule is that it may be the case that the top-ranked alternative by C_1 is simultaneously the *bottom*-ranked alternative by criteria $C_2, \ldots, C_n$. An ordered dictatorial rule disallows any give and take with respect to the criteria being used for evaluation.

We argue that settings in which criteria can be hierarchically ranked represent decision-making scenarios that are not particularly complex. Accordingly, our appeal to the no dictator axiom is quite modest and empirical: to the degree that real-world collective choice depends on aggregation rules that can achieve compromise with respect to various goals, the implications of the impossibility theorems must be granted significance. We now turn to the final of Arrow's axioms, transitivity.

3.6 TRANSITIVITY

An accurate description of the "goal" of Arrow's theorem is the construction of a collective decision maker that mimics its components in terms of (classical) rationality. Specifically, as discussed earlier, Arrow's Theorem adopts a strong starting point in terms of the inputs to the problem – every criterion is presumed to be "rational" in the sense that it is a complete and transitive ordering of the alternatives – and then asks whether an IIA, Pareto, and nondictatorial aggregation rule exists that always produces a similarly "rational" collective output. However, while the result is disturbing only insofar as one thinks that this notion of collective rationality is desirable, the result is relevant regardless of how one feels about the desirability of producing a transitive collective ordering. This is because the result indicates that we still need to concern ourselves with the (nontrivial) construction of choices from the outputs of aggregation rules.

The need to construct choices from inputs and to defend those choices is inarguably a necessity of any desirable collective choice procedure. Transitivity is a compelling condition because it provides the strongest possible defense of a collective choice; it ensures that the choice procedure generates a comparison of alternatives akin to a "greater than or equal to" relationship, as used to describe numbers on a line. At the same time, we find transitivity to be the least compelling of Arrow's axioms from the standpoint of constructing a legitimate collective choice procedure. Why?

Transitivity is fundamentally different than Pareto efficiency, no dictator, and IIA. The latter three axioms concern how the choice procedure responds to its inputs – the goals or criteria that the procedure is designed to respond to and, more strongly, that it is designed to further. These three axioms each impose a condition on the process of comparing alternatives that ensures that the procedure is faithful to the criteria it is intended to promote and that it reasonably responds to changes in the criteria. We have spent this chapter defending these axioms in this way: the Pareto axiom ensures that the procedure is responsive in a minimally positive way to the criteria, no dictator ensures compromise with respect to two or more criteria, and IIA preserves the fidelity of a comparison of a subset of alternatives to information concerning only those alternatives. Conversely, transitivity solely concerns the *output* of aggregation and says very little about how the procedure should respond to its inputs. If anything, transitivity requires the procedure to ignore potentially useful information about the inputs to the aggregation problem. For example, if it is known that the procedure produces $a \succ b$ and $b \succ c$, then transitivity requires that $a \succ c$, and it requires this *without using any knowledge of how a and c actually fare with respect to the criteria that the procedure is designed to further.*[56]

As discussed before, a violation of transitivity by an aggregation rule can imply that there is no well-defined "best" element. Arrow's Theorem implies that this possibility is endemic to any nondictatorial procedure that aggregates heterogeneous criteria (in the sense of unrestricted domain) and that satisfies IIA and Pareto efficiency. The conclusion, however, should not be interpreted as implying that an intransitivity undermines the legitimacy of the procedure or its output. Rather, it simply implies that the procedure may not provide a conclusive answer on the basis of aggregation alone.

In light of the defense we have offered for Pareto, no dictator, and IIA, we think a reasonable conclusion is that the acknowledgment of intransitivity is itself informative. That is, when a procedure satisfying Pareto, no dictator, and IIA fails to produce an unambiguously "best" alternative, the implication is clear and simple: there is no "best" outcome according to the plural criteria that served as inputs for the aggregation problem. In such cases, the procedure is revealing inherent conflict among the criteria. The implication is that resolving the choice problem requires more work.

This implication is the basis for an important conclusion about the possibility of multiple legitimate outcomes. In other words, Arrow's Theorem can be seen as a statement about the multiplicity of legitimate outcomes. Arrow's Theorem does not imply that the output of a nondictatorial, IIA, and Pareto efficient preference aggregation rule should be accorded no deference. Indeed, we believe that the opposite is true. Insofar as the inputs to the aggregation rule are themselves legitimate, the arguments we have presented in favor of Arrow's axioms imply that the output of such a procedure is necessarily "good" in some sense, even in the face of Riker's contention that the output is simply a product of the details of the aggregation procedure.

The use of aggregation methods in collective choice situations illuminates how Riker's criticism of the legitimacy of aggregation-based decision making misses the point. Democratic governance, whether represented narrowly as the

---

[56] This argument bears some similarity to Saari's argument (e.g., Saari, 2001) that IIA forces important "connecting information" about irrelevant alternatives to be disregarded, as it requires that the procedure ignore absolute rankings of alternatives in favor of relative rankings within subsets. Conversely, we have argued in Section 3.3 that the information lost through IIA is actually quite minimal.

aggregation of individuals' preferences or broadly as the aggregation of more general empirical criteria in the formation of public policy, produces legitimate outcomes precisely *because* of the details of the aggregation procedure(s). However, simply leveling this objection to Riker's criticism is unsatisfying in that it omits the important details of how one can instantiate democratic governance through the use of a nondictatorial aggregation rule satisfying unrestricted domain, IIA, and Pareto efficiency. If Riker's criticisms are to be satisfactorily answered, one should present a means by which effective and legitimate governance can be reconciled with the fact that what one might term "populist aggregation" will necessarily, in some cases, produce an intransitive or cyclic collective ranking. In other words, there is a need for a theory of how one can take the next step of refining a potentially cyclic collective ranking in order to select a policy to be implemented. In the next part of the book, we present a theory of how this "next step" can be defined and characterized in terms of a notion of legitimacy based on the output of such a procedure.

PART II

A THEORY OF LEGITIMATE CHOICE

4

Legitimacy and Choice

In the first part of this book, we argued that social choice–theoretic results such as Arrow's theorem and the Gibbard-Satterthwaite theorem motivate the study of democratic politics by illuminating the difficulties inherent in accommodating multiple goals within a single decision framework. The theorems tell us that democratic procedures really *matter*; they must do more than simply select a best outcome, because such an outcome will often not exist. In such cases, it follows, collective choices must be justified, or *legitimated*, on a basis other than being the unambiguous product of popular will. According to the theory we present and develop in this part of the book, the legitimacy of a collective decision is based on the provision of an explanation (reason, justification, rationale, etc.) for it.

The social choice arguments presented in Part I establish that cycles and intransitivity are endemic to decisions based on the aggregation of multiple criteria (regardless of whether these criteria are directly based on individual preferences). Specifically, the notion of "the best choice" is frequently ill-defined in such settings so that, even after criteria have been duly aggregated, the question of what to choose may not have yet been answered. Such cases are exactly those in which a *legitimate* choice requires an additional explanation above and beyond the details of the aggregation.

In the chapters that follow, we first discuss the notion of legitimacy and its various conceptualizations, definitions, and applications. We then present our notion of legitimate choice. Our theory is predicated on a form of consistency. To be legitimate in our framework, a collective decision must be consistent with an underlying principle that allows comparison of some, if not all, possible choices with each other. Some principles identify a unique decision in any given situation, but many do not. Nonetheless, maintaining consistency with both a given principle or set of principles and previous decisions will in general constrain what might be chosen in a legitimate fashion. Viewed from one angle, our theory of legitimacy is more a theory of *il*legitimacy insofar as it is easily defined in terms of the types of policies that *cannot* be chosen in a legitimate fashion.

At first, such an approach might seem at odds with itself or at best setting itself too modest a goal. After all, one wants a legitimate government, not just one that is not illegitimate. As Meyer and Scott describe it, "perfect legitimation is perfect theory, complete (i.e., without uncertainty) and confronted by no alternatives,"[1] and, indeed, our theory will speak to this point: there are situations in which "perfect" legitimacy may be obtained. However, as we have argued earlier in this book, the search for a collective choice or judgment that is perfectly legitimate in this sense may be fruitless. In such situations, we will show, the search for what one might call imperfect legitimacy is not fruitless. Furthermore, one can argue that the necessity of imperfect legitimacy is itself a cornerstone of the notion's empirical import. For example, Pfeffer and Salancik describe the dilemma of detecting or observing legitimacy as follows: "Legitimacy is known more readily when it is absent than when it is present. When activities of an organization are illegitimate, comments and attacks will occur."[2]

Before moving on to the discussion of our theory, we address a few foundational questions about legitimacy. First, the concept of legitimacy may be (and has been) applied to a variety of things, including organizations, social relations, collective decisions, and individual choices. In Section 4.1, we clarify how we are using the notion: since we are interested in general problems of aggregation and choice, we are agnostic about the subject of evaluation. That said, our empirical focus in the book is closely tied to collective governance. Accordingly, we generally speak about the concept as it is applied to institutions and procedures. In other words, while one could apply our arguments to the evaluation of individual choices or social relationships, we do not actively explore this direction; our discussion and presentation is consciously oriented toward what is broadly referred to as organizational legitimacy.

We then move on in Section 4.2 to discuss the foundations of legitimacy. Almost every definition of legitimacy of which we are aware depends on congruence between the object being evaluated and an underlying condition, such as social norms, fairness, equality, or popular acceptance. (An important exception to this characterization is the notion that legitimacy is equivalent to deference, as we discuss later.) In Section 4.2, we attempt to clarify how we, and our theory, remain agnostic about the nature of the underlying condition. Specifically, the combination of our arguments about the general applicability of social choice in the first part of the book and the main results presented in the ensuing chapters allow us this freedom.

---

[1] Meyer and Scott (1983), p. 201.
[2] Pfeffer and Salancik (1978), p. 194.

4.1 LEGITIMACY OF WHAT?

Legitimacy is a broadly applied concept. As Johnson writes, legitimacy can be ascribed (or denied) to "an act, a rule, a procedure, a routine, a distribution, a position, a group or team, a group's status structure, teamwork, a system of positions, an authority structure, an organization, organizational symbols, an organization's form, practices, services, programs, a regime, a system of power, and a system of inequality (to name a few)."[3] Put more succinctly, Deephouse and Suchman state that "at this point, it appears that almost anything can be a subject of legitimation."[4] Put simply, whatever one is deciding is or is not legitimate is the *subject* of the legitimacy judgment.

Subjects of Legitimacy Judgments: Organizations and Relationships

A useful distinction between existing theories of legitimacy is based on the subject of the legitimacy judgment: Is one judging the legitimacy of an organization or a social relationship? We refer to theories based on the first as *organizational* and those focused on social relationships as *social*.[5] The two categories are not mutually exclusive, of course, but nonetheless exhibit significant differences.

The first significant difference between social and organizational theories of legitimacy centers on how one should measure legitimacy. In particular, social theories of legitimacy are typically more subjective in nature. A central question in these theories is whether an individual ought to obey the commands of another individual.[6] Thus, scholars working within the social tradition frequently equate legitimacy with receiving deference: legitimate relations are those that are obeyed.[7]

A practical and theoretical difficulty with this subjective basis for legitimacy is that it potentially conflates legitimacy with (de jure or de facto) authority. Although one might argue that authority ought to be respected if and only if the authority is legitimate, it is also true that self-interest often dictates that authority should be obeyed regardless of its legitimacy and, similarly, one might measure (or define) authority as possessing the power to have one's dictates obeyed. Even setting these measurement issues aside, equating legitimacy with receiving deference is an unsatisfactory stance from a normative perspective. After all, many regimes and sociopolitical relationships receive deference and are sustained despite clearly questionable moral, legal, or ethical motivations;

---

[3] Johnson (2004), pp. 10–11.

[4] Deephouse and Suchman (2008), p. 54.

[5] The terms are ours, but the schematic was developed by Tost (2011).

[6] In terms of relationships, note that the question of whether one ought to obey another is often answered by reference to the existence of a superior-subordinate relationship between the two individuals. This then naturally leads social legitimacy theorists to consider the question of whether such a relationship is itself legitimate.

[7] For a related discussion of the role of deliberation in producing this form of legitimacy, see Fearon (1998), pp. 55–58.

justifications; or actions. Put another way, a relationship that achieves deference by successfully appealing to the notion that the relationship is legitimate
(e.g., "obey the law because it is the law") is tautologically legitimate from this
viewpoint.

Furthermore and more substantively, our viewpoint is that deference to
the collective decision of the group requires the plausibility that the group
made its decision *for a reason*. In other words, a legitimate policy choice must
be justifiable. Furthermore, deference to a long-standing decision will require
more than a purely procedural justification. For example, although it may be
quite legitimate for a candidate to claim victory in one election because he or
she won more votes than each of the other candidates, this particular argument
does not seem on its face to be up to the challenge of justifying why the decisions
of that candidate should be deferred to by members of the society twenty years
in the future.

A second important difference between organizational and social theories
of legitimacy is the frequency with which legitimacy is equated with fairness in
the social approach. The two concepts should be treated as logically distinct
for several reasons. First, many organizational arrangements (i.e., procedures)
exist precisely because fairness is at least arguably impossible to achieve. A
classic class of such procedures is tie breakers. In many situations, a winner
must be chosen from a set of otherwise equally qualified contestants. A common
solution to this practical problem is the use of a randomizing device, such as
flipping a coin. Setting aside minutiae such as how one ensures that the coin
in question is, and is believed to be, "fair" in the statistical sense, one might
ask whether all such randomizing devices are equally fair in the legitimacy
sense. For example, suppose that there are two equally qualified contestants
of different genders. Instead of flipping a coin that decides the identity of the
winner, one could decide the winner based on the flip of a (statistically fair)
coin with "man" printed on one side and "woman" printed on the other. From
a fairness standpoint, these two procedures are equivalent. From a legitimacy
standpoint, however, we assert that the two approaches would be viewed very
differently; labels matter. Alternatively, one could have the two contestants
engage in a duel, with the survivor being declared the winner (and the loser
dying). Even supposing the duel were known and perceived to be fair in a
statistical sense, the greatly increased cost of losing under this procedure would
presumably decrease its perceived legitimacy.[8]

Subjects of Legitimacy Judgments: Processes and Outcomes

Even within an organizational legitimacy framework, the subjects of legitimacy judgment can be fruitfully divided into two further categories: *internal*

---

[8] One might ask whether it would be better to set aside the issue of perceived legitimacy and ask
whether either of the alternative procedures should be accorded different "objective" legitimacy.
We would answer this question in the negative: each of the two alternatives are objectively
dominated by the classic "coin flip between contestants" approach.

processes by which the organization operates (i.e., by which outcomes are selected) and the *external actions* of the organization (i.e., the *outcomes* that are chosen by the organization's processes). The fact that these two categories are simultaneously distinguishable and inextricably linked by nature is well known. Furthermore, even though "good decision making" can lead to bad decisions and, conversely, good decisions sometimes result from "bad decision making," a general supposition is that good decision-making processes tend to produce good outcomes and bad processes tend not to do so.

Analogously, an illegitimate process might produce a legitimate outcome, and a legitimate process might produce an illegitimate outcome, but legitimate processes do (or at least should) promote the selection of legitimate outcomes. Thus, our theory purposely includes both process and outcome in the definition of legitimacy. However, in addition to the descriptive accuracy of such an approach, the discussion of social choice in Part I also motivates this separation of process and outcomes: an important implication of Arrow's Theorem is that any theory of legitimacy that wholly restricts attention to outcomes will necessarily be incomplete.

Aiming Our Theory

At least from the practical standpoint of simplifying our presentation, we think it is useful to "pick a side" and focus on organizational subjects of legitimacy evaluations. Because our empirical referents are (formal) governmental processes and institutions, organizational legitimacy is a natural framework for our discussion. Just as important, however, our theory of legitimacy is designed to be objective in the sense that legitimacy within our theory is independent of subjective evaluations. There is no "observer" within our framework. Similarly, our theory contains no notion of "agency." The concept of an "individual" is orthogonal to our setting in the sense that the results are meaningful regardless of whether one populates our model with individual actors.

By ignoring notions such as individual and agency, our theory is simultaneously both quite "thin" and very general. It is thin in that little of the theory's "axiomatic weight" is devoted to discriminating between good and bad. For example, there is little to no recognition of, or demand for, notions such as "autonomy" or "rights." We do not bring such concepts into our theory for two reasons. First, we do not need them; as we discuss from time to time throughout this part of the book, a powerful implication of the generality of our framework is that the results we obtain – in particular, our existence result (theorem 6) – imply that such notions can be brought in later as appropriate. Second, it is well known that including such notions leads to impossibility results that are analogous to the theorems of Arrow and Gibbard & Satterthwaite.[9]

Another explanation for our theory's thinness is somewhat more ideological in nature. We believe that a proper definition of legitimacy is objective. That is,

[9] For example, see Sen (1970*b*) and Gibbard (1974).

legitimacy should be at least theoretically verifiable. We believe this precisely because we believe in the notion that individuals "ought" to defer to legitimate policies and commands. It would be ironic to suggest that another individual ought to follow (say) a law that he or she otherwise finds objectionable because it represents a "legitimate" law if the legitimacy of that law was based entirely on some individual's perception of that law's legitimacy.[10]

Similarly, as discussed in Section 1.3, our goal in this book is theoretical: our discussion of empirical referents in Part III is intended to provide traction for understanding how institutions and decisions can emulate the characteristics of legitimate procedures and choices, respectively. We do not claim that our definition of legitimacy is predictive of securing deference or even broadly descriptive of real-world institutions or policies. Returning to the analogy between our theory and that of Nash equilibrium discussed in Section 1.3, we offer a theory of legitimacy that describes and discriminates. It is valid theoretically regardless of whether it predicts behavior. Thus, we think it appropriate to place our theory within an organizational legitimacy framework and to realize that the proper and relevant framing of legitimacy judgments are as a combination of the policy in question and the processes that produced it. The policy is the initial product of interest, and the description of the process leading to it provides the explanation for why that policy – and not some other one – was ultimately chosen.

Before continuing, however, it is important to note that although our discussion of the foundations of our theory accords closely with formalized institutions, one could also apply the theory to informal, or "less institutional," settings and arrangements. The main difficulty with extending the theory to such environments is the frequency with which informal institutions are less transparent. That is, as we discuss in the chapters that follow, a key component of legitimacy in our framework is the linkage between the ultimate choice and the decision process leading up to it. From a practical standpoint, providing this linkage requires some kind of record keeping. Regardless of whether such record keeping is more or less formalized, the notion of an informal institution immediately suggests that such records are less likely to be created or retained. For example, although legislatures typically maintain accounts of their deliberations such as transcripts and recorded votes, such records are rarely maintained for decisions made in informal institutions such as families and social groups. Of course, this is not to say that the decisions of informal arrangements are necessarily less legitimate than those of formal institutions. Indeed, the opposite might very well be true to the degree that the formality of an institutional arrangement is itself endogenously determined. Formality is, at least in a direct sense, more costly than informality. Thus, the formality

---

[10] To put it another way, relegating legitimacy judgments to the subjective evaluation of one or more observers merely pushes back the origin of true legitimacy. Namely, which observers are proper judges of legitimacy? Presumably not the promulgator of the policy being evaluated, of course, but then who? And who gets to say who the proper judge is?

of an institutional arrangement may itself be an indicator of the participants' perception of the need to legitimize the institution's choices. Unfortunately, these interesting and important questions are beyond the scope of our project, and we accordingly set them aside. With that said, we now proceed to consider organizational legitimacy in more detail.

Organizational Legitimacy

Applying our theory to organizations requires traversing the divide between processes and organizations. That is, how do an organization's constituent processes and procedures compose the organization as a whole? How does the introduction or adoption of a single illegitimate procedure affect the legitimacy of the organization? In a sense, we sidestep this important question by abstracting from the range of various moving parts of which an organization might be composed. Rather, the theory considers a decision and the process by which it was chosen in isolation. The question of how one aggregates multiple decisions and the corresponding constitutive processes into a cohesive judgment of "aggregate" legitimacy is purposely left unaddressed.[11]

Our approach is consonant with others' views regarding organizational legitimacy. For example, Scott describes organizational or institutional legitimacy as "not a commodity to be possessed or exchanged, but rather a condition reflecting perceived consonance with relevant rules and laws, normative support, or alignment with cultural-cognitive frameworks."[12] More generally, one should inquire as to whether a proposed means of measuring legitimacy (i.e., comparing varying degrees of legitimacy) is itself legitimate. By virtue of generating comparisons between subjects, any "legitimacy metric" is itself a mechanism by which choice could be produced. That said, research on organizational legitimacy has identified some key components of its procurement and sustenance. To explain why they do not factor into our treatment of the topic, we briefly discuss two of these – external linkages and isomorphism – before turning to consider the sources of legitimacy.

External Linkages

Individual perceptions of an organization's legitimacy are highly influenced by perceptions of how others perceive it (both individually and collectively). Successfully identifying the organization with cultural symbols or legitimate external figures (by, for example, securing endorsements from, or donating resources to, other legitimate figures or organizations) generally enhances the

---

[11] Tackling this question is possible within the framework developed here but would in a sense merely replicate the structure and notions we develop in the ensuing chapters. After all, aggregating legitimacy judgments is clearly an aggregation problem to which one can directly apply the social choice arguments presented earlier in the book.

[12] Scott (1995), p. 45.

organization's legitimacy.[13] In addition, linking the organization and its actions with successful or efficient pursuit of its ends can promote perceptions of its legitimacy.[14] In general, individual perceptions of an organization's legitimacy tend to be based on the perceived relationships between the organization with referents external to the organization that are perceived to be legitimate. From an empirical standpoint, then, external linkages represent evidence about the nature of these relationships. A high-profile way in which such linkages are inferred and categorized is described by the notion of isomorphism, which we now briefly describe.

Isomorphism

Isomorphism describes the degree to which the procedures, structures, and strategies used by an organization are similar to other procedures, structures, and strategies that are deemed legitimate.[15] There are numerous arguments for why isomorphism with other legitimate organizations tends to support perceptions of legitimacy, including uncertainty about linkages between means and ends, emulation of successful predecessors and competitors, and inferences about commonality of purpose or intent. However, measuring isomorphism is in the end no easier than measuring legitimacy: comparing the structures of any two organizations is generally an aggregation problem in its own right. For example, how does one compare and trade off the various possible dimensions of isomorphism? Two organizations may use very similar procedures for hiring employees and very different processes for internal promotion. Is the isomorphism between these two organizations stronger or weaker than that between two other organizations that use identical promotion schemes but very different hiring practices?

4.2 THE BASES OF LEGITIMACY

Although legitimacy is frequently linked to a consonance between an organization and *something*, scholars differ on what that something is. Broadly speaking, the various candidates for what this something is can be divided into three categories, which we refer to as legal, social, and moral bases.[16]

Legal Bases of Legitimacy

Legal bases of legitimacy include factors such as whether the leaders are selected in accordance with preexisting procedures, endorsement of the organization by

---

[13] Galaskiewicz (1985), pp. 296–297.

[14] Meyer and Rowan (1977) and Deephouse (1996).

[15] For more on isomorphism see, among many others, DiMaggio and Powell (1983) and Deephouse (1996).

[16] As we discuss in more detail later, these categories are not mutually exclusive, and many scholars require consonance with multiple bases in order for an organization to possess full or perfect legitimacy. An excellent example of such an approach is provided by Beetham (1991).

the state, and linkage of the organization's activities with the sustenance of the rule of law. Few scholars treat these bases of legitimacy as entirely dispositive, if only because such an approach leaves open the question of whether the laws in question were themselves legitimate. However, such bases are commonly treated as a necessary condition for legitimacy; discarding them arguably broadens the scope of legitimacy too much. Without a legal basis of legitimacy, the dictates of a clearly invalid government would be accorded the same legitimacy as they would if rendered by a government selected in a procedurally appropriate fashion.

Social Bases of Legitimacy

Social bases of legitimacy focus on the norms and traditions of a group. In the discussion of such bases of legitimacy, the term "cultural" is broadly synonymous with "social." Social bases of legitimacy focus on whether the organization or its practices are generally viewed as acceptable, where acceptability is demonstrated by individual and collective actions in settings apart from the organization. Thus, in a very informal sense, an organization has a stronger social basis of legitimacy if it "looks" and "acts" in ways similar to how society does.[17]

Perhaps unsurprisingly, many sociologists have focused on this form of basis for legitimacy. Indeed, social and cultural bases were central to many early studies of legitimacy.[18] Meyer and Scott describe legitimacy as "the degree of cultural support for an organization – the extent to which the array of established cultural accounts provide explanations for its existence, functioning, and jurisdiction, and lack or deny alternatives."[19] Similarly, Suchman writes: "Legitimacy is a generalized perception or assumption that the actions of an entity are desirable, proper, or appropriate within some socially constructed system of norms, values, beliefs, and definitions."[20] Similar to legal legitimacy, social legitimacy can in some cases be conferred through endorsement of the organization by social actors.[21]

An example of a policy that can be clearly judged in terms of its consonance with social norms and traditions is differentiation between individuals on the basis of gender (e.g., organizations such as the Boy Scouts and Girl Scouts

---

[17] It is beyond our scope to thoroughly explore the distinction between objective and subjective definitions of legitimacy, but it is worth noting that one can replace the notion that a social basis of legitimacy depends on the organization looking and acting like society with "looking and acting like people's perceptions of society." This distinction is unimportant for our purposes but has important implications for how legitimacy is related to social welfare.

[18] For example, Parsons (1956, 1960) and Weber (1968). For an overview, see Powell and DiMaggio (1991).

[19] Meyer and Scott (1983), p. 201.

[20] Suchman (1995), p. 574.

[21] Deephouse (1996).

and policies prohibiting women from certain positions, such as those held by some churches and nations' militaries). An explicit policy of gender distinction is arguably more consonant with the social practices of eighteenth-century America than it is with those of twenty-first-century America. Accordingly, in terms of the social basis and holding all other factors constant, an organization in the United States using such a policy would be more legitimate 300 years ago than it would be now.

Moral Bases of Legitimacy

The final category of legitimacy bases, the "moral" bases, refers to dictates of how things ought to be or be done. Relative to legal and social bases, moral bases of legitimacy are generally more "absolute" or, perhaps, context free than legal and social bases of legitimacy. Specifically, although a moral basis may provide conditional legitimation (e.g., killing is wrong unless it is in self-defense, stealing another person's food is wrong unless it is to prevent one's own starvation), a moral basis of legitimacy is itself *universal*.[22] That is, a moral basis of legitimacy is itself legitimated on the basis of reasons that themselves need not be scrutable (e.g., faith, tradition).

Our Agnostic Approach

In this book, we are in some sense agnostic about the basis of legitimacy insofar as we presume that there is an underlying principle by which some or all of the feasible alternatives may be compared. Our theory is independent of the origins of this principle. For example, one could use as the principle any of the following:

- a purely legal basis for legitimacy in which a legislature has rendered pairwise comparisons for some or all of the pairs of feasible alternatives,
- a purely social, populist basis for legitimacy in which some or all of the pairs of feasible alternatives have been compared according to results of a plebiscite, or
- a moral basis of legitimacy by which some or all of the pairs of feasible alternatives have been compared according to (say) which of the two alternatives offers a greater absolute level of resources to the worst-off member of society.

On the other hand and regardless of the nature of the underlying principle, our approach to legitimacy is moral in nature insofar as it is adopts a logical

---

[22] This is arguably the heart of the reason that it is controversial to reference moral bases of legitimacy in public spheres. To countenance such a basis as a proper judge of what "ought" to be implies a countenancing of that as a basis of what "ought" to be in all situations, even those extending beyond the public sphere.

and context-free system of axioms as its starting point. In terms of the bases of legitimacy, an additional virtue of our approach in this book is that it provides a precise conception of consistency between an organization – conceived as a combination of processes used and choices made – and an underlying principle that the organization is presumed to be pursuing. In the next chapter, we provide an informal exposition of our theory and its representation of both processes and their consonance with an underlying principle.

5

Principles and Legitimate Choice

In this chapter, we describe and explicate the theory of legitimacy in informal terms. However, while our discussion is much less formal than the presentation in the following chapter, a bit of notation will make the discussion here more precise and succinct. Specifically, the basic primitives of our theory are a set of feasible *policies*, denoted by X, and a set of *principles*, denoted by $\mathcal{P}$. In addition, when we are discussing a particular principle in $\mathcal{P}$, we will denote it by p. As described in more detail in this chapter, a principle $p \in \mathcal{P}$ is simply a generalized description of how the various possible policy choices are compared or ranked. The principle is akin to the collective ordering denoted by $\succ$ in the first part of the book, which we used to denote the output of an aggregative process, f. Thus, a principle represents a method of comparing alternatives that may take many factors into account and that may have been generated via an aggregative procedure. However, in the remainder of the book, we deliberately set aside the question of how the aggregative process of generating a principle worked, the axioms it satisfied, etc. What we take as given is that the principle, as it stands, is the standard by which alternatives are measured and represents the accepted way of choosing alternatives. By "the accepted way of choosing alternatives," we mean that the principle is accepted as the basis for justifying or explaining why one alternative was chosen as opposed to another. In the first part of this book, we have hopefully convinced the reader of the difficulties of aggregation insofar as the principle ultimately produced by the aggregation of multiple criteria might not be transitive. We now move on to discuss the possibility of rendering choices that respect a potentially cyclic principle that does not yield a unique and unambiguous best choice.

In our theory, a principle represents whatever means by which two alternatives would be compared and ranked. For example, consider comparing applicants for admission to college. Admitting students involves assigning each

TABLE 5.1. *Example of Competing Principles*

	Three Policies		
Policy	Wealth of i	Wealth of j	Wealth of k
x	10	10	10
y	8	15	11
z	9	9	13

	Three Possible Principles	
Principle	Ranking	Properties of Ranking
Wealth maximization	$y\ p\ z, z\ p\ x, y\ p\ x$	*Complete and transitive*
Majority rule	$z\ p\ y, y\ p\ x, x\ p\ z$	*Complete and cyclic*
Makes both j & k better off	$y\ p\ x$	*incomplete*

applicant to one of two categories (admit or reject).[1] Several criteria might be used for this problem, including standardized test scores and grade point average. Many, if not most, of these criteria, if applied individually, would provide a transitive ordering of all applicants for whom the information is available. Using any of these alone to make one's decision (what we referred to as a dictatorial aggregation rule) would generate an essentially unambiguous ranking of all applicants.[2] Of course, it is arguable whether one would want to allocate spots (i.e., admit students) based on any one of these yardsticks alone. However, if one uses two or more criteria to make the admissions decisions, then the resulting principle may not be capable of deeming one potential entering class uniquely and unambiguously "best."

From a theoretical perspective, a principle is simply *any* method of comparing the possible choices that might be used to justify a collective decision. One can replace the term "justify" with "explain," "provide a reason for," or any similar concept. For example, consider the choice between three policies, x, y, and z, each of which represents a different distribution of wealth among the citizenry, which consists of three individuals, i, j, and k. The wealth of each individual under each of the three policies is displayed in Table 5.1. Table 5.1 also describes three potential principles, two of which are straightforward and yield complete binary relations (wealth maximization and majority preference)

---

[1] That is, the admission decision is best viewed as a choice between different sets of admitted applicants (i.e., "entering classes") as opposed to as a choice between admitting or rejecting individual applicants. That is, in line with the discussion in Part I, the alternatives confronting an admission committee are different possible entering classes. The principle describing this choice problem, then, ranks pairs of entering classes.

[2] The only ambiguity resulting from the possibility of ties between two or more applicants.

and a third (mutual gain for individuals j and k) that yields an incomplete relation: it does not give an unambiguous ranking for all pairs.[3] Supposing that one grants that these principles might be used as reasons to justify decisions within a democratic institution, one must allow for cyclic or incomplete principles within a theory of legitimate deliberative decision making.

Our definition of a principle as a binary relation carries an important implication and is in some sense not without loss of generality.[4] It implies that principles rank (or, for incomplete principles, possibly *fail* to rank) each pair of alternatives and that the ranking of alternatives by any given principle is set. Is this realistic? The notion of *situational ethics* represents one type of objection to this conceptualization of principles. Put succinctly, proponents of situational ethics argue that there is rarely an applicable absolute standard: the choice one ought to make is inherently and inextricably dependent on the details of the situation at hand.[5] However, such an objection is based on a distinction that lies outside of our theory: our representation of principles implies that any principle is absolute only in the sense that the principle provides a definite and fixed ranking (or nonranking) of any given pair of alternatives. In other words, we assume that any relevant elements of the situation or context have been incorporated into the principle: our theory does not require one to take a position on whether the principle is absolute in a universal sense or situationally dependent.

While representing principles as binary relations is arguably restrictive, an important implication of our definition is that we are quite permissive with respect to what we term a principle. Specifically, we denote as a principle binary relations that are ill behaved insofar as they are cyclic or incomplete. By not ruling out cyclic principles, we are allowing for principles that may not be well behaved as prescriptions for behavior. As illustrated in Table 5.1 and the accompanying discussion, a potential example of such a principle is majority preference. More important, our theory shows how the process of collective decision making (at least as conceptualized here) can itself render ill-behaved principles useful as sources of legitimation for policy choices. From a technical standpoint, the inclusion of such ill-behaved, cyclic principles presents our theory with a greater challenge. After all, any acyclic principle will be consistent with at least one internally consistent and unobjectionable choice.

---

[3] The third principle in this example yields an incomplete relation because it relies essentially on a supermajoritarian rule (or, equivalently, gives veto or blocking power to some individuals). This type of reliance is frequently sufficient to generate incomplete orderings of the alternatives but is of course not a necessary condition for such a principle. In particular, if one considers policies with multiple attributes (or characteristics) and principles that consider only strict differences between these characteristics (e.g., the "Elimination by Aspects" heuristic proposed by Tversky, 1972), incompleteness results in many situations.

[4] See p. 56 for an informal discussion of binary relations. A more formal treatment is provided in the following chapter.

[5] For example, Fletcher (1966).

The main argument in favor of allowing principles to be incomplete is empirical: many popular principles (e.g., Pareto optimality and supermajority preference, as in Table 5.1) can provide incomplete rankings. As will become clear, our theory provides a vivid portrait of one undesirable property of choice according to an incomplete principle. In particular, the fact that incomplete principles are indecisive between some pairs of alternatives implies that, in general, more choices can be legitimated with such principles, thereby undermining the notion of legitimacy as a refinement on the set of possible outcomes.

The Origins of Principles

Throughout much of our discussion, we take the principle to be given (i.e., exogenously determined). That is, some principle $p \in \mathcal{P}$ is assumed to have been formed, chosen, or accepted before the decision situation under examination.[6] The principle represents the structure (or, perhaps, logic) with respect to which a collective decision must be justified.

In simple terms, a principle compares pairs of possible choices. By taking the principle as given, we do not inquire more deeply into how the comparisons are formed. However, the discussion of aggregation in Part I is our starting point: principles are frequently the product of aggregating various criteria. In this part of the book, we presume that the principle is the output of an aggregation process that has already occurred before the process by which an alternative is chosen. For example, in choosing the set of regulations governing air pollution in the United States, the Environmental Protection Agency is responsible for using an aggregation of various criteria as set forth in statute by Congress. Similarly, when evaluating districting plans, a District Court judge applies the aggregation of a set of criteria set forth in the Constitution, applicable federal statutes, and relevant judicial precedents.

The social choice arguments discussed in Part I imply that nontrivial aggregation of multiple factors (preferences, judgments, or other criteria) can create ill-behaved principles for comparison. Our main results, as presented and discussed in Chapter 6, ensure that our theory of legitimacy will produce a nonempty set of legitimate processes and decisions for *any* ultimate product of this a priori aggregation.

Comparing Principles

For the most part, we consciously avoid the question of whether one should (or can) rank principles. Because of our decision to sidestep this question, the ensuing discussion in this chapter and that contained in the next takes on a distinctly "thin" feel. This is unfortunate – after all, a direct reading of our theoretical framework as presented suggests that processes and policies can

---

[6] In terms of the first part of the book, we are assuming now that the primitive criteria have already been aggregated – before the choice process – in some fashion to form a principle.

(or might) be as easily rendered legitimate by reference to *Mein Kampf* as by reference to the U.S. Constitution – but we believe that this thinness is, in a sense, unavoidable. We fervently believe that one can and should evaluate principles on their merits – it is just not the case that this theory is primarily designed to do so.[7] Nonetheless, in this book, we adopt an agnostic position with respect to how the principles are chosen. As we return to at various points, one of the most powerful aspects of our theory's conclusions about legitimacy is the degree to which they are not dependent on beginning with specially chosen principles. In concluding, our approach to legitimacy and choice mirrors that of Nonet (1980), who notes that

> the choice of a purpose may pose even greater problems of legitimacy than do conclusions drawn from an accepted purpose. But our concern here is only with institutional arrangements regulating the subordinate decisions that carry out an established mandate.[8]

5.1 CHARACTERIZING LEGITIMACY

As discussed at the beginning of this book, we conceive of a legitimate choice as a choice that conforms to a recognized principle or standard. The difficulty we have set forth concerns how a decision can conform to such a principle when the principle is ill behaved. Taking the principle as given, legitimate choice in our theory involves selecting a series of $n \geq 1$ alternatives, $\delta = (x_1, \ldots, x_n)$ – the *decision sequence* – that justifies (or rationalizes) the final choice, x_n, via the established principle, p. The decision sequence is intended to represent the (perhaps hypothetical) progress of collective reasoning leading to the final decision x_n. Roughly, the sequence δ can be thought of as a sequence of proposals culminating in the ultimate acceptance of x_n as the collective choice. To justify the final policy, x_n, the reasoning process, as represented by decision sequence δ, must itself be consistent with the principle p. Thus, the decision sequence represents the link between the collective choice and the underlying principle. We now turn to a recent example that demonstrates the important of consistency between a choice and an underlying principle.

---

[7] One could use our theory to rank principles, broadly construed as bases of legitimacy as discussed in Section 4.2. In particular, our framework is based on two axioms, each of which imposes conditions on the relationship between various alternatives and giving pride of place to the alternative that is ultimately chosen (and hence part of the object of the legitimacy evaluation). To the degree that one accepts either of these two axioms as primitive to the notion of legitimacy, one should then consider whether a principle attempts to preclude the comparisons between alternatives called for by the axioms themselves. Principles that do so are necessarily less legitimate *as principles*. Conversely, one could also argue that principles that promote the individual and collective consideration of such comparisons as possessing greater legitimacy, again *as principles*. In the interest of maintaining a sustained focus, however, we do not explore this topic in this book.

[8] Nonet (1980), p. 279.

Example 1 (*Citizens United*) In *Citizens United v. Federal Election Commission*[9], the Supreme Court ruled that the freedom of speech guarantees of the First Amendment prohibited the government from limiting political expenditures by unions and corporations. The specific issue at hand was whether advertisements for a documentary film entitled *Hillary: The Movie* could be shown on television shortly before an election or whether such airings violated the 2002 Bipartisan Campaign Reform Act (BCRA), which prohibited certain electioneering communications during this preelection period. By a five to four majority, the Court ultimately found that parts of the BCRA violated the First Amendment, a contentious decision that overturned a high-profile ruling on campaign finance law, *Austin v. Michigan Chamber of Commerce*.[10]

Interestingly for the purposes of our argument, Chief Justice Roberts issued a 14-page concurrence to discuss "important principles of judicial restraint and *stare decisis* . . . " One focus of Roberts's concurring opinion was to discuss the precedent established in *Austin*,[11] a case which ruled that corporate money can unfairly influence elections and that was overturned by the decision in *Citizens United*. Both the majority in *Citizens United* and the minority in *Austin* argued that banning corporate money from politics was akin to attempting to "level the political playing field," a concept rejected as illegitimate under the First Amendment in *Buckley v. Valeo*.[12] In her attempt to convince the Court to uphold *Austin*, Solicitor General Elena Kagan abandoned the "equality rationale" underlying the *Austin* decision, arguing instead that first, corporate spending would corrupt, or appear to corrupt, politicians, and second, that corporate spending in elections is a possible misuse of shareholders' money. Referring to the argument in *Austin*, Kagan stated "We do not rely at all on that."[13]

In his concurrence, Chief Justice Roberts defended the Court's decision to overturn *Austin* in part by noting that the government had abandoned the original reasoning behind the *Austin* decision:

> To the extent that the government's case for reaffirming *Austin* depends on radically reconceptualizing its reasoning, that argument is at odds with itself. . . . There is therefore no basis for the Court to give precedential sway to reasoning that it has never accepted, simply because that reasoning happens to support a conclusion reached on different grounds that have since been abandoned or discredited.

> Doing so would undermine the rule-of-law values that justify *stare decisis* in the first place. It would effectively license the Court to invent and adopt new principles of constitutional law solely for the purpose of rationalizing its past errors, without a proper analysis of whether those principles have merit on their own. . . .[14]

[9] *Citizens United v. Federal Election Commission*, 558 U.S. 310 (2010).
[10] *Austin v. Michigan Chamber of Commerce*, 494 U.S. 652 (1990).
[11] 494 U.S. 652 (1990).
[12] *Buckley v. Valeo*, 424 U.S. 1 (1976).
[13] "Stints in Court May Yield Clues to a Style," *The New York Times*, April 15, 2010, A1.
[14] 558 U.S. 310 (2010) (Roberts, C.J., concurring).

In this statement, Roberts notes that *stare decisis* is compelling because it privileges the principles used in past decisions; he argues that past use of these reasons is evidence of their merit, as it demonstrates that the reasons have been given thoughtful consideration. At the same time, in overruling *Austin*, the *Citizens United* decision overruled decades of campaign finance law. In part (we have argued) because the Supreme Court is unelected, it must convince people of the legitimacy of its decisions.

Roberts takes time to illustrate the reason behind his decision by arguing that rejecting the government's case is not as blatant a violation of *stare decisis* as they claim it is: the government has defended *Austin* via a line of reasoning that was never used as a defense in the first place. In fact, Roberts goes even further to say that according to Austin, precedential sway on the basis of Kagan's argument would actually undermine the logic behind *stare decisis* because it would "... license the Court to invent and adopt new principles of constitutional law solely for the purpose of rationalizing its past errors...." In other words, Roberts argues, the ruling in *Austin* cannot be disentangled from the reasoning that initially supported it.

Roberts writes that the strength of the majority opinion lay, in part, on the fact that the government had defended *Austin* using reasoning that differed dramatically from what had originally been argued in that case: in other words, the government abandoned the *principle* that the case it was defending had rested upon. As Roberts wrote,

> the Government never once even *mentions* the compelling interest that *Austin* relied upon in the first place: the need to diminish "the corrosive and distorting effects of immense aggregations of wealth that are accumulated with the help of the corporate form and that have little or no correlation to the public's support for the corporation's political ideas.[15]   Δ

The above example describes a scenario in which the government attempted to defend an outcome – the *Austin* decision that upheld restrictions on corporate speech – while dismissing the decision sequence and guiding principle that had led to that outcome. In overturning *Austin*, the Court rejected the original principle underlying *Austin* and rendered a decision consistent with a different principle – one consistent with corporations having First Amendment rights of free speech.

In our theory, a decision sequence is consistent with a principle if and only if it satisfies two requirements. The first of these consistency requirements is referred to as being *internal* in nature, as it refers to the relationship between the alternatives explicitly included in the justification – i.e., the decision sequence. The second consistency requirement regards the choices *not* included in the decision sequence and consequently is referred to as being *external* in nature. We now briefly describe each of these two requirements.

---

[15] 558 U.S. 310 (2010) (Roberts, C.J., concurring).

Internal Consistency

The internal consistency requirement is satisfied only if the decision sequence does not use any alternative that is ranked strictly lower by the principle than some alternative considered earlier in the decision sequence. In words, this requirement captures the idea that to justify the collective decision with the underlying principle, p, the decision process was indeed guided and constrained by that principle. Each step in the process of collective reasoning refined the set of possible choices with respect to the guiding principle. Internal consistency is productively discussed in terms of two foundational components, *sensibility of outcome* and *sequence coherence*, which we now discuss in turn.

Sensibility of Outcome

A decision process has not produced a sensible outcome if the process at some point rejected an alternative that is obviously superior to the chosen alternative. Accordingly, a decision sequence is legitimate only if no alternative in the sequence is strictly superior to the final choice.

Sensibility is really a minimal requirement for a decision-making process to be described as rational (with respect to the principle p). Consideration of this point clarifies our approach to legitimacy. Using the classical meaning of rationality as an accurate correspondence between means and ends, the notion of the principle in our theory is a generalized portrait of the ends and the decision sequence is a generalization of the means. A decision sequence that fails to be sensible with respect to the outcome it produces necessarily fails the most minimal test of whether it represents a rational attempt to optimize with respect to p: the final choice is not the best alternative under p *even among those choices that have been explicitly rejected in favor of it*. As a minimal test, it is not surprising that this requirement is simple to satisfy and imposes very minor restrictions on the set of legitimate procedures. The real bite of internal consistency as a foundation for legitimacy is provided by sequence coherence, to which we now turn.

Sequence Coherence

Sensibility of outcome distinguishes the alternative that is ultimately chosen from the alternatives explicitly rejected in favor of it and compares each such alternative with the final choice according to the underlying principle, p. Aside from this minimal relationship, the sensibility of an outcome of a decision sequence does not depend on how the sequence is structured. *Sequence coherence* describes our requirement that the order of the decision sequence (i.e., the order of consideration) not contradict the presumption that reasoning was guided by the underlying principle.

By "guided," we mean that a coherent decision sequence always "follows" the underlying principle p in the sense (1) that each alternative is ranked as superior to the immediately previously discussed alternative by p and (2) the decision sequence never uses an alternative that is ranked as inferior by p to an alternative considered and refined earlier. Sequence coherence is a strengthening of outcome sensibility – a coherent decision sequence is necessarily sensible – and it can be much harder to satisfy. This strengthening is desirable in its own right insofar as legitimate choices – choices demonstrably consistent with an underlying principle – should be made based on a demanding set of criteria. In addition, coherent arguments are more persuasive: they are more likely to engender deference from the governed. Specifically, individual perceptions of legitimacy are enhanced by the provision of logical rationales for an organization's actions.[16] To the degree that legitimacy is a product of reason giving, as we portray it in this book, coherence is a necessary condition for legitimate choice: reasons are not simply aggregated chunks of excuses. Rather, a reason is analogous to a linear argument, consisting of propositions and conclusions, tied together by connectives such as "because," "from which it follows that," and "therefore."[17] Arguments are intended to persuade. Thus, our theory portrays the added (i.e., legitimating) value of the decision sequence as providing in some sense the structure of an argument. In other words, the set of alternatives may very well be known to all observers. When this is the case, the decision sequence explains not only why the final choice was chosen but also why the other alternatives were not. (We return below to a fuller description of this second aspect of what the decision sequence explains.)

Viewed as an argument provided to justify the chosen alternative, constructing a coherent argument generally requires effort unless there is a self-evident policy choice (i.e., a policy that is inferior to no other alternative under the guiding principle). Sequence coherence captures one purpose (or product) of the exertion of such effort. However, one can justify our requirement of coherence from a slightly different empirical standpoint if one thinks of the decision sequence as mimicking or recording the deliberations leading to the selection of the chosen alternative. A deliberative choice process should exhibit some nontrivial structure, and coherence represents a general representation of such structure. There are many possible ways (e.g., temporal, grammatical, logical) one might conceptualize deliberative structure, of course, and we do not distinguish among any of them.

With that noted, there are at least two reasons that we think the possibility of presenting a linear depiction of the justification for a choice is important for legitimation of that choice. First, such a format is in line with the presumption that the decision sequence rationalizes the final choice. A good analogy is the structure of formal proofs in mathematics: starting from a set of axioms – in

---

[16] Elsbach (1994), Kernisky (1997), and Elsbach and Elofson (2000).
[17] For example, see Walton (1990) and Johnson (2000).

this case, the principle p and the initially proposed alternative – one proceeds, without violating the principle, to propose alternatives and extend the decision sequence until no further alternative can be added to the decision sequence without violating sensibility of outcome. Following this analogy, a second argument for requiring coherence is one of perceived fidelity to the underlying principle. The principle is, in our theory, offered alongside the final choice as the foundation of the decision sequence. Each alternative in the sequence serves to refine the outcome with respect to the principle; as the decision sequence proceeds, choices become increasingly consistent with the principle as each choice refines its predecessors with respect to p. The choice of principle clearly matters in determining whether a given alternative can be legitimated and, if so, what such legitimation requires in terms of the decision sequence that justifies the alternative's selection.

Before continuing, it is important to recognize that requiring coherence of a decision sequence for legitimacy does have some downsides. For example, coherence may be too demanding in that it amplifies the degree to which alternatives already considered and refined foreclose consideration of some not-yet-considered alternatives. More suggestively, the inclusion of an alternative that cannot itself be a feasible final choice (i.e., a policy that is unable to be chosen legitimately) can nevertheless foreclose the legitimate selection of one or more otherwise feasible alternatives. Thus, requiring coherence amplifies the importance of agenda power. In other words, requiring coherence focuses attention on the importance of "the agenda" (defined here as constructing the decision sequence) in establishing or foreclosing legitimate choice of a given alternative. In this sense, history matters.

History Mattering and Sequential Choice Methods

We now turn briefly to consider for a moment – in terms of the relationship between our theory and real-world selection procedures – the notion of "history mattering." In particular, our theory is consistent with what one might call "elimination-based" processes of choice. Specifically, many methods of choosing involve whittling down the set of possible choices in a sequential fashion. For example, a wide menagerie of run-off systems are used in electoral settings as well as other selection systems. In such procedures, all and only those alternatives receiving sufficient support (points, votes, etc.) in the "first round" are passed on to the second round, at which point the scoring or voting occurs again (sometimes instantaneously, with ballots being rescored according to a predetermined formula), and the process is applied iteratively until the desired number of choices – often one, but sometimes more than one (e.g., elections to multimember districts) – remain.

These procedures are superficially different than our description of decision sequences: the difference is that one needs to think of alternatives in the decision sequence as being subsets of the set of possible alternatives. In each step of a legitimate decision sequence produced by such procedures, the succeeding "alternative" – i.e., the set of retained possible choices – is ranked as above or superior to the preceding superset of possible choices – i.e., the set of possible choices that had been retained from the previous round – by virtue of a principle that can be described as "scored at least the required threshold of points/votes relative to the remaining possible choices."[18]

A prominent example of such a procedure is provided by single-elimination tournaments.[19] In such competitions, the "winner of the tournament" is analogous to the "final choice" in our setting, and the decision sequence is a round-by-round description of the contestants who were not yet eliminated as of that round. Thus, the first "alternative" in the decision sequence is the set of all entrants, the second "alternative" is the set of all entrants who were not eliminated in the first round, and so forth. Finally, the analogue for the principle in such a conception can be described in words as "has not yet lost a match to any entrant." Eventually, the structure of single-elimination tournaments (in terms of having winners play other winners) returns a unique entrant – the final choice or "winner" of the tournament.

In each of these types of choice procedures, note that the corresponding principle is acyclic and the final choice (or choices, as in the case of multi-winner electoral systems) are ranked as inferior to no other possible choices. That is, these elimination-based methods can be easily construed as being based on a nonvacuous principle and producing a decision sequence that is internally consistent with respect to that principle. Of course, a weakness of these systems is that the observed principle does not necessarily rank the losers against each other. This is consistent with our theory and, we believe, an important point: these systems are practical instantiations of collective choice. Accordingly, they have been designed to (or, arguably, sustained because they) guarantee the production of an acyclic binary relation from which the final choices (i.e., winners) are deduced. However, returning to the point of history mattering, it is well recognized that the details of the scheduling (in, say, a sports tournament) and the calculation of the points and thresholds (in electoral systems) can play a significant role in determining which alternative is the winner.

Of course, this dependence has bothered some. In pithy terms, one can think of Riker (1982) as casting an extremely skeptical eye on the idea that we should defer to the winner of a tournament or election as being "the best" simply because he or she won the tournament or election. After all, since it is entirely possible that a different team, party, or candidate might have won a reordered version of the same kind of tournament or election, selection by these

---

[18] Arguably, in light of the discussion in Part I, one might think that a better analogy for the principle is the scoring rule itself, which might aggregate various objective criteria. However, as discussed earlier in this chapter, space and time constraints lead us to consciously (and regretfully) sidestep the question of comparing or choosing principles.

[19] In this short passage, the term "tournament" is used in its colloquial sense. In addition, the passage focuses on single-elimination tournaments merely for succinctness and clarity: the analogy extends to more exotic variants such as round-robin and double-elimination tournaments.

procedures cannot confer legitimacy or "bestness" in and of itself. We believe that the analogy between these selection procedures and our theory suggests a more measured (and positive) conclusion. In particular, simply saying that the team, party, or candidate "won a tournament or election" leaves little to conclude much from. However, the combination of (1) a description of the tournament or election in terms of both the scoring method (i.e., the principle) and (2) a detailed description of how the application of this scoring method ultimately resulted in the victory of the team, party, or candidate (i.e., the decision sequence) represents a broader and more secure foundation for claims of the legitimacy of the winner's victory. Indeed, one of the more important theoretical conclusions obtained in the following chapter is that this is "as much as one can expect" in terms of an axiomatic approach to legitimacy. Simultaneously, the arguments in Part I suggest that this is as much as one *should* demand of *any* notion of legitimacy in the sense of the selected alternative being (one of) "the best" according to some latent objective ordering. The essential objection to the legitimacy-conferring quality of well-designed and faithfully implemented procedures (regardless of their nature) is predicated on the proper underlying principle – i.e., the latent objective ordering – being cyclic. As political pundits and sports fans alike are keenly aware, it is exactly in these cases when one *must* choose a procedure if one wants to select a "winner." With that analogy between our theory and real-world selection procedures explored, we now summarize the notion of internal consistency before turning to a discussion of stability.

Summarizing Internal Consistency

Internal consistency requires that the decision sequence, or deliberative process, exhibit a logical structure with respect to the underlying principle. Specifically, internal consistency requires that the considered alternatives be ordered in a "linear" fashion with respect to the underlying principle. In this conception, public reasoning or deliberation is in a clear sense unidimensional: each alternative considered could be assigned a unique number, with the alternatives assigned higher numbers having been considered later in the deliberative process and being more consistent with the principle than alternatives with lower numbers.[20]

Of course, simply requiring that there is some such structure to the decision-making process imposes no restriction unless we require that this ordering be consonant with the principle, p. Requiring such consonance means that satisfaction of internal consistency has some bite in that *failure* of internal consistency suggests that the principle did not in fact guide the decision process. To the degree that observers desire concurrent justification – as opposed to

---

[20] Echoing the discussion above concerning the generality of our notion of structure, our use of the term "later" in this sentence is shorthand for a general notion of succession: the sequencing of the alternatives need not be temporal in nature.

an ex post rationalization – of the collective decision, internal consistency is a necessary requirement of (an observer-based definition of) legitimacy. Internal consistency views the principle and decision sequence as acting in conjunction as a form of argument justifying the final choice. In this way, internal consistency precludes arguments containing any steps in which the argument proceeds contrary to the principle or doubles back on itself.

The most significant weakness of the internal consistency requirement is that it is trivially satisfied by a decision sequence containing a single policy. In other words, choosing the only alternative considered in the decision process is both sensible with respect to outcome and sequentially coherent. We address this weakness with the stability requirement.

Stability

We require that a legitimate decision be accompanied by a decision sequence that justifies the exclusion of each alternative not included in the decision sequence. The possible justifications for exclusion of an alternative depend on the principle, p. Specifically, exclusion of an alternative y is justified if and only if there is some element of the decision sequence, x that is ranked strictly superior to y by the principle p.

As we discuss in more detail later in the book, this stability requirement demands that the decision sequence include "enough" alternatives to justify the conclusion of the decision process. In particular, satisfaction of the stability requirement implies that the inclusion of any new alternative in the decision sequence would either introduce a policy that is incomparable to the final policy choice or violate internal consistency as discussed earlier. This requirement is most relevant when the underlying principle is cyclic. Indeed, when faced with a "sufficiently cyclic" principle – i.e., when each alternative is inferior to some other alternative under the principle – an internally consistent decision sequence *must exclude* at least one alternative from the decision sequence.

An important difference between internal consistency and stability is the set of alternatives that are being compared. Whereas internal consistency concerns the relationship between the principle and the alternatives used in the decision sequence, stability uses the principle to compare the decision sequence and all of the other (i.e., unutilized) alternatives. Stability is related to the notion that the principle and decision sequence represent a logical argument justifying the chosen policy. Specifically, stability requires that for any objection to the conclusion of the argument (i.e., an alternative not considered that is better than the chosen policy under the selected principle), there is a counterobjection that defends the final choice.[21]

Requiring stability recognizes that our theory is agnostic about – or, independent of – the exact form by which challenges to potential collective policy

---

[21] We discuss this interpretation in more detail later.

choices are raised within a group. Thus, stability represents a demand that legitimate decisions must be in some sense institution free, similar to the arguments forwarded by McKelvey (1986). While including a more precise delineation of how decision sequences are (or should be) constructed would clearly offer the possibility of generating a more precise characterization of legitimate governance, this agnosticism is reasonable to the degree that the exact structure of the dynamic collective reasoning process is potentially a response to practical and theoretical demands other than legitimacy.[22] Stability requires that, regardless of how the process of collective choice is structured, the final decision must be in some sense "challenge proof," where a challenge is represented by the proposal of an alternative policy to replace the final choice and *a successful challenge must be superior under the principle currently used to justify the final choice*.

The requirement that a successful challenge must respect the principle being used to justify the incumbent final choice is one of two advantages our theory grants to the incumbent final choice. The second is that the incumbent final choice may be "protected" from challenges by earlier incumbents within the decision sequence that have since been refined. The notion of stability, to the degree that one believes that the principle is dispositive with respect to such challenges, represents the maximally demanding analog of a "challenge-proof" requirement that is guaranteed to be satisfied by at least one process that is sensible with respect to outcome. Furthermore, requiring joint satisfaction of stability and sensibility significantly refines requiring sensibility of outcome alone. On the other hand, requiring only satisfaction of stability is trivial. Any decision sequence that includes all feasible alternatives is tautologically stable, as there are no unconsidered alternatives. However, such a vacuous approach to satisfaction of stability will fail to satisfy sensibility if no principle p in the set of available principles, $\mathcal{P}$, yields one or more top-ranked alternatives. That is, if there is no available principle p that can on its own suffice to justify the unilateral selection of some alternative x (in the sense that pairing x and the principle p is both sensible with respect to outcome and stable), then joint satisfaction of sensibility and stability is nontrivial.

5.2 LEGITIMATE DECISION SEQUENCES

With our three criteria – stability, sensibility of outcome, and sequence coherence – in hand, we can now informally characterize the decision sequences that

---

[22] For example, should all participants in the process (say, all duly elected legislators) be guaranteed an opportunity to propose alternatives prior to the rendering of a final choice? Should they be guaranteed *equal opportunity* to offer such proposals? These questions are interesting and difficult. Our approach allows us to sidestep these debates in the interest of space and focus. Our results directly imply that there exists a set of procedures that will satisfy our requirements for legitimate governance.

satisfy various combinations of them. Our main result is that all three criteria can always be satisfied, but the presentation and discussion of this result is aided by first discussing several intervening steps. The first of these regards how decision sequences can satisfy both sensibility and stability. These two criteria are agnostic about how the decision sequence is structured (aside from the identity of the final policy choice) – they depend only on the relationship between the alternatives included and, respectively, excluded from the decision sequence leading up to the selection of the final choice. After that, we turn our attention to the internal structure of the reasoning process. We discuss how a sensible and stable decision sequence might fail to be coherent and present an argument in favor of requiring sequence coherence for legitimacy.

Sensibility and Stability

Sensibility of outcome, which requires only that no alternative in the decision sequence is strictly better – according to the principle p – than the final choice, is easy to satisfy: simple promulgation without justification of any policy is trivially sensible. The potential difficulty, then, is finding a sensible decision sequence that is simultaneously stable with respect to the principle p. Leaving aside the question of whether a given policy can be chosen via a sensible and stable decision sequence (in general, there will be some policies for which no such decision sequence can be constructed for a given principle), construction of such a sequence is equivalent to the construction of an *externally stable set*. In other words, a set of policies Y is externally stable with respect to a principle p if Y contains a counterobjection (under p) to every alternative not in Y.[23]

The notion of an externally stable set lies at the center of our conception of legitimacy and accordingly deserves some discussion. Intuitively, external stability of a set of reasons for a decision is equivalent to "covering one's bases" before arguing in support of the decision: every possible objection to the choice can be refuted with something already provided in one's argument. Of course, our theory substitutes potential choices, or alternatives, for reasons. In such a representation, an objection to a proposed choice is simply any other alternative, and an objection that would at least at first blush be "sustained" is any alternative that the principle ranks as strictly superior to the proposed choice. Finally, "refuting" an objection is equivalent to the proposer pointing out that, if the objection were sustained, one or more alternatives already considered and implicitly refined would themselves then represent successful refinements of the resulting (new) final choice.

Precluding the inclusion of such an alternative as a successful counter-objection may seem arbitrary at first blush: why should an objector care about the previous refinement of an ultimately unchosen alternative, after all? Our justification for this assumption relies upon the presumption that a final choice

---

[23] Note that there is always at least one externally stable set for any principle p by the fact that the entire set of policies, X, is trivially externally stable.

cannot be disentangled from the decision sequence leading up to it. The final choice is, by definition, a refinement of its predecessors. Overriding a choice x with a different alternative y that is superior to x via p when the new alternative y does not itself constitute a refinement of the decision sequence leading to x pursues a line of reasoning that is inconsistent with that which heretofore guided the decision process (i.e., the preexisting decision sequence leading up to and including x). In this respect, stability complements sensibility of outcome in the sense that it helps preserve sensibility in the face of potential challenges to the final choice.

Maintaining Sensibility of Outcome

Just as sensibility of outcome is simple to achieve by including no alternatives other than the final choice in the deliberative process, stability is trivial to guarantee by excluding no alternatives from the deliberative process. However, just as offering no alternatives frequently does not yield a stable decision sequence, rarely does including all possible alternatives in the decision sequence satisfy sensibility of outcome. The challenge for legitimating a policy as the final choice under a given principle, p, involves finding an externally stable set of alternatives in which the chosen alternative is also unbeaten by any alternative in the decision sequence under p.

A central theoretical result undergirding our theory of legitimacy is that – *for any given principle p* – one can find at least one alternative x for which there is a sensible and stable decision sequence with x as the final choice (Theorem 6). Furthermore, the set of such policies can be characterized in a straightforward way with previously defined solution concepts. Specifically, for a given principle p, the set of policies that can be associated with a stable decision sequence that is sensible with respect to outcome is equal to the *uncovered set* under p. Uncovered alternatives are not dominated by any other alternatives. Specifically, one alternative y is covered by another alternative x under a principle p if x is ranked higher than y by p and if every alternative z that is ranked higher than x under p is also ranked higher than y under p. Equivalently, an alternative y is covered by another alternative x under p if x defeats y under p, and y defeating an alternative z under p implies that x also defeats z under p. The uncovered set under a principle p is equal to the set of alternatives that are not covered by any other alternative. Thus, the uncovered set is defined by the alternatives that it does *not* contain.

The set of alternatives that can be associated with a stable decision sequence that is sensible with respect to outcome under a given principle p is *equal* to the uncovered set under p. Thus, the set of alternatives that can be rendered legitimately – i.e., with decision sequences satisfying all three of our criteria – is a subset of the uncovered set.[24] Before we move to consideration of the final

---

[24] At this point in the presentation of the results, we have not yet discussed the implications of requiring sequence coherence. Sequence coherence will frequently result in a further nontrivial refinement of the uncovered set.

criterion of sequence coherence, however, it is useful to pause and consider in some detail what this result, combined with some facts about the structure of the uncovered set, implies in our framework.

First, the uncovered set is in general a strict subset of the available choices. Thus, as one would desire, our notion of legitimacy is in general discerning in terms of limiting what policies satisfy it with respect to a given principle. Second, as hinted at by the discussion of its definition in terms of domination, the uncovered set satisfies an appealing efficiency criterion: it includes no alternative that is Pareto dominated by another alternative under the principle. An interesting implication of this is that, considering any pair of elements of the uncovered set that are each ranked by p against at least one other policy (this need not necessarily be the same alternative), each member of the pair defeats an alternative under p that the other does not. A third suggestive fact is that the structure of a principle p among the elements of its uncovered set is almost unconstrained.[25] Finally, moving beyond the alternatives that can be rendered with sensible and stable decision sequences to consider the decision sequences themselves, another important implication of the notion of covering in our framework emerges. Specifically, if an alternative y is covered by another alternative x under a principle p, the consideration of y has no effect on either the sensibility or the stability of a decision sequence offered to legitimate x as the final policy choice.

We now turn to the requirement of coherence. As we discuss below, sensibility and stability of the decision sequence are not enough to ensure that the policy choice can be the conclusion of an internally consistent set of arguments. As our notion of legitimacy is intended to represent the characteristic of a policy choice and process that are jointly able to be rationalized with one another, such a property is desirable. Requiring that the decision sequence be coherent guarantees this.

Sequence Coherence

As discussed earlier, requiring that decision sequences be coherent implies that the decision sequence has a specific structure. We interpret this structure as linear, in line with the ideal of being able to present the reasoning process in a single-threaded, narrative form. In other words, coherence requires that it be plausible that the deliberative sequence was indeed guided by the principle in the sense that it does not contradict itself at any point *and* the discussion responds to the principle in a positive or direct fashion at each step.

---

[25] The only restriction is that the uncovered set can contain a Condorcet winner (among its members) only if the uncovered set is a singleton. Formally, for any tournament that lacks a Condorcet winner, there is some other tournament for which that tournament is the subtournament induced on the tournament's uncovered set. See, for example, Moulin (1986) and Laslier (1997).

While the actual form of the presentation might not be particularly important, we believe that it is important to be able to represent the deliberations leading to a final decision as having such a structure. That is, whether the sequence represents an actual record of the sequence of deliberations is not particularly important from our perspective – it must merely be plausible that the deliberations indeed reflected an abiding concern about the principle that is proffered as the link between the deliberations and the rendered decision.

As described earlier, coherence encompasses two related properties. The first of these requirements is that no alternative is ever strictly inferior, or less consistent with principle p, to any alternative discussed earlier. The second requirement is that each alternative after the first be directly comparable (and accordingly superior via p) to the alternative it directly succeeds. We now briefly revisit each of these.

Monotonicity

Monotonicity describes the requirement that a coherent decision sequence not contain an alternative that is strictly inferior to any of the preceding alternatives. This requirement is based on a general preclusion of cycles in the principle within the decision sequence.[26] Empirically, one can portray monotonicity as follows. Upon observing the inclusion of an alternative that is strictly inferior to something considered and refined earlier in the decision sequence, an observer might ask, "Well, if you are trying to create a decision sequence that is sensible with respect to outcome, why did you include this alternative *now*, when something considered earlier implies that the decision sequence will not be sensible if it is concluded *at this point*?" Another way of putting this is that monotonicity is implied by requiring that every (ordered) subset of the decision sequence be sensible with respect to outcome. In particular, there is no point in the decision sequence, with respect to its ordering, at which rendering the alternative under consideration at that point would not be sensible with respect to the underlying principle.

Connectedness

In our terminology, a decision sequence satisfies connectedness with respect to the underlying principle p if each successive pair in the sequence is related according to p. This requirement has bite in the sense that it can preclude the legitimate choice of one or more alternatives. As we discuss in more detail later (Example 3), requiring connectedness for legitimacy differentiates among

---

[26] It is a "general" preclusion in the sense that it precludes many decision sequences in which there is no cycle as well. However, the effect of the preclusion, given the additional requirement of connectedness for sequence coherence, is to preclude cycles: acyclic decision sequences that violate monotonicity necessarily also violate connectedness.

alternatives on the basis of how they are related to *groups of* other alternatives that are considered superior to them. In other words, connectedness is an imposition that binds only on alternatives that are ranked inferior to *more than one* other alternative according to the underlying principle, *p*. This is part of an important point in understanding what connectedness brings to the table in terms of how it refines our notion of legitimacy. Specifically, when combined with the requirement of stability, connectedness is in a clear sense more demanding of alternatives that are ranked as inferior to larger sets of other alternatives. Legitimately rendering such alternatives requires the provision of more counterobjections along the decision sequence (holding all else constant): connectedness requires that one find a "path" through the underlying principle *p* that defends against each objection.

More strongly, connectedness requires that the path be directed according to *p*. One could weaken connectedness to require only that each alternative in the decision sequence after the first be comparable under *p* to *some* alternative considered earlier in the sequence. We neither adopt nor explore the implications of this weaker approach. Clearly, our approach yields a definition of legitimacy that is theoretically more demanding. From an empirical perspective, the weaker notion of connectedness differs from our approach only insofar as it admits decision sequences in which one or more arguments is distinctly *ad hoc* in the sense that each newly admissible decision sequence has at least one step in which there is an interim decision that is connected to the argument, but not in a linear fashion. Thus, such decision sequences can be described as containing essential digressions: tracing a path along the principle through one or more counter-objections requires a line of reasoning that is not directly implied by *p*.

Characterizing Coherence

Joint satisfaction of sensibility with respect to outcome, stability, and sequence coherence is feasible for any principle and is satisfied by a generalized version of the Banks set (Banks, 1985) defined and explored by Banks and Bordes (1988).[27] In addition to generating a decision sequence that is compatible with the claim that the collective reasoning process was indeed "guided by" the principle, the requirement of sequence coherence has the advantage that the decision sequence was sensible with respect to outcome *at every step of the process*. Of course, it is possible (indeed, in an informal sense, likely) that *none* of the interim decision sequences were stable. Put together, requiring coherence not only refines the set of possible legitimate outcomes; it also focuses attention

---

[27] Specifically, in their terminology, Banks and Bordes refer to a decision sequence that satisfies sensibility, stability, and coherence as a "maximal T_4-trajectory." Theorem 3.3 of Banks and Bordes (1988) thus implies that the set of all decision sequences that satisfy sensibility, stability, and coherence is nonempty.

on outcomes that were the product of decision sequences that were, at each step, themselves offering plausibly legitimate choices.

This is most easily pictured by thinking of the requirement of stability within a dynamic framework. Specifically, suppose that new policies are introduced into the set of feasible choices by an exogenous process. Furthermore, suppose that after each new alternative is added to the set of existing feasible alternatives it is compared with a preexisting sensible, stable, and coherent decision sequence in a simple fashion: if the new alternative renders the existing decision sequence unstable, it is added to the end of that decision sequence as the new policy choice. Otherwise, the decision sequence and policy choice remain unchanged (and a new alternative is possibly generated). It is simple to verify that this process, if begun with a sensible, stable, and coherent decision sequence, will continue to return a sensible, stable, and coherent decision sequence.

Before concluding, a useful way of thinking about sequence coherence is to consider the implications for alternatives for which there exists at least one sensible and stable decision sequence but for which no decision sequence is simultaneously sensible with respect to outcome, stable, and coherent. The fact that a coherent decision sequence is necessarily acyclic directly yields that the alternatives that are ruled out by the additional requirement of sequence coherence above and beyond sensibility and stability are exactly those for which sensible, stable decision sequences exhibit unambiguously "circular reasoning" with respect to the structure of the principle among the alternatives. In other words, the requirement of coherence is equivalent to ruling out exactly those policy choices for which there is no sensible, stable, and internally consistent set of justifications.[28] Furthermore, there are situations in which the set of policies that can be associated with sensible and stable decision sequences but that cannot be similarly associated with a sensible, stable, and coherent decision sequence, is nonempty. In other words, imposing coherence results in a meaningful refinement of the set of outcomes that can be legitimately rendered. We now proceed to a more formal treatment of these concepts.

[28] As throughout, the principle p represents the underlying "logic" of any decision sequence offered as justification for a final choice.

6

A Social Choice Theory of Legitimacy

In this chapter, we formally define our theory of legitimacy and characterize both the sets of policies that may be chosen legitimately and the decision sequences that may be used to legitimate a policy choice. As discussed in the previous chapter, our theory of legitimacy views a legitimate choice as being, for the most part, inseparable from the decision sequence that legitimates the choice. It is arguably not enough to know simply that a policy choice *can* be legitimated; an observer might reasonably demand to know *how* the choice in question was legitimately rendered. In this way, our characterization of the decision sequences that legitimate their associated final choice is analogous to a characterization of legitimate procedures.

PRIMITIVES AND NOTATION. Let $\mathcal{X}$ denote the set of all finite nonempty sets of alternatives and, for any set $X \in \mathcal{X}$, let $\mathcal{P}_X$ denote the set of all asymmetric binary relations (principles) on X. An asymmetric binary relation on a set X, $p \in \mathcal{P}$, is a subset of $X \times X$. If $(x, y) \in p$, we write $x \, p \, y$ and say that "x is related to y through p." Asymmetry implies that if $x \, p \, y$ then not $y \, p \, x$. As discussed earlier with respect to social aggregators, a binary relation p is *complete* if, for all $(x, y) \in X^2$ with $x \neq y$, $(x, y) \in p$ or $(y, x) \in p$. Finally, a binary relation is a *tournament* if it is asymmetric and complete and we denote the set of all tournaments on a set X by $\mathcal{T}_X \subset \mathcal{P}_X$. For any binary relation $p \in \mathcal{P}_X$ and any $x \in X$, we use the following notation:

$$p(x) = \{y \in X : (y, x) \in p\},$$
$$p^{-1}(x) = \{y \in X : (x, y) \in p\}.$$

CHOICE SITUATIONS. A pair (X, p) with $p \in \mathcal{P}_X$ is a parsimonious representation of a choice situation: X represents a set of possible choices and p represents a principle (binary relation) relating some or all of the alternatives to each other. A *decision sequence* is simply a finite sequence of elements within X. An arbitrary decision sequence is denoted by $\delta = (x_1, \ldots, x_n)$ and the set of all decision sequences within a set X is denoted by Δ_X. For any decision sequence $\delta \in \Delta_X$, we represent the ordering of δ by $x_i \succ_\delta x_j$ if $i > j$. Thus, $x_i \succ_\delta x_j$ if x_i and x_j are both in δ and x_i "comes after" x_j in δ. The last element of δ, denoted by $c(\delta)$, is referred to as the *final decision*: $c(\delta)$ is the unique policy $x \in X$ such that $x = x_n$. This represents the policy choice or, in other words, the decision that is to be legitimated.

INTERNAL CONSISTENCY AND STABILITY. As discussed in the previous chapter, our theory partitions alternatives into those that are included in the decision sequence and those that are not. Internal consistency requires that the alternatives in the decision sequence possess a certain structure with respect to the underlying principle, p. In other words, internal consistency requires that the content and ordering of the decision sequence be consonant with the underlying principle. Thus, internal consistency is a function of the structure of the principle *restricted to the alternatives in the decision sequence*. In formal terms, this is a focus on the *subrelation* induced by the principle on the decision sequence. For any subset of alternatives $Y \subseteq X$ and principle $p \in \mathcal{P}_X$, we write $p|_Y$ to denote the "subrelation" induced by p on the points in Y, which is defined as follows for any subset of alternatives $Y \subset X$:

$$x \, p|_Y z \Leftrightarrow \left[\{x, z\} \subseteq Y \text{ and } x \, p \, z \right].$$

Axiom 1 (Internal Consistency) *A decision sequence δ is internally consistent with respect to a principle p if*

1. *for each pair $x, y \in \delta$,*

$$y \succ_\delta x \Rightarrow \neg[x \, p \, y],$$

and
2. *for each $i \in \{1, \ldots, |\delta| - 1\}$ we have $x_{i+1} \, p \, x_i$.*

Satisfaction of Axiom 1 implies that the decision sequence δ is acyclic with respect to the principle, p. The second requirement of the axiom[1] is the connectedness requirement we discussed earlier: each alternative must be, in terms of the principle p, comparable to the alternative it succeeds, or replaces, in the decision sequence.

Axiom 1 can be described as a "weak" requirement because later alternatives in the decision sequence are only required to not be strictly inconsistent with prior alternatives according to the stated principle and connectedness (i.e., comparability with respect to p) is required only between successive alternatives. In other words, no considered alternative is strictly inferior to any alternative considered before it, but the final choice $c(\delta)$ is not necessarily related to every alternative in the decision sequence. Of course, the connectedness

---

[1] Namely, that for each $i \in \{1, \ldots, |\delta| - 1\}$ we have $x_{i+1} \, p \, x_i$.

requirement implies that one can construct a chain of comparisons through the decision sequence between any pair of alternatives in the decision sequence, but the shortest such chain might include all intervening alternatives. We discuss strengthening this requirement along these lines in Section 6.3. On the other hand, the axiom can be criticized as being too strong, a point that we defer until Section 6.2.

Axiom 2 (Stability) *A decision sequence δ is stable with respect to a principle p if, for each $y \notin \delta$,*

$$y \ p \ c(\delta) \Rightarrow c(\delta) \succ_\delta z \ \text{and} \ z \ p \ y \ \text{for some} \ z \in \delta.$$

Axiom 2 clarifies one reason we refer to this requirement as stability. Specifically, satisfaction of Axiom 2 by a decision sequence δ implies that the decision sequence is *externally stable* (von Neumann and Morgenstern, 1947) with respect to the principle p. As we will discuss again later in the chapter, stability is attractive because it rules out attempts to satisfy Axiom 1 simply by selecting a single choice with no accompanying decision sequence. Satisfaction of the axiom implies that, if an alternative not considered is proposed as a replacement for the final choice, a justification for the final choice can be constructed using the underlying decision sequence and the selected principle to obtain a special form of counterargument. As with Axiom 1, one can describe this axiom as "weak" because it does not impose any restriction on the types of alternatives that can be included to provide exactly such a justification. In particular, Axiom 2 does not require that the final choice actually be directly comparable to the counterargument(s) used to justify it relative to alternatives not considered.

Before proving that legitimate procedures always exist and characterizing them, we note two simple facts about satisfying Axioms 1 and 2. The first fact is that internal justification is guaranteed to be satisfied by any one-element decision sequence *regardless of the principle chosen to justify it* and the second fact is that stability is guaranteed to be satisfied by any decision sequence that contains all alternatives.

TRIVIAL INTERNAL CONSISTENCY. A choice that is promulgated without an accompanying decision sequence can clearly not be inconsistent with it. Put another way, it is in some sense impossible to check if the process used to select an alternative is infirm without a description of the decision-making process itself.[2] This is formally stated below.

---

[2] We say "in some sense" because our theory does, in general, provide some leverage in terms of ruling out certain alternatives as being capable of being rendered legitimate for a given principle p. Thus, if one knows the principle p, there will in general be alternatives such that, regardless of whether such an alternative is accompanied by a decision sequence or not, one can infer with certainty that any decision sequence that led to it would fail to satisfy either internal consistency or stability. Furthermore, in the truly extreme case of putting forward a "Condorcet loser" under p – an alternative that is strictly inferior to every other alternative under p – one can infer

Fact 1 *If δ contains exactly one alternative, δ necessarily satisfies Axiom 1, regardless of p.*

In logical terms, Fact 1 highlights a tautology. Inconsistencies between pairs of distinct alternatives cannot arise if there are no distinct pairs of alternatives: it is impossible to argue that a decision process is not sensible if no process exists. At the same time, it is hard to defend a choice if no supporting evidence is provided with which to back it up. In terms of the substantive application of the theory, this conflict highlights the legitimating value of giving serious consideration to multiple alternatives, as this consideration can be used to defend a final choice. At the same time, allowing free-ranging discussion and deliberation within a collective can create a situation in which *no* final choice can be reconciled with a principle – that is, legitimacy can ultimately be stymied without requiring that the decision-making process proceed in a sensible way that is consistent with the underlying principle. This is demonstrated by the following simple example.

Example 2 (Too Much Deliberation) Suppose that there are three policies, A, B, and C, and the principle, p, generates a Condorcet cycle among the three alternatives, with $A \, p \, B \, p \, C \, p \, A$. Now consider the decision sequence $\delta = (C, B, A)$. Clearly, such a procedure does not satisfy Axiom 1 with respect to p because the final choice, A, loses to an alternative considered earlier in the decision sequence (i.e., C). Furthermore, this is true for any decision sequence containing all elements A, B, and C. $\triangle$

Several important points follow from Example 2. First, unstructured or unconstrained deliberation can undermine the legitimating feature of principle-based deliberative decision making: the discussion itself may extend so far as to make it impossible to rationalize *any* final choice. Accordingly, limits on the scope of discussion may be central to the provision of legitimate policy decisions, a point we return to in Chapter 9. Another way of interpreting Fact 1 is as implying that legitimate decision making may require abstraction from certain comparisons, similar to what Cass Sunstein terms an *incompletely theorized agreement*.[3]

TRIVIAL STABILITY. If the decision process fails to exclude any alternatives, then clearly one does not need to justify why any alternative was excluded from consideration. This trivial satisfaction of stability serves a useful purpose in the sense that it links the stability requirement, Axiom 2, with various notions of deliberation, fairness, and representation: while Axiom 1 values an orderly and logical decision process, Axiom 2 acknowledges the importance of an inclusive one, valuing broad-ranging discussion insofar as it might affect the final decision.

that such an alternative cannot be accompanied by any internally consistent decision sequence containing any other alternatives.

[3] Sunstein (2001).

Fact 2 *If a decision sequence δ contains every policy, δ necessarily satisfies Axiom 2.*

While Fact 1 highlights the importance of Axiom 2 in refining the set of possible legitimate sequences, Fact 2 highlights the formal importance of Axiom 1 for our theory. Specifically, Axiom 2 is satisfied by *any* decision sequence containing every alternative in X – stability requires only that excluded alternatives be properly defeated by a previously considered object. Accordingly, if one does not exclude any alternatives, stability is trivially satisfied.

THE COMPLEMENTARY NATURE OF AXIOMS 1 AND 2. Fact 2 highlights the substantive importance of Axiom 1 and one way in which Axioms 1 and 2 complement each other. After all, intuition suggests that simply considering every option is insufficient to bestow legitimacy upon the final decision. If this were the case, then *any* feasible choice could be rendered legitimate, which would negate both the theoretical and empirical value of the corresponding notion of legitimacy. Thus, according to Axiom 1, the decision-making process must proceed in a linear fashion with respect to the principle that will be used to justify the final decision. Combining Facts 1 and 2 results in an important conclusion: if one can legitimate some policy choice x with a decision sequence that encompasses every possible alternative, one can render it legitimate with a unitary decision sequence containing only the final choice x. Thus, somewhat paradoxically, if a policy decision x is unambiguously "the best" under a principle p in the sense that one does not need to exclude any other alternatives in order to legitimately choose x, one similarly does not need to consider any alternatives in order to legitimately choose x. This is formally stated in the following theorem.

Theorem 5 *If a decision sequence δ contains every policy and satisfies Axiom 1, then $\delta' = (c(\delta))$ also satisfies both Axioms 1 and 2.*

Proof: Suppose that δ contains all elements of X and satisfies Axiom 1 with respect to a principle $p \in \mathcal{P}_X$. Then for each $x \in X$, $\neg[x \ p \ c(\delta)]$. Accordingly, $\delta' = (c(\delta))$ satisfies Axiom 2, as there is no alternative $y \in X$ such that $y \ p \ c(\delta)$. ∎

An implication of Theorem 5 is that when internal consistency can be satisfied by the inclusion of every alternative in the decision sequence (e.g., when the principle is a complete and transitive ordering of the alternatives or the principle has a nonempty core), then the inclusion of multiple alternatives is also unnecessary for satisfaction of Axioms 1 and 2. Again, somewhat ironically, when internal consistency can be satisfied without excluding any alternatives, external stability can be achieved with the briefest of decision processes.

6.1 EXISTENCE OF LEGITIMATE PROCEDURES

We now demonstrate that our theory is nonvacuous in the sense that our axioms can always be satisfied by some decision sequence. This technical result has substantive import because it demonstrates that our response to the objections of both Riker and his critics – namely, that choices can be legitimately rendered even when made according to intransitive goals or criteria (e.g., majority preference) – is not nonsensical.

For any set $X \in \mathcal{X}$ and any principle $p \in \mathcal{P}_X$, let $\mathcal{L}(X, p) \subseteq \Delta_X$ denote the set of decision sequences in X that satisfy Axioms 1 and 2 with respect to p. We will refer to $\mathcal{L}(X, p)$ as the set of *legitimate procedures* for X and p. The next result establishes that the set of legitimate procedures is always nonempty.

Theorem 6 *For any set $X \in \mathcal{X}$ and principle $p \in \mathcal{P}_X$,*

$$\mathcal{L}(X, p) \neq \emptyset.$$

Proof: The proof is constructive. Fix any finite and nonempty set X, any binary relation $p \in \mathcal{P}_X$ and construct δ as follows. First, choose any element $x_1 \in X$. If $p(x_1) = \emptyset$, then $\delta = (x_1)$ satisfies Axioms 1 and 2: Axiom 1 is satisfied trivially and Axiom 2 is satisfied by the supposition that $p(x_1) = \emptyset$. If $p(x_1) \neq \emptyset$, choose any element $x_2 \in p(x_1)$. If $p(x_2) \subset p^{-1}(x_1)$, let $\delta = (x_1, x_2)$. Axiom 1 is satisfied since $x_2 \, p \, x_1$. To see that Axiom 2 is satisfied, notice that $z \in p(x_2) \Rightarrow z \in p^{-1}(x_1) \Rightarrow x_1 \, p \, z$.

If $p(x_2) \not\subset p^{-1}(x_1)$, choose any $x_3 \in p(x_2) \setminus p^{-1}(x_1)$. If $p(x_3) \subset p^{-1}(x_1) \cup p^{-1}(x_2)$, let $\delta = (x_1, x_2, x_3)$. Axiom 1 is satisfied since $x_3 \, p \, x_2$, $x_2 \, p \, x_1$ and $x_3 \notin p^{-1}(x_1)$. To see that Axiom 2 is satisfied, notice that $z \in p(x_3) \Rightarrow [x_1 \, p \, z$ or $x_2 \, p \, z]$. Otherwise, if $p(x_3) \not\subset p^{-1}(x_1) \cup p^{-1}(x_2)$, choose an $x_4 \in p(x_3) \setminus p^{-1}(x_1) \cup p^{-1}(x_2)$ (as above) and iterate the procedure.

Finally, note that this iterative procedure can be continued at most a finite number of times since X is finite. Once this iterative construction is complete, we have constructed a $\delta = (x_1, \ldots, x_k)$ satisfying Axioms 1 and 2. Accordingly, because X and p are each arbitrary up to the requirement that $X \in \mathcal{X}$ (X is nonempty and finite), the result follows: $\mathcal{L}(X, p) \neq \emptyset$. ∎

6.2 CHARACTERIZATION OF LEGITIMATE PROCEDURES

As discussed earlier, a key aspect of how or whether a given decision sequence justifies or legitimates the final policy choice is the degree to which it is consistent with the underlying principle, p, that the decision-making process is intended to promote and refine. This aspect is the subject of our internal consistency requirement (Axiom 1). We now discuss in more formal terms the implications of this requirement for the structure of legitimate procedures (i.e., decision sequences) and its relationship with other concepts in choice theory.

Covering and the Uncovered Set

The notion of *covering* is central to the modern theory of choice and has attracted significant interest in political science and economics.[4] In general, covering is a form of dominance: informally, if alternative x covers y then x both defeats y and everything that defeats x also defeats y. When the underlying principle p is complete and asymmetric, the definition of covering is unambiguous: since every alternative x can be directly compared to every other alternative y by p (i.e., either xpy or ypx, and only one, must hold), stating that x defeats y implies that y does not defeat x and, conversely, stating that x does not defeat y implies that y *does* defeat x. When the principle is incomplete, however, various notions of covering have arisen. We use a definition of covering that follows directly from the definition above, which is called *Gillies covering*.[5]

Given a principle p, an alternative $y \in X$ is (Gillies) *covered* under p by another alternative $x \in X$, denoted by $x\mathbf{C}_p y$ if the following hold:

$$x\mathbf{C}_p y \Leftrightarrow x \, p \, y \text{ and } z \, p \, x \Rightarrow z \, p \, y. \tag{6.1}$$

With this definition of covering in hand, an alternative x is *uncovered* under p if it is not covered by any other alternative y under p. The set of alternatives in a set X that are uncovered under a principle $p \in \mathcal{P}_X$ is denoted by $UC(X, p)$.

Miller (1980) examined the uncovered set using graph theoretic tools and shows a nesting relationship among various solution concepts. Perhaps most famously, Miller demonstrated that when p is a tournament, uncovered points are precisely those that can beat all other alternatives in at most two steps. More generally, Miller showed that the core is a subset of the uncovered set and the uncovered set is in turn a subset of the top-cycle set. Penn (2006*a,b*) studied general complete (but not necessarily asymmetric) binary relations and demonstrated that the equivalence of several different definitions of the uncovered set disappears in this larger set of binary relations. In this book, we consider principles to be drawn from the set of all incomplete and asymmetric binary relations, and in this respect, the closest works to ours include Schwartz (1986) and Banks and Bordes (1988).[6]

---

[4] In addition to the seminal developments of Fishburn (1977) and Miller (1980), see also Bordes (1983); Shepsle and Weingast (1984); Banks (1985); McKelvey (1986); Feld, Grofman, Hartly, Kilgour, and Miller (1987); Feld and Grofman (1988); Miller, Grofman, and Feld (1990); Epstein (1997); Schofield (1999); Tsebelis (2002); Bianco, Jeliazkov, and Sened (2004); Dutta, Jackson, and Breton (2004); Bianco and Sened (2005); Bianco, Lynch, Miller, and Sened (2006); Jeong (2008), and Miller (2007).

[5] As described in Bordes (1983, p. 127), this notion of covering was defined as early as 1959 by D. B. Gillies.

[6] In Banks and Bordes (1988), the primitive binary relation (i.e., the "principle") is complete, but not necessarily asymmetric (i.e., some alternatives can be tied: $xRyRx$). Because we consider asymmetric relations, some of their results can be translated into ours by relabeling incomplete comparisons in our setting with "ties."

As alluded to earlier, the uncovered set is the set of alternatives that are undominated in a specific sense. In particular, for any alternative x in the uncovered set, if there exists some y that defeats x, then there also exists some z such that z defeats y but z does *not* defeat x.[7]

The next result states that legitimate procedures must return final choices within the uncovered set of their selected principle. We denote the set of alternatives that may be legitimately rendered under p – alternatives for which there exists a decision sequence $\delta \in \mathcal{L}(X, p)$ returning it as the final choice, $c(\delta)$ – by $\Lambda(X, p)$, which is formally defined as follows:

$$\Lambda(X, p) \equiv \bigcup_{\delta \in \mathcal{L}(X,p)} c(\delta).$$

With this in hand, our first conclusion about this set is stated formally in the next result.

Theorem 7 *For any $X \in \mathcal{X}$ and any principle $p \in \mathcal{P}_X$,*

$$\Lambda(X, p) \subseteq UC(p).$$

Proof: Fix a finite set of alternatives X and a principle $p \in \mathcal{P}_X$. For the purpose of obtaining a contradiction, suppose that there exists a legitimate decision sequence $\delta \in \mathcal{L}(X, p)$ for which some x covers $c(\delta)$ under p. Axiom 2 says that for any x with $x \, p \, c(\delta)$, it must be the case that there exists a $z \in \delta$ with $z \, p \, x$. By $x C_p c(\delta)$ we know that $x \, p \, c(\delta)$ and we know that that $z \, p \, x$ implies $z \, p \, c(\delta)$. Thus, there exists a $z \in \delta$ with $z \, p \, c(\delta)$. However this violates Axiom 1, a contradiction. Thus $\delta \in \mathcal{L}(X, p)$ implies that $c(\delta)$ is uncovered. ∎

When the principle p is complete, satisfaction of Axiom 1 by a decision sequence δ implies that p is *transitive* on the alternatives in δ. This stronger conclusion implies that the set of alternatives that can be legitimated is identical to the *Banks set* (Banks, 1985).[8] For any finite set X and tournament $t \in \mathcal{T}_X$, let $B(X, t)$ denote the Banks set under t. The next result follows directly from Theorem 7 and the internal consistency requirement (Axiom 1).

---

[7] Note that uncovered alternatives under this definition satisfy a weakened version of the two-step principle: if x is Gillies uncovered it cannot necessarily reach any y in two steps via p (as in $x \, p \, z$ and $z \, p \, y$), but it is guaranteed that there is a z such that $z \, p \, y$ and *not* $z \, p \, x$. As Bordes (1983); Banks and Bordes (1988); Dutta and Laslier (1999); Peris and Subiza (1999); Penn (2006a), and others have noted, there are at least four closely related (but not equivalent) definitions of covering that one might use in this setting. The definition described by (6.1) corresponds to the C_u notion of covering as defined in Banks and Bordes (1988).

[8] The Banks set was originally defined only for complete and asymmetric binary relations (i.e., tournaments). Extending the definition of the Banks set to all complete binary relations is considered in detail by Banks and Bordes (1988). They discuss four possible extensions of the Banks set in this setting. We return to this point later in the book when we examine refinements of our notion of legitimacy (Section 6.3).

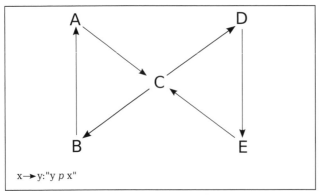

FIGURE 6.1. An Incomplete Principle p for which $B(X, p) \neq UC(X, p)$.

Corollary 1 *For any $X \in \mathcal{X}$ and any tournament $t \in \mathcal{T}_X$,*

$$\Lambda(X, t) = B(X, t).$$

Because there are complete principles for which the Banks set is a strict subset of the uncovered set (i.e., t such that $B(X, t) \subsetneq UC(X, t)$),[9] it follows that Corollary 1 implies that Theorem 7 cannot be strengthened to provide an equivalence result. In other words, for any given principle p, Theorem 7 ensures that every legitimate policy outcome belongs to the uncovered set under p, but the converse need not hold: there may be elements of the uncovered set that cannot be rendered legitimate under p. The following examples illustrate how this strict inclusion of the set of legitimate outcomes within the uncovered set can occur with both complete and incomplete principles.

Example 3 (Illegitimate Uncovered Alternative: Incomplete Principle)
Consider a set of five alternatives, $X = \{A, B, C, D, E\}$, and the following principle, p:

$$p(A) = \{C\},$$

$$p(B) = \{A\},$$

$$p(C) = \{B, D\},$$

$$p(D) = \{E\}, \text{ and}$$

$$p(E) = \{C\}.$$

The principle is pictured in Figure 6.1. Note first that every alternative is uncovered under p: $UC(X, p) = \{A, B, C, D, E\}$. The set of legitimate decision sequences under p is

$$\mathcal{L}(X, p) = \{(C, D), (A, C, D), (B, A), (E, C, B), (C, B), (D, E)\},$$

[9] For example, Banks (1985); Dutta (1988); Schwartz (1990), and Laslier (1997).

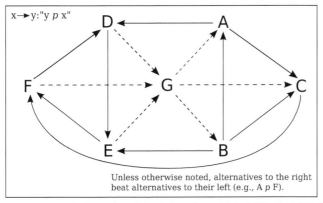

x→y:"y p x"

Unless otherwise noted, alternatives to the right
beat alternatives to their left (e.g., A p F).

FIGURE 6.2. A Complete Principle p for which $B(X, p) \neq UC(X, p)$.

but there is no decision sequence satisfying both Axioms 1 and 2 that yields C as the final choice. Thus, the set of alternatives that can be rendered legitimately under p is

$$\Lambda(X, p) = \{A, B, D, E\}.$$

To see that C cannot be rendered legitimate, first note that the two alternatives that defeat C are B and D. Thus, any legitimate sequence yielding C as the outcome must contain alternatives that defeat B and D; therefore, the sequence must contain A and E. However, A and E are not related to each other via p, so no decision sequence containing A, E, and C exists that satisfies Axiom 1. △

The difference between $\mathcal{L}(X, p)$ and $UC(X, p)$ in Example 3 is a direct result of the incompleteness of the underlying principle: if $A \ p \ E$ or $E \ p \ A$ held, then C could be rendered legitimate. The following example illustrates that incompleteness of the underlying principle is not necessary for the set of alternatives that can be legitimately rendered, $\Lambda(X, p)$, to be a strict subset of the uncovered alternatives, $UC(X, p)$. Rather, the two can differ even when the underlying principle is complete.

Example 4 (Illegitimate Uncovered Alternative: Complete Principle)
Consider a set of seven alternatives, $X = \{A, B, C, D, E, F, G\}$, and the following complete principle, p, which is pictured in Figure 6.2:

$$p(A) = \{C, D\} \quad p(D) = \{B, C, E, G\},$$
$$p(B) = \{E, A\} \quad p(E) = \{A, C, F, G\},$$
$$p(C) = \{F, B\} \quad p(F) = \{A, B, D, G\}, \text{ and}$$
$$p(G) = \{A, B, C\}.$$

Because p is complete, one can use the "two-step principle" (Miller, 1980; Shepsle and Weingast, 1984) to confirm that every alternative is uncovered under p.[10] However, every stable decision sequence with G as the final choice must contain D, E, and F, which violates internal consistency, as p is cyclic on $\{D, E, F\}$. (In other words, G is not an element of the Banks set under p.)   △

Example 4 highlights a hurdle for rendering a given choice legitimately: some final choices might require that one uses as counterobjections a set of alternatives on which the underlying principle is cyclic. Such choices are not legitimate in our theory because they cannot be produced by a stable decision sequence that satisfies internal consistency (Axiom 1). Defending such policies from all challengers under the principle p requires that one use circular reasoning (with respect to the underlying principle p). As discussed with respect to the excluded alternative C in Example 3, we do not classify decision sequences containing such circular reasoning as legitimate, and Theorem 6 ensures that we do not need to allow for them in order to ensure that legitimacy is a nonvacuous concept. In Example 4, every alternative other than G can be justified by a stable decision sequence that is a chain in p. For example, selection of the alternative D is legitimated by the decision sequence $\delta = (F, A, D)$; the first alternative, F, is essentially a counterobjection to alternative C (because $F \; p \; C \; p \; D \; p \; F$), and the second alternative is a counterobjection to alternatives B, E, and G. Note that p is transitive on δ: $D \; p \; A \; p \; F$ and $D \; p \; F$. Thus, it is logical to conclude that D is, and perhaps even *should be*, the final choice given the principle p and the consideration, in turn, of F followed by A.

Before continuing, it is useful to note that while the set of legitimate policy choices can exclude some uncovered alternatives in some situations, the classic Condorcet cycle on three alternatives ($A \, p \, B \, p \, C \, p \, A$) illustrates that Theorem 7 is "tight" in the sense that there are principles p such that $\mathcal{L}(X, p) = UC(X, p)$.

6.3 STRENGTHENED NOTIONS OF LEGITIMACY

We now explore a number of directions in which one might extend or refine our notion of legitimacy. In general, we argue that, while refinement is possible, strengthening our notion leads to situations in which (i.e., principles such that) legitimacy is forestalled in the sense that no alternative can be rendered legitimate by a decision sequence satisfying the strengthened notion of legitimacy.

As discussed earlier, Axioms 1 and 2 are not particularly strong. For example, because the principle p may be incomplete, Axiom 1 does not require that the rationale generated to justify the policy be transitive: this implies that the conclusion may not be directly related or comparable to all of the elements of

---

[10] The "two-step" principle states that the uncovered set is the set of alternatives that can "reach" any other alternative in two or fewer steps. Thus, when p is asymmetric and complete, then x uncovered implies that for any $z \neq x$ either $x \, p \, z$ or there is some $y \in X$ such that $x \, p \, y$ and $y \, p \, z$.

the decision sequence through the principle, p. Somewhat similarly, Axiom 2 does not require that the justification offered for the failure to consider an alternative be straightforward in any sense. These points raise the question of whether Axioms 1 and 2 can be strengthened in pursuit of a more demanding (and, arguably, more appealing) notion of legitimacy. To answer this question (unfortunately in the negative), consider the following strengthened versions of Axioms 1 and 2.

Axiom 1* (**Strong Internal Consistency**) *A decision sequence δ is strongly internally consistent with respect to a principle p if, for each alternative in the decision sequence, $x \in \delta$ with $x \neq c(\delta)$,*

$$c(\delta) \ p \ x.$$

and for each $i \in \{1, \ldots, |\delta| - 2\}$ we have $x_{i+1} \ p \ x_i$.

Axiom 2* (**Strong Stability**) *A decision sequence δ is strongly stable with respect to a principle p if, for each unconsidered alternative, $y \notin \delta$,*

$$y \ p \ c(\delta) \Rightarrow c(\delta) \ p \ z \text{ and } z \ p \ y \text{ for some } z \in \delta.$$

For any $X \in \mathcal{X}$ and principle $p \in \mathcal{P}_X$, let $\mathcal{L}^*(X, p) \subseteq \mathcal{L}(X, p)$ denote the set of decision sequences satisfying Axioms 1* and 2* under p. The next result demonstrates that these axioms cannot be satisfied for some principles when there are 4 or more alternatives. In particular, some principles provide so little structure that *no* decision sequence will satisfy the conditions of both Axioms 1* and 2*.

Theorem 8 *For all $X \in \mathcal{X}$ such that $|X| > 3$, there exists $p \in \mathcal{P}_X$ such that $\mathcal{L}^*(X, p) = \emptyset$.*

Proof: Note that demonstrating the result for $X \in \mathcal{X}$ with $|X| = 4$ is sufficient because additional elements can always be added so as to be ranked strictly lower, via the p constructed here in this proof, than each of the elements of a subset of X containing exactly four elements. Accordingly, let $X = \{A, B, C, D\}$ and consider the following principle p:

1. $A \ p \ B$, $B \ p \ C$, $C \ p \ D$, $D \ p \ A$, and
2. No other pairs are related via p.

Now note the following, each of which can be verified directly.

1. Any decision sequence δ that is a singleton violates Axiom 2*.
2. Any decision sequence that has exactly two elements must also violate Axiom 2*.
3. Any decision sequence with exactly three distinct elements must violate Axiom 1*.
4. Any decision sequence that contains all four elements, A, B, C, and D violates Axiom 1 and hence violates Axiom 1*.

Accordingly, there is no decision sequence satisfying both Axioms 1^* and 2^*, as was to be shown.   ∎

Before continuing, we note that Axiom 1^* alone is sufficient to obtain Theorem 8 in the sense that strengthening only Axiom 1 but leaving Axiom 2 unchanged results in a notion of legitimacy that is equivalent to imposing both Axioms 1^* and 2^*. For any $X \in \mathcal{X}$ and principle $p \in \mathcal{P}_X$, let $\mathcal{L}_1^*(X, p)$ denote the set of decision sequences satisfying Axioms 1^* and 2 under p.

Theorem 9 *For any $X \in \mathcal{X}$ and principle $p \in \mathcal{P}_X$,*

$$\mathcal{L}_1^*(X, p) = \mathcal{L}^*(X, p).$$

Proof: Fix a set $X \in \mathcal{X}$ and a principle $p \in \mathcal{P}_X$ and then consider first a decision sequence $\delta \in \mathcal{L}_1^*(X, p)$. We show that $\delta \in \mathcal{L}^*(X, p)$. (Note that the opposite inclusion follows immediately.) Choose any $y \notin \delta$. (If there is no such y, then $\delta \in \mathcal{L}^*(X, p)$ by trivial satisfaction of Axiom 2^*.) Satisfaction of 1^* implies that $c(\delta) \, p \, z$ for all $z \in \delta$ such that $z \neq c(\delta)$. Accordingly, by the presumed satisfaction of Axiom 2 by δ,

$$y \, p \, c(\delta) \Rightarrow c(\delta) \, p \, z \, p \, y \text{ for some } z \in \delta,$$

which is equivalent to Axiom 2^*, so that $\delta \in \mathcal{L}^*(X, p)$.   ∎

The previous results establish that strong internal consistency, Axiom 1^*, is too strong. To finish our argument, let $\mathcal{L}_2^*(X, p)$ denote the set of procedures satisfying Axioms 1 and 2^* for a given $X \in \mathcal{X}$ and principle $p \in \mathcal{P}_X$. The following result states that imposing Axiom 2^* along with Axiom 1 yields a notion of legitimacy that similarly cannot be satisfied for all sets of principles. This is a slightly different result than Theorem 9 because the set $\mathcal{L}_2^*$ is a superset of $\mathcal{L}^*$ (and for some principles p, a strict superset), but the "enlargement" accomplished by relaxing Axiom 1^* is not sufficient to alleviate the conclusion of Theorem 8. Thus strong stability (Axiom 2^*) is too strong as well.

Theorem 10 *For all $X \in \mathcal{X}$ such that $|X| > 3$, there exists $p \in \mathcal{P}_X$ such that $\mathcal{L}_2^*(X, p) = \emptyset$.*

Proof: Consider the example provided in the proof of Theorem 8. As stated in the proof of Theorem 8, any δ consisting of only one or two alternatives cannot satisfy Axiom 2^*. Similarly, no decision sequence with exactly four alternatives can satisfy Axiom 1. Last, it can be directly verified that no decision sequence with exactly three alternatives that satisfies Axiom 1 also satisfies Axiom 2^*. ∎

Taken together, the results in this section have a substantive implication beyond our notion of legitimacy being "as strong as possible." In particular, the potential emptiness of these refinements of our notion of legitimacy is due to the fact that the underlying principle might be incomplete. Substantively, this suggests an important desideratum for legitimating processes, one that we turn to in the next section.

6.4 COMPARING PRINCIPLES

While we remain deliberately agnostic about the (empirically or theoretically) "correct" structure for the set of possible principles, the results presented and discussed in the previous section set up one abstract and neutral basis for comparing different principles in terms of their legitimating "power." In particular, some principles can legitimate choices under more demanding notions of legitimacy than others. We approach this question in two different ways in this section.

The first and main conclusion about comparing principles concerns the degree to which a given principle is incomplete. Formally, an incomplete principle does not compare (or, rank) every pair of alternatives. Such principles are incomplete in a colloquial sense, too, as they may be "completed" by including comparisons for the unranked pairs.

Definition. *A principle* $p \in \mathcal{P}_X$ *is a* completion *of another principle* $q \in \mathcal{P}_X$ *if it satisfies two requirements:*

- *p is complete and*
- $q \subseteq p$: $x \ q \ y \Rightarrow x \ p \ y$.

The first requirement of the definition of a completion simply requires that a completion be its own completion. The second requirement is substantive: a completion of a principle does not change any of the original principle's determinations. Thus, a completion of a principle p can be thought of as simply p extended so as to "break all ties."

The classic case of a completion is provided by the canonical representation of a majority preference relation: an odd number of three or more voters, each with strict preferences over each pair of alternatives. This setting yields a complete social preference under majority rule, in which an alternative x is ranked strictly higher than another alternative y if and only if x is preferred by a strict majority of voters. Of course, one could use such a decision rule to complete some exogenous and incomplete principle as well. For example, in the deliberative ideal described by Joshua Cohen, majority rule is forwarded as the correct mechanism to break ties when consensus does not emerge from deliberation.[11]

> Even under ideal conditions there is no promise that consensual reasons will be forthcoming. If they are not, then deliberation concludes with voting, subject to some form of majority rule. The fact that it may so conclude does not, however, eliminate the distinction between deliberative forms of collective choices and forms that aggregate non-deliberative preferences.[12]

---

[11] One could similarly use a coin flip or other exogenous means of breaking the tie or completing the incompleteness. Majority voting is focused on here simply because the potential pathologies of majority rule are often forwarded as motivation for discussing and adopting deliberative decision processes.

[12] Cohen (1997), p. 75.

The next result illustrates the power of tie breaking (regardless of whether it is by majority rule or some other method) for refining the set of legitimate outcomes.

Theorem 11 *For any principle $p \in \mathcal{P}_X$ and decision sequence $\delta \in \mathcal{L}(X, p)$, there exists a tournament $t \in \mathcal{T}_X$ that is a completion of p such that $\delta \in \mathcal{L}(X, t)$.*

Proof: Fix $p \in \mathcal{P}_X$ and $\delta \in \mathcal{L}(X, p)$. Construct $t \in \mathcal{T}_X$ as follows for each distinct pair $y, z \in X$:

1. If $y \, p \, z$, then set $y \, t \, z$.
2. If neither $y \, p \, z$ nor $z \, p \, y$ hold, then
    (a) if $y \in \delta$, and $z \notin \delta$, set $y \, t \, z$,
    (b) if $y \in \delta$, $z \in \delta$, and $y \succ_\delta z$, set $y \, t \, z$, and
    (c) if $y \notin \delta$, and $z \notin \delta$, fix either $y \, t \, z$ or $z \, t \, y$ arbitrarily.

It can be verified that t so defined is a tournament and, more importantly, that δ is an externally stable chain with respect to t, so that $\delta \in \mathcal{L}(X, t)$, as was to be shown.   ∎

In addition to establishing that tournaments provide in a certain sense the most restriction on the set of outcomes that might be rendered legitimate, Theorem 11 also implies something important about the observability of cycles when decisions are made by legitimate procedures. Namely, Theorem 11 implies that legitimate decisions from acyclic principles are always consistent with some cyclic principles as well. Accordingly, the observation of seemingly transitive decisions is not sufficient evidence that the underlying principles guiding that choice are themselves transitive. This point represents a serious challenge to the claims of scholars that the well-ordered operation of democratic choice in the real world can be used to refute claims that majority preference cycles are present or, perhaps, relevant to the study of democracy or democratic institutions.[13]

The discerning nature of complete principles at the heart of Theorem 11 also reflects the importance of commensurability to the *stability* of legitimacy of institutions within a dynamic setting. As Beetham describes this issue,

> ... both the evidence and the interests of the subordinate are so structured that the justifications advanced for the rules of power prove plausible to them within the given social context. Their plausibility can only be challenged from a position or standpoint outside that context, e.g. by comparison with alternative rules of power, or when social changes have come to undermine from within the

---

[13] Foremost among such work are the arguments offered by Mackie (2003), who criticizes the focus on majority preference cycles by social choice and rational choice theorists. In many ways, we are sympathetic with Mackie's goal insofar as he is skeptical of claims by some that democratic choice fails to provide some form of legitimation for the selected policies. Despite, this, however, his arguments fail to provide proper accounting for the importance of the institutional details of democratic choice.

evidence on which they are based. It is a characteristic of the modern period that such comparisons are more readily available, and substantial social change is more continuous, than in the pre-modern world. It follows that the legitimacy of any society's power rules is now more open to question, and its legitimating principles and procedures have to be more capable of withstanding comparison and challenge, if they are to provide a credible support for the rules of power.[14]

6.5 CONCLUSION

In this book, we have equated "legitimacy" with "adherence to an accepted principle" and, in so doing, have asked a deceptively simple question: if the concept of adhering to a principle is ill behaved, how can one legitimize democratic outcomes? Our approach has been procedural in the sense that a policy is legitimate if the process through which it was rendered is consistent with the underlying principle. In this chapter, we have conceived of *process* as a sequence of intervening decisions (i.e., considered, but rejected policies) that justify the final choice. The consistency of this sequence of alternatives with the principle is based on two characteristics: internal consistency and stability. We have formally demonstrated first that the set of legitimate choices is always well defined and nonempty – in other words, there is *always* a legitimate choice, regardless of the underlying principle. In addition, we have characterized the set of decision sequences that satisfy the two requirements for any given principle p and, accordingly, the policies that may be chosen with such a sequence (i.e., the policies that may be legitimated). While our theory in general does not identify a unique policy as legitimate, it does allow us to characterize these policies in terms of their welfare properties. Policies that can be legitimately rendered in our theory are guaranteed to be undominated (i.e., Pareto efficient and uncovered) with respect to the underlying principle that is used to rationalize the choice.

Because the principles need not be weak orders of the alternatives, the theory represents a notion of legitimacy that can be satisfied even when the guiding principles are potentially cyclic or incomplete, each of which presents a unique challenge to producing a legitimate choice. First, the ability of our theory to account for cyclic principles contrasts with the tenor of the arguments of Riker (1982) and others, who argue in various ways that the possibility that majority preference can produce cyclic orderings undermines the degree of deference one ought to accord to majoritarian collective decisions. By incorporating a representation of the process by which such choices are made, our theory provides a nontautological means by which majority rule decisions can be rendered legitimate. In other words, majority rule may not in and of itself be a sufficient basis for rendering a policy legitimate, but our notion of legitimacy establishes that majority rule can be used as a key part of such a basis. An important point in

---

[14] Beetham (1991), p. 62.

establishing this connection is that majority rule (or any other potentially cyclic principle) need not be consistent with a uniquely legitimate outcome. Indeed, the possible multiplicity of outcomes consistent with basic tenets of democratic choice lies at the heart of Riker's challenge to liberal hopes for democratic legitimacy. The inclusion of process into the foundation of legitimacy nonetheless delineates a nontrivial boundary on both the set of policies that might be legitimately chosen and the methods by which they may be produced.

While not as commonly forwarded as a challenge to legitimate governance, incomplete principles also generally share the multiplicity problem exhibited by cyclic principles. In addition to serving as a basis for characterization of legitimacy in these settings, our theory also – somewhat ironically – highlights the power of majority preference in refining the set of legitimate outcomes. In so doing, while our approach is agnostic about the admissibility of various principles, we have explored the implications of the approach for comparing principles in terms of their legitimating power.

7

Theory and Method

As noted in the introduction of this book, our theory is not intended to be predictive. Much of modern social science research centers on an idealized version of the scientific method in which a model is built on first principles, predictions are derived from this model, and these predictions are then subjected to empirical verification. The driving force in this approach is falsification: while a theory can rarely if ever be shown to be true, sufficient empirical data can conclusively reveal if the theory is false.

While Arrow's Theorem has served as the principal theoretical motivation for our theory, we note again that our main results have more in common with Nash's Theorem (Nash, Jr., 1950) than with Arrow's. In the preceding chapter, we established that our notion of legitimacy is theoretically nonvacuous for any principle p, and we characterized the types of decisions that satisfy it. Note that, just as the Nash equilibria of a game are entirely determined by the preferences of individuals, the choices (and decision sequences) that satisfy our notion of legitimacy are entirely determined by the principle by which choice is intended to be structured, p. Neither Nash equilibrium nor our theory of legitimacy provide any guidance about either what the primitives (preferences or principles, respectively) are from an empirical perspective or even about how these primitives "should" be configured.

This point is central to our approach in the third part of this book: rather than attempting to determine how often our notion of legitimacy describes any particular decision, we instead argue by drawing analogies between our theoretical framework and the processes and structures of various political institutions that are (at least partially) justified in terms of their legitimating influence on outcomes. The primary goal of this exercise is to put some meat on the bones of an admittedly abstract theory: while we do not believe that many decisions are perfectly legitimate as we have defined it, we do believe that the foundations of our theory – that some choices must be made in situations where conflicting goals admit no "best" choice and such choices are or should be accompanied by a justification based on those competing goals – are descriptive of mechanisms and processes by which groups have chosen to vet and validate contentious policy choices.[1]

In the remainder of this chapter, which concludes Part II of this book, we address three important gaps between the theoretical framework and actual instances of collective decision making. In addition to clarifying the context of the empirical discussion in the ensuing chapters, each of these gaps impedes any attempt to apply our theory in a predictive fashion. In other words, each of these gaps – disagreements about the principle, incomplete knowledge of the set of possible choices, and the distinction between actual decision sequences and how they are portrayed – is related to individual decision making, preferences, or beliefs, none of which factor in our theory. To be a predictive theory of collective decision making, however, these elements would need to be included. Thus, discussing them in turn can hopefully clarify how our theory *can* be useful in interpreting and understanding political institutions and processes.

7.1 DISAGREEING ABOUT PRINCIPLES

Perhaps the most glaring disconnect between our theory and the empirical reality of collective choice is the theoretical presumption of a single latent principle according to which choices must be justified and the empirical reality that such principles are often essentially contested. For example, Supreme Court justices may each agree about the implications and meaning of free speech precedents and yet disagree over whether they are relevant (or, at least, should be considered dispositive) when considering a statute regulating campaign spending.[2] Similarly, justices can disagree about the proper definition of a "public use,"[3] the distinction between a tax and a financial penalty,[4] and whether white voters should be granted standing to pursue an equal protection claim with respect to redistricting plans designed to promote minority representation.[5]

Disagreements about the principle that should govern collective choice do not undermine our theory as we are presenting it. Indeed, when viewed in the context of the discussion contained in Chapters 2 and 3, these disagreements highlight the importance and power of our theory. In particular, the main

---

[1] Our approach and focus in Part III is analogous to and inspired in many ways by the excellent treatment of the founding within the context of social choice theory by Schofield (2006).

[2] See *Buckley v. Valeo*, 424 U.S. 1 (1976), *McConnell v. Federal Election Commission*, 540 U.S. 93 (2003), and *Citizens United v. Federal Election Commission*, 558 U.S. 310 (2010).

[3] *Kelo v. City of New London*, 545 U.S. 469 (2005).

[4] *National Federation of Independent Business v. Sebelius*, 567 U.S. ___ (2012), upholding the Patient Protection and Affordable Care Act as a constitutional application of Congress's tax power.

[5] *Shaw v. Reno*, 509 U.S. 630 (1993).

results of our theory indicate that there is at least a theoretical possibility for reconciling these differences. This conclusion is made possible by the fact that the theory takes seriously the impossibility theorems and, accordingly, can account for *any* aggregation of the heterogeneous principles that the members may bring to a situation.

To see this even more clearly, consider again the Supreme Court and note that any individual justice's "principle" – that is, his or her ordering of the relevant alternatives at hand in a case – is equivalent to a generalized individual preference (generalized in the sense that our theory explicitly allows for cyclic principles). Thus, creating a common principle among any collection justices can, at least in theory, be accomplished by aggregating the members' principles (e.g., by majority rule with respect to each pair of alternatives). Our theory of legitimacy then provides a method by which this potentially cyclic common principle can be used to render a final legitimate decision through the provision of both the common principle and a decision sequence that justifies the decision (i.e., satisfies Axioms 1 and 2 with respect to that common, aggregated principle).

With this possibility established, it is appropriate to note that our theory does not provide any particular reason to expect that all individuals will be equally happy (or, perhaps, happy at all) with the conclusions reached by such a process. But that is arguably the point of legitimacy: a legitimate decision is one that makes sense in spite of not being universally acclaimed. As the results of Chapter 6 indicate, our theory is in some sense redundant when there is one policy that satisfies everyone (or, perhaps, is uniquely rationalizable or explicable) in the sense of uniquely satisfying Pareto efficiency. In such cases, simply announcing the decision satisfies Axioms 1 and 2. Thus, cases in which there is nontrivial disagreement between individuals or principles are exactly the cases in which one might suspect to see decisions accompanied by explanations (i.e., decision sequences) similar to those at the heart of our theory.

This point is important, and we have discussed it earlier.[6] When bringing our theory to bear on the dynamics of observed collective choice, it is important to note that deliberation, choice, and explanation are inherently costly activities. Accordingly, one should not be surprised that the situations in which we see extended efforts to select and explain a policy choice are those in which there is some disagreement between the individuals or goals on which the choice depends. Further, even if the selection of the policy is fortunate enough to occur in an environment in which the goals or individuals are broadly in agreement, in many situations there is always the possibility that the choosers are concerned with securing deference from either the governed or subsequent

---

[6] Section 2.4.

decision makers. This point is made concrete by situations in which a unanimous court provides a lengthy reasoning behind its decision.[7] In summary, the reality is that many, if not most, extended collective choice processes are characterized by conflicting goals and concomitant disagreement about the construction of the proper principle to guide the ultimate decision. While this reality imposes a daunting hurdle that must be overcome if one is to use our theory in a predictive fashion, it highlights both the power of our theory's conclusions and the degree to which Mackie's objections to Riker, discussed in Chapter 2, fall short. To be clear, the conclusion one would draw from a straightforward reading of Mackie's assertion that single-peakedness describes most political choices would imply that a simple reporting of pairwise votes would be a sufficient (i.e., legitimating) explanation for any decision in such a situation. The effort expended by justices, politicians, and others in providing rationales for their desired choices strongly suggests that such a common latent, order-inducing structure is absent. With that in mind, we now move to the second gap between the parsimony of our theoretical framework and the muddy waters of real-world choice situations: ambiguity about the set of possible choices.

7.2 DEFINING THE SET OF POSSIBLE CHOICES

Stability, as captured in Axiom 2, is a very demanding criterion. Indeed, simply verifying that any given decision sequence satisfies the condition can be a daunting task when the set of possible choices is large. This reality alone suggests that real-world choices and decision sequences are unlikely to satisfy stability. Stability is better thought of as an "ideal" upon which legitimacy rests rather than as a practical imperative. The question this raises is whether and to what degree this divide between theory and practice undermines the usefulness of our theory.

The short answer is that the failure of real-world policymaking to satisfy stability is entirely consistent with our theory, particularly when we observe policy change. To the degree that an observed choice is replacing or refining a

---

[7] Some high-profile historical examples are *Marbury v. Madison*, 5 U.S. 137 (1803), *A.L.A. Schechter Poultry Corp. v. United States*, 295 U.S. 495 (1935), *Brown v. Board of Education*, 347 U.S. 483 (1954), *Gideon v. Wainwright*, 372 U.S. 335 (1963), and *United States v. Nixon*, 418 U.S. 683 (1974), each of which required or presupposed deference by other political actors in order to have instrumental effect. While arguably less grand in scope, two very recent examples are *Hosanna-Tabor Evangelical Lutheran Church and School v. EEOC*, 565 U. S. ___ (2012), affirming a ministerial exemption from federal discrimination laws on Establishment Clause and Free Exercise Clause grounds, and *Sackett v. United States Environmental Protection Agency*, 566 U.S. ___ (2012), affirming a citizen's standing to seek review of the Environmental Protection Agency's compliance orders under the Administrative Procedure Act. Each of these decisions centered on a classical aggregation problem in the sense of considering conflicting and long-standing goals.

prior one without a change in the governing principle, the current observed act of choice suggests that the prior one was not stable or, more appropriately, that the decision sequence leading to the prior one is not stable. Our discussions of judicial review in Chapters 8 and 10 are clear illustrations of this. Barring statutory or constitutional changes, "new" judicial decisions (are supposed to) replace or refine earlier ones precisely when a new policy is found to be both superior to the existing policy in question and not inconsistent with other precedents. Thus, stability should not be satisfied by evolving real-world policymaking because, in a very intuitive sense, the decision sequence is not yet complete: new policies are being constructed and compared with the existing decision sequence. In other words, the practical achievement of stability will in many cases occur only following what might be best described as a search process.[8]

Of course, the search dynamic in these settings can be interpreted as relaxing the assumption that the set of feasible alternatives is static and known. After all, introduction or recognition of a previously unknown alternative can of course overturn the stability of a decision sequence. In such situations, a proper "test" of our theory would consider whether a newly chosen alternative is accompanied by an internally consistent decision sequence. The strongest version of this would add an ancillary assumption that the preexisting decision sequence must be carried forward as a whole and incorporated into the decision sequence accompanying the new alternative.[9]

The practical difficulty of being aware of all possible choices, not to mention how the principle compares (or does not compare) each pair of them, points out a subsidiary value of advocacy or adversarial-based approaches to collective choice. Whether one considers legislatures, courts, or bureaucracies, a common thread among political institutions is that the onus of proposing, shepherding, and defending potential policy choices is generally explicitly assigned to one or more individuals (e.g., lawyers in judicial settings, committee members within legislatures, "affected parties" in bureaucratic rulemaking proceedings). In some cases, these individuals are within the body (as in some legislatures), sometimes explicitly outside the body (as in many courts), and sometimes both (as in many bureaucracies). The relationship between a collective choice body and those to whom it looks for proposals is intimately tied to the body's legitimacy bases, as discussed in Chapter 4.

The practical difficulties with achieving stability – finding and comparing alternatives to the currently prevailing policy – highlights the potential impact

---

[8] In addition to the practical reality that policymaking often requires "searching" through the set of possible policies, of course a change in the latent, underlying principle can lead to an apparent violation of stability, too. However, for the reasons discussed in the previous section, we simply note this and set it aside.

[9] Strictly speaking, our theory does not take a position on whether this need be the case, particularly insofar as the new alternative is chosen much later in time by a different set of agents or after other relevant facts may have evolved in significant ways.

of identifying and enabling multiple individuals to propose alternatives on the legitimacy of an institution and its decisions. In general, no single individual will have sufficient incentive to provide a comprehensive accounting of the full set of possible choices. Instead, any proposer's primary (policy) interest when making a proposal is to secure his or her favored policy or policies. Thus, providing access to multiple individuals with varied policy interests can play an intuitive and practical role in achieving and verifying stability in the institution's decision making. In other words, while internal consistency (Axiom 1) captures the notion that legitimate policies "make sense," stability (Axiom 2) is intended to capture the notion that legitimate policies are "good." Confronting prevailing policies with as broad a range of competing policies as is practically possible is one practical mechanism to pursue this goal.

7.3 ACTUAL VERSUS PERCEIVED DECISION SEQUENCES

Our theory is agnostic about what, in practice, constitutes a decision sequence. The analogy with a transcript of the actual proceedings leading to the ultimate choice is a useful one, but such a record is only one of several possible instantiations of the decision sequence. The role of the decision sequence in our theory is to provide an explanation for the final choice that accords with the principle. This role could be just as well served by a simplified, perhaps even hypothetical, version of events or arguments leading to the final choice. To the degree that the principle and the set of feasible choices are known by an observer, such a construction could suffice in the sense that its satisfaction of Axioms 1 and 2 would be verifiable.

The empirical relevance of this point is brought out by considering the frequency of what one might charitably refer to as "selective memory" in a wide variety of choice settings. Whether it is a judicial opinion or a campaign platform, it is common for advocates and commentators alike to refine the history of events and decisions leading to a final choice. Again, this phenomenon represents a serious impediment to formulating our theory in a predictive (or even "postdictive") fashion. However, this difficulty does not undermine the theory as it is presented here. In particular, what is important in this regard is that selective memory that operates through omission – removing some decisions that occurred but not creating any decisions or judgments that did not in fact happen – can salvage a literal decision sequence that violates internal consistency but cannot transform a decision sequence that violates stability into one that is stable.

This highlights an ancillary value of a specific kind of "fable" when attempting to legitimize or explain prevailing policy choices. In particular, refining the past by omitting certain steps avoids taking too close a look at "how the sausage is made" and may generate a hypothetical story line or explanation from the actual series of events that provides a more direct (in the sense of involving both fewer steps and removing cycles) rationale for the decision in terms of the governing principle. After all, an arguably important part of the subjective appeal of providing a rationale for the selection of a contentious policy is the degree to which it satisfies a natural human desire to ascribe motivations or rationality to an otherwise amorphous collection of individuals or criteria. In other words, it is common to ask, "Why did Congress pass that law?" or "Why did the Supreme Court uphold the Affordable Care Act?" The decision sequence and underying principle are one representation of attempts by the decision maker to provide an answer to such a question.

This point highlights an important potential implication of our theory. To the degree that one subscribes both to our theory of legitimacy and the notion that a policy can be legitimated by the construction of a verifiably legitimate but admittedly hypothetical decision sequence, the results can be interpreted as suggesting that, when the alternatives and principle are known, there is no need to bother with the cost and expense of engaging in deliberative policymaking at all. After all, why not randomly choose a policy that can be legitimately rendered under the principle and call it a day? Would such a process itself be legitimate?

The simplest response to this is that, first, there should be no objection to calling such a selection process legitimate and, second, this thought experiment is useful in highlighting the nature of principles. In many, if not all, political decisions, the principle is itself at least partially dependent upon privately observed factors, such as individuals' political preferences. For example, whenever a decision is wholly or partially guided by democratic notions such as the common good or popular will, it is not the case that the principle is commonly known. Rather, the principle itself must be elicited. Drawing forth and, perhaps just as important, publicizing the principle in such settings is a primary justification for participatory and deliberative political institutions. In other words, the frequency with which real-world policy decisions are preceded and accompanied by the costly creation, provision, and publication of actual decision sequences is arguably evidence of the ubiquity of the challenges of aggregation discussed in Part I of this book. With that in mind, we now turn to the final part of the book and consider the analogy between our theory and a few examples of real-world policymaking.

PART III

LEGITIMATE POLICY MAKING IN PRACTICE

8

Legislative Legitimacy and Judicial Review

When considering legislative policymaking, legitimacy is important in two related ways. First, most statutes are generally applicable: there is no guarantee of fit between the requirements of the statute and the facts of each and every covered case. Furthermore, many statutes derive their ability to impact policy outcomes through potentially coercive methods: failure to behave in accordance with the statutory provisions can result in various forms of punishment. In such cases, and as discussed in Section 4.1, the legitimacy of the statute is at best imprecisely gauged through observing compliance. The state's authority, which may be based simply on sufficient strength, can substitute for legitimacy of its policies in eliciting "deferential" behavior by the governed.

Second, legislatures are collective bodies – the statutes they enact are not necessarily transparent in either their consequences or motivations. As the extent of public law and the impact of statutes on everyday life have each grown over the past two centuries, the importance of judicial review – for both verification and explication of the purposes and justifications of legislative action – has concomitantly expanded as well. Thus, while the legitimacy of enigmatic legislative pronouncements is inherently suspect, modern judicial review is theoretically well suited to render both origins and implications of statutes scrutable to the governed.

In what follows, we focus on the relationship between federal judicial review and our notion of legitimacy. Our goal is to demonstrate a tight linkage between our notion of legitimacy and modern judicial review of equal protection and due process claims – essentially, review of claims that a statute is inconsistent with the rule of law – under the Fifth and Fourteenth Amendments of the United States Constitution. The relevant provisions of each of these are:

> No person shall be...deprived of life, liberty, or property, without due process of law; nor shall private property be taken for public use, without just compensation.[1]

---

[1] Amendment V, U.S. Constitution.

and

> No State shall...deprive any person of life, liberty, or property, without due
> process of law; nor deny to any person within its jurisdiction the equal protection
> of the laws.[2]

From the standpoint of the U.S. Constitution, equal protection and due
process are key components of legitimacy. In particular, each is a bulwark
against abuse of legislative power. In colloquial terms, these two concepts
ensure that law is fair in both design and application: equal protection requires
that laws be uniformly applicable, and due process is intended to make the
application of the law precise.[3] Of course, as with the concept of legitimacy, it
is easier to detect violations of either equal protection or due process than it is
to make fine-grained comparisons of the degree to which particular statutes or
policies adhere to these notions.

In more practical terms, both concepts are undermined by arbitrary classification or action. Equal protection, for example, is largely concerned with
how citizens, property, and actions are grouped together. Classic examples of
equal protection issues include drawing legally relevant distinctions between
citizens based on race, gender, or religious beliefs, imposing different burdens
on the exercise of free speech based on the content of the speech, and allowing
or denying couples a marriage license based on whether they are of the same
gender. Equal protection is complicated precisely because the point of many
government policies is drawing distinctions among various classes of citizens,
property, and actions. That is, the state (or, perhaps, "the people") will not be
able to fulfill principal missions – such as securing the safety of its citizens' lives,
limbs, and property – and preserve the ideal of truly equal protection. After
all, few convicts will voluntarily remain in prison. Accordingly, the gravest
disputes about equal protection typically center on the question of what interests of the state are sufficiently important to warrant society countenancing
statutory recognition of potentially invidious distinctions.

Due process concerns typically focus more on process and are particularly
relevant when the government allocates benefits, levies taxes, grants (or denies)
licenses, or exercises eminent domain.[4] Consistency with due process requires
making sure that the governmental action does not infringe in impermissible
ways on individual rights. The question of what infringements should be considered permissible is generally the locus of the most heated debates about
satisfaction of due process.

---

[2] Section 1, Amendment XIV, U.S Constitution.
[3] Furthermore, due process is a form of legitimacy validation in its own right. We return to this
   topic in Chapter 10.
[4] A related and important set of concerns focus on the delegation of legislative authority to other
   groups or individuals. We return to this topic in more detail when we discuss the delegation
   doctrine in Chapter 10.

8.1 LEGISLATIVE RATIONALITY AND JUDICIAL REVIEW

When considering the question of what constitutes due process, an essential starting point from a judicial perspective is whether the power being exercised properly lays in the legislature's hands. As the twentieth century dawned, federal courts tended to view the landscape of powers as being divided into regions according to the proper claimant thereof: some powers were Congressional, some presidential, others reserved for the states, and still others ("rights") held by the people and properly not interfered with.[5] In such a construction, courts "afforded no justification for greater or lesser degrees of deference to other institutions' judgments concerning where the boundaries lay."[6] Accordingly, during this time period, courts focused much of their statutory review power on the question of whether the right(s) interfered with were properly directable through statute. In practice, this was mostly concerned with review of state laws, and the court did not "view itself as weighing or accommodating competing public and private interests."[7] Whether a statute was constitutionally permitted or not was simply a matter of whether the power to regulate the behavior in question was constitutionally permitted to the legislature. In most cases, once this question was resolved, the courts considered their job to be complete.

This stance began to change slowly in the early 20th century, as legislative mandates began to take aim at broader social ills and desires. Such statutes necessarily drew a starker contrast between the collective goals of society and the individual rights and freedoms of the citizens. The landmark opinion in this respect is provided in *Lochner v. New York*,[8] in which the Court invalidated a state statute restricting the scope of private employment contracts. Indeed, in the majority opinion of the case, Justice Rufus W. Peckham describes the dilemma as one of weighing the interests of the many against the rights of the individual:

> ...the question necessarily arises: is this a fair, reasonable and appropriate exercise of the police power of the State, or is it an unreasonable, unnecessary and arbitrary interference with the right of the individual to his personal liberty...?[9]

Peckham describes the proper way of answering this question as depending on two factors: the relationship between the statute in question and its goal, and the nature of the goal itself. In essence, Peckham describes what is now referred to as *rational basis review*:[10] to the degree that they interfere with personal liberty, legislative enactments are subject to review in terms of both

---

[5] See, for example, Kennedy (1980).
[6] Fallon, Jr. (2006), p. 1286.
[7] Ibid., p. 1285.
[8] 198 U.S. 45 (1906).
[9] 198 U.S. 45, 56 (1906).
[10] This notion of review goes by several names in both the scholarly literature and judicial opinions, including "rationality review," "minimal scrutiny," and sometimes "means-ends analysis."

their means and their ends. Specifically, he describes the question and its proper resolution as follows:

> It is a question of which of two powers or rights shall prevail – the power of the State to legislate or the right of the individual to liberty of person and freedom of contract. The mere assertion that the subject relates though but in a remote degree to the public health does not necessarily render the enactment valid. The act must have a more direct relation, as a means to an end, and the end itself must be appropriate and legitimate, before an act can be held to be valid which interferes with the general right of an individual to be free in his person and in his power to contract in relation to his own labor.[11]

The outcome in *Lochner* was decided by the slimmest of margins, but there was unanimity on a key doctrinal point: the state's police powers had nontrivial limitations and, perhaps most important, these boundaries were both unclear and subject to judicial review.[12] Given the salience of the *Lochner* decision as the hallmark and perhaps high-water mark of the Supreme Court's reliance on a doctrine of "substantive due process," the unanimous construction of the dilemma faced by the Court is notable. In particular, this construction has served as the foundation for the standards of review that would emerge and evolve over the ensuing century.

While one can read Peckham's opinion in *Lochner* as describing rational basis review, the doctrine was first explicitly applied by the Court in *Nebbia v. New York*.[13] In *Nebbia*, the Supreme Court upheld a New York state law that regulated the price of milk, stating:

> So far as the requirement of due process is concerned, and in the absence of other constitutional restriction, a state is free to adopt whatever economic policy may reasonably be deemed to promote public welfare, and to enforce that policy by legislation adapted to its purpose. The courts are without authority either to declare such policy, or, when it is declared by the legislature, to override it. If the laws passed are seen to have a reasonable relation to a proper legislative purpose, and are neither arbitrary nor discriminatory, the requirements of due process are satisfied, and judicial determination to the effect renders a court *functus officio*.[14]

Nebbia signaled a clear break with the doctrine of substantive due process as interpreted and leveraged by the Court in the late nineteenth and early twentieth centuries, most famously associated with the ruling in *Lochner v. New York*.[15]

---

[11] 198 U.S. 45, 57-58 (1906).

[12] For example, Justice Peckham states "the exact description and limitation of [police powers] have not been attempted by the courts." From the dissenting viewpoint, Justice Harlan's dissent begins by acknowledging that the Court "has not attempted to mark the precise boundaries of what is called the police power of the State...." (198 U.S. 45 at 65).

[13] 291 U.S. 502 (1934).

[14] 291 U.S. 537 (1934).

[15] 198 U.S. 45 (1905).

With the benefit of hindsight, it also marked the beginning of an increasingly deferential judicial stance toward social and economic legislation.[16] The Court soon extended and clarified the stance it took in *Nebbia* when it declared that legislatures could regulate economic activity if their selection rested on a "rational basis."[17] A more modern and oft-quoted description of rational basis review was offered in the Court's opinion in *McGowan v. Maryland*:[18]

> The constitutional safeguard is offended only if the classification rests on grounds wholly irrelevant to the achievement of the State's objective. State legislatures are presumed to have acted within their constitutional power despite the fact that, in practice, their laws result in some inequality. A statutory discrimination will not be set aside if any state of facts reasonably may be conceived to justify it.[19]

The Court's application of rational basis review has been described by both commentators and occasionally Justices themselves as "tantamount to no review at all."[20] For example, surviving rational basis review does not require that the government defend, or even state, the purpose of the statute in question.[21]

In *FCC v. Beach Communications, Inc.*,[22] Justice Thomas makes the minimal nature of rational basis review clear when he writes for the Court that

> [w]hether embodied in the Fourteenth Amendment or inferred from the Fifth, equal protection is not a license for courts to judge the wisdom, fairness, or logic of legislative choices. In areas of social and economic policy, a statutory classification that neither proceeds along suspect lines nor infringes fundamental constitutional rights must be upheld against equal protection challenge if there is any reasonably conceivable state of facts that could provide a rational basis for the classification.

Rational basis review is intended to be minimal for a number of reasons, of course. From the standpoint of legitimacy, this minimality is consistent with concerns about the "countermajoritarian difficulty,"[23] which focuses on the proper role of an unelected judiciary in reviewing policies enacted by popularly elected legislatures. Simply put, freely elected bodies have a greater claim to legitimacy than do unelected judges, and the low, but still extant, hurdle of rational basis review acknowledges this reality while still offering the hope of checking unconstitutional usurpations of power by the legislature.

[16] For a discussion of the economic side of this development, see Riker and Weingast (1988).
[17] *United States v. Carolene Products Company*, 304 U.S. 144 (1938).
[18] 366 U.S. 420 (1961).
[19] 366 U.S. 420, 425–426 (1961), citations omitted.
[20] Hershkoff (1999), p. 1136, quoting *FCC v. Beach Communications, Inc.*, 508 U.S. 307, 323 n.3 (1993) (Stevens, J., concurring).
[21] For example, *Flemming v. Nestor* 363 U.S. 603 (1960). More generally, see Farrell (1992), pp. 22–25, 38–40.
[22] 508 U.S. 307 (1993).
[23] Bickel (1986) and Friedman (1998).

8.2 RATIONAL BASIS REVIEW AND LEGITIMACY

Regardless of how one views its application by the Court,[24] the basic structure of rational basis review involves verifying an initial part of the internal consistency requirement of our notion of legitimacy. Namely, rational basis review involves verifying that upholding the policy in question is preferable to reversing it according to some *admissible principle*. By "an admissible principle," we mean simply any method of comparing policy outcomes – that is, any justification for choosing one policy over another or, equivalently, any justification for a government policy – that the Court considers an appropriate basis for legislative action. In other words, an admissible principle is equivalent to the ranking of policies induced by a permissible legislative end or purpose. Because this concept is central to this chapter, we now turn briefly to the empirical question of how courts have distinguished between permissible and impermissible legislative ends and purposes.

Admissible Principles for Legislative Action

What we refer to as an admissible principle is referred to by courts in a variety of ways, but perhaps the most frequent term used to describe it is a "legitimate state interest."[25] In line with the variety of terms used by the Court to describe it, the notion of a legitimate state interest is ambiguous.[26] For our purposes, it is enough that the notion does have limits: statutes have been overturned for lacking a legitimate state interest.[27]

---

[24] For example, Wadhwani (2005) sketches three basic versions of rational basis review. Each of these requires that there be some goal (i.e., a "legitimate state interest," as discussed later) to rationalize or justify the statute being reviewed. Under the most demanding of these versions, "a court may not conjure up conceivable purposes but must ask about the legitimacy of the actual purposes. If the actual purposes are deemed rational, a court must then examine whether the governmental action at issue bears a 'fair and substantial relation' to the realization of those purposes." (Wadhwani, 2005, p. 803.)

[25] Other phrases used to describe this concept (or close facsimiles thereof) include "substantial government purpose," "legitimate public purpose," and "legitimate governmental interest." We acknowledge but leave to the side the theoretical and practical difficulties of the notion of a legislature having an "intent" when enacting a statute. For more on this issue see, among many others, Brilmayer (1980); Farber and Frickey (1988); Shepsle (1992); Easterbrook (1994); and McCubbins, Noll, and Weingast (1994).

[26] As Farrell (1992) writes, "[a]lthough the Supreme Court speaks frequently of permissible or impermissible purposes (i.e., every time it states the doctrine of rationality review), it has not systematically articulated the criteria that distinguish permissible from impermissible legislative purposes" (Farrell, 1992, p. 43).

[27] Examples include *Korematsu v. United States*, 323 U.S. 214 (1944) (racial hostility impermissible); *Regents of the University of California v. Bakke*, 438 U.S. 265 (1978) (racial preference impermissible); *Zobel v. Williams*, 457 U.S. 55 (1982) (awarding government benefits on basis of length of residence impermissible); *Metropolitan Life Ins. Co. v. Ward*, 470 U.S. 869 (1985)

The Court has stated that the "congressional desire to harm a politically unpopular group cannot constitute a *legitimate* government interest."[28] Statutes infringing on religious freedom, placing limits on speech, and drawing racial distinctions have been particularly vulnerable to rational basis review, for a variety of reasons.[29] Thus, while courts have been and remain clearly cautious in presuming to offer an explicit construction of the boundaries of proper legislative purposes, these boundaries undoubtedly exist in both theoretical and practical senses.

Furthermore, even if the scope of legitimate state interests is incredibly broad, the need for a statute to fulfill such an interest can nonetheless be restrictive if the various components of the law are expected to be consistent with the same purpose. While the courts have historically been reluctant to engage in explicit or finegrained discussion of "purpose" reasoning, they have on some occasions imposed more general consistency tests under the rubric of "rationality tests." In general, such consistency tests require that the (stated or hypothesized) legislative purpose not only justifies the statute but is also consistent with the specific provision or provisions of the statute being challenged. For example, in *Morey v. Doud*,[30] Illinois had imposed general licensing requirements for the sale of money orders but provided a specific exemption to the American Express Company. Upon reviewing the statute, the Supreme Court acknowledged that while the purpose of the statute was "to protect the public when dealing with currency exchanges,"[31] the specific exemption was unconstitutional since "a statutory discrimination must be based on differences that are reasonably related to the purpose of the Act in which it is found."[32]

Formally, rational basis review asks whether there is some admissible principle, p, for which the current policy is strictly better than the policy that would occur if the court overturned the statute(s) in question. To make the language precise, let P denote the set of admissible principles, s denote the policy resulting from upholding the statute, and r denote the policy that would follow from the court overturning the statute. Then a statute s survives rational basis review

(discrimination against nonresidents to further domestic business interests impermissible); *City of Cleburne v. Cleburne Living Center, Inc.*, 473 U.S. 432 (1985) (discrimination against people with intellectual disabilities impermissible); *Romer v. Evans*, 517 U.S. 620 (1996) (sexual orientation animus impermissible); and *Lawrence v. Texas*, 539 U.S. 558 (2003) (regulating private consensual sex between adults impermissible). See Farrell (1998) for a more extended discussion.

[28] *United States Department of Agriculture v. Moreno*, 413 U.S. 528, 534 (1973), quoted in Farrell (1992).

[29] We return later to more demanding notions of review (in particular, "strict scrutiny") that have emerged as focal standards for judicial review of statutes in these and related areas.

[30] 354 U.S. 457 (1957), cited in Bennett (1979).

[31] 354 U.S. 457, 464 (1957).

[32] 354 U.S. 457, 465 (1957).

if and only if there exists an admissible principle, $p \in P$, that ranks s higher than r:

$$\text{"s has a rational basis"} \Leftrightarrow \exists p \in P \text{ such that } s \; p \; r. \qquad (8.1)$$

Viewing rational basis in this way makes clear how and why it is a minimal (i.e., undemanding) notion of review: a statute will be overturned only if there is *no* admissible principle (i.e., no $p \in P$) that ranks the current policy as better than the alternative. Put another way, rational basis review essentially involves the court verifying that there is some admissible principle p for which the decision sequence, δ, satisfies the following:

1. the statute, s, is the final choice from δ,
2. δ contains the policy following from the statute's reversal, r, and
3. δ is internally consistent with respect to p.

Note that if such a decision sequence can be found, then the decision sequence $\delta = (r, s)$ satisfies each of these three properties as well. Thus, rational basis review need not inquire too deeply into how the statute was enacted. Considerations such as legislative history, the true intent of the legislators while debating the statute, and other contextual features of how the statute came to be enacted are unnecessary for carrying out rational basis review.

This formulation clarifies the fact that rational basis review becomes less and less demanding as the set of permissible principles grows (i.e., more principles are added to or included in P). Accordingly, the question at hand when one inquires as to how much bite rational basis review actually has in practice is how many principles are considered admissible by the court (i.e., how many principles are in P). As discussed above, while the set of admissible principles is bounded, it is quite broad. Accordingly, rational basis review can be thought of as verifying a necessary condition for legitimacy, a point to which we now turn.

Rational Basis as Necessary for Legitimacy

Rational basis review is clearly *less* demanding than our notion of legitimacy. That is, a law that passes rational basis review might still be illegitimate from the standpoint of our theory. This is for two related reasons. First, rational basis review does not require that the rational basis be provided by the state. Thus, from a procedural standpoint, rational basis review does not require that the policy be *accompanied* by a decision sequence and principle. Rather, it requires (at most) that there be some decision sequence and principle justifying the final choice. Furthermore, rational basis review is very permissive in the sense that it essentially puts the burden of proof on the litigant who seeks to overturn the statute in question. This is a high bar indeed, as the litigant must persuade the Court that there is *no* principle that justifies the challenged policy.

The second reason that successfully passing rational basis review is less demanding than our notion of legitimacy concerns stability. That is, when applying rational basis review, the Court is typically unconcerned with the question of whether the legislature has justified *not* choosing the unchosen policies. For example, the Court's use of rational basis review is described by Justice Hugo Black as being based on a

> constitutional principle that states have power to legislate against what are found to be injurious practices in their internal commercial and business affairs so long as their laws do not run afoul of some specific federal constitutional prohibition or of some valid federal law. Under this constitutional doctrine, the due process clause is no longer to be so broadly construed that the Congress and state legislatures are put in a strait jacket when they attempt to suppress business and industrial conditions which they regard as offensive to the public welfare.[33]

In a very direct sense, survival of rational basis review is a necessary condition for legitimacy as defined in our framework. This conclusion implies that there will be government policies that pass muster under rational basis review, but would not be considered legitimate. Our axiomatic framework implies that there are two ways in which this can happen: the policy might fail to satisfy internal consistency or stability (or both). However, we believe that any proper construction of rational basis review (i.e., any review posture that offers a non-trivial possibility of overturning a statute) must at least verify that the policy can be supported by some internally consistent decision sequence containing both the policy and the alternative policy that would follow from overturning the statute(s) in question.[34]

One should not be surprised that failure to find a rational basis for a statute justifies judicial intervention and negation of the statute. Rather, the potentially surprising aspect of rational basis review is how lax a standard it represents. This reality is useful in illuminating the different bases or origins of legitimacy. In justifying its use of rational basis review, justices have frequently made explicit mention of legitimacy. In particular, the Court has referenced (electoral) accountability in justifying judicial deference to legislative and executive policy decisions in a wide array of situations. As Justice Stevens wrote for the Court in the seminal case of *Chevron U.S.A., Inc. v. Natural Resources Defense Council, Inc.,*[35]

> ... federal judges – who have no constituency – have a duty to respect legitimate policy choices made by those who do. The responsibilities for assessing the wisdom of such policy choices and resolving the struggle between competing views of the public interest are not judicial ones....[36]

---

[33] *Lincoln Union v. Northwestern Co.,* 335 U. S. 525, 536-537 (1949), citations omitted.

[34] As discussed earlier, any decision sequence consisting of a single policy is trivially internally consistent. Accordingly, any real notion of review must subject the policy under review to comparison with at least one other policy.

[35] 467 U.S. 837 (1984).

[36] 467 U.S. 837, 866 (1984)

In general, judicial review is (and arguably should be) highly deferential to the choices of elected branches so long as the chosen policies are not unduly coercive. If a statute imposes no requirements on the citizenry, it is arguable that the question of whether the statute is legitimate is essentially moot – what would be the effect of overturning such a statute?[37] Accordingly, the deference accorded by a court is (and arguably should be) generally decreasing in the degree to which the statute coerces individuals to behave in certain ways. In other words, the legitimating power of having been adopted by a duly elected representative body is finite and at least potentially insufficient to warrant abrogation of individual and collective liberties.

While there are multiple ways one might attempt to legitimate significantly coercive legislation, all reasonable approaches would impose greater demands in terms of the sets of admissible principles or purposes for which coercion might be legitimately mandated. This relationship is reflected in the notion of strict scrutiny, to which we turn in the next section.

8.3 TWO-TIERED REVIEW

In *Carolene Products*, the Court upheld a federal law regulating the interstate shipment of dairy products, applying a presumption of constitutionality to the statute in question, and agreeing that the prohibition was related to the legitimate legislative interest of protecting public health. The majority opinion in the case is most famous for "footnote 4," in which Justice Harlan Stone laid out a basic two-tiered structure of review. In addition to the already understood notion of rational basis review, Stone's footnote notes the possibility of a more searching and demanding form of review for legislation that "tends seriously to curtail the operation of those political processes ordinarily to be relied upon to protect minorities."[38] While the Court did not apply a higher standard of review in *Carolene Products*, the footnote provided the framework within which the Court would eventually develop a more intricate form of inquiry in equal protection cases – a form of inquiry that would be more directly responsive to the need to weigh various individual liberties and social goals against one another.

The doctrine that evolved from Justice Stone's "footnote 4" is now known as *strict scrutiny*. Strict scrutiny is a less deferential stance called for when the government infringes upon certain "preferred" rights.[39] The doctrine of strict

---

[37] This raises the question of how to properly review laws that allocate benefits to some, but not all, citizens while imposing per se burdens on none. In terms of equal protection jurisprudence, the denial of a tangible benefit can be construed as an imposition.

[38] 304 U. S. 144, 152, n. 4.

[39] The Court has developed a family of intermediate forms of scrutiny that are more deferential than strict scrutiny and less deferential than rational basis review. A detailed discussion of these is beyond the scope of this chapter. Galloway (1988) provides a useful summary and discussion of some of these standards.

scrutiny emerged from the Warren Court, which famously adopted a broadly interventionist stance with respect to judicial review of both administrative and legislative action. Fallon, Jr. (2006) describes the doctrine as reflecting

> a set of assumptions that defined both a series of problems worth solving and a framework within which to seek answers. Seen in this light, the strict scrutiny test invited the Court to think about whether particular claimed rights might deserve more than rational basis review, for it framed manageable issues regarding which infringements of those rights should nevertheless be permitted.[40]

The "series of problems" that Fallon alludes to can be broken down into two categories, each of which corresponds to an interpretation of how the Court has applied strict scrutiny. These categories are protection of near-absolute rights and illicit governmental motives.[41] The problem of protecting near-absolute rights is best exemplified by the Court's longstanding approach to free speech cases. For example, in *United States v. Playboy Entertainment Group, Inc.*,[42] Justice Kennedy's opinion for the majority pointed out that a content-based speech restriction

> can stand only if it satisfies strict scrutiny. If a statute regulates speech based on its content, it must be narrowly tailored to promote a compelling Government interest. If a less restrictive alternative would serve the Government's purpose, the legislature must use that alternative. To do otherwise would be to restrict speech without an adequate justification, a course the First Amendment does not permit.[43]

While similar arguments have been forwarded for the application of strict scrutiny to statutory recognition of racial distinctions, uncovering illict governmental motivations is also commonly cited as a goal of strict scutiny in such cases. For example, the Court applied strict scrutiny in reviewing an affirmative action program.[44] In the majority opinion in this case, Justice Sandra Day O'Connor described the application of strict scrutiny as follows:

> Absent searching judicial inquiry into the justification for ... race-based measures, there is simply no way of determining what classifications are "benign" or "remedial" and what classifications are in fact motivated by illegitimate notions of racial inferiority or simple racial politics. Indeed, the purpose of strict scrutiny is to "smoke out" illegitimate uses of race by assuring that the legislative body is pursuing a goal important enough to warrant use of a highly suspect tool. The

---

[40] Fallon, Jr. (2006), p. 1293.

[41] *Cf.* Fallon, Jr. (2006), pp. 1303–1311. Fallon describes a third category of application, "weighted balancing," but then attacks this use as incompatible with the traditional understanding of strict scrutiny. In addition, strict scrutiny is rarely described in this way by Justices and, typically, only in dissent (see in particular Fallon, Jr. 2006, pp. 1306–1308). Accordingly, we focus on the protection of near-absolute rights and detection of illict motives.

[42] 529 U.S. 803 (2000).

[43] 529 U.S. 813. (Citations omitted.)

[44] *City of Richmond v. J. A. Croson Co.*, 488 U.S. 469 (1989).

test also ensures that the means chosen "fit" this compelling goal so closely that there is little or no possibility that the motive for the classification was illegitimate racial prejudice or stereotype.[45]

A subtle but important distinction between rational basis review and strict scrutiny is alluded to by Justice O'Connor's phrasing, "assuring that the legislative body *is* pursuing a goal" (emphasis added). In particular, strict scrutiny inquires more deeply about the role of legislative intent *qua* the purpose of the statute. Ideally, the compelling state interest that justifies the statute should have been (part of) the legislature's purpose for enacting it. This position implies that the legislature should be able to demonstrate that this was indeed the case. Thus, while the Court is generally content to hypothesize about the possible rationale for a statute being subjected to rational basis review, the government is generally required to provide an explicit justification or purpose when the statute is subjected to strict scrutiny.

The goals of these two categories are poorly served by rational basis review primarily because of the presumption of constitutionality that serves as the starting point for such review. Furthermore, while the tests differ in practical terms such as the language adopted by the Court in offering guidance to the legislature upon overturning the statute in question, all of the categories overlap in terms of looking to the question of whether there is a *justification* of the statute's infringement on individual liberties. The Court's opinion in *Adarand Constructors, Inc. v. Pena*[46] describes strict scrutiny as "determin[ing] whether a compelling governmental interest justifies"[47] the injuries inflicted by a statute on individuals' rights.

The phrase "compelling government interest" is of vital importance in theoretically distinguishing between strict scrutiny and rational basis review. As with "legitimate state interest," this notion essentially refers to what we term principles in our theory. Indeed, compelling state interests are necessarily legitimate state interests, but the converse does not hold: there are legitimate state interests that are not compelling. As we discuss in more detail later, this is a principal way – from the standpoint of our theory – in which surviving strict scrutiny review is more legitimating than is surviving rational basis review.

8.4 STRICT SCRUTINY AND LEGITIMACY

Logically more demanding than rational basis review, strict scrutiny is also more closely consistent with our notion of legitimacy. Strict scrutiny is more demanding than rational basis in two broad ways: it admits a narrower set of legitimate state interests (i.e., a smaller set of admissible principles) and imposes a more demanding requirement on the relationship between the legislative

---

[45] 488 U.S. 493.
[46] 515 U.S. 200 (1995).
[47] 515 U.S. 200, 230 (1995).

purpose and the statute's provisions. On the first count and regardless of the goal motivating its use by the Court (i.e., regardless of whether its purpose is protection of near-absolute rights or the ferreting out of illicit motives), strict scrutiny is based on a more refined notion of an admissible principle. That is, internal consistency is more difficult to satisfy under strict scrutiny review – there are reasons or purposes that the Court might accept as justification under rational basis review but reject as sufficient under strict scrutiny, while there are no purposes that satisfy strict scrutiny review but would not pass muster if rational basis were to be applied. Thus, referring back to the representation of rational basis review in Section 8.1, we can refine this representation for strict scrutiny by letting $P^* \subset P$ denote the set of principles that the Court accepts as "compelling state interests," each of which it necessarily also accepts as a "legitimate state interest."

Second, the structure of strict scrutiny review requires more than there being a principle that is a compelling state interest, p, such that the decision sequence containing the statute in question, s, and the policy following from the statute's reversal, r, is internally consistent with respect to p. In addition, it requires that the statute is narrowly drawn in the sense of there not being an alternative formulation of the statute, a, that fulfills the statute's compelling state purpose *and* that is less invasive of individual and collective rights. Strict scrutiny requires that statutes be "narrowly drawn" but, more important, the notion is intended to inquire as to whether the infringing aspects of the statute are necessary to accomplishing the statute's stated purpose.

This aspect of strict scrutiny can be formally represented as follows. The notion of a preferred or protected right implies that when comparing two possible statutes, s and a, differing *only* in that one (a) is less invasive than the other (s), any (judicially) admissible principle – including compelling state interests (P^*) – must rank the less invasive statute strictly higher than the more invasive one: $a \; p \; s$. Viewed in this way, requiring that a statute be narrowly drawn is equivalent to a form of stability. Formally, let $N(s)$ denote the alternatives that are more narrowly drawn (i.e., less invasive) than s: these are the hypothetical statutes that differ from s in that they do not infringe on individual and collective liberty as much as s does.[48] Then one can represent this requirement as requiring that, for any more narrowly drawn alternative form of the statute, a,

---

[48] Note that we do not condition $N(s)$ on the purpose of (i.e., principle p used to justify) s. Thus, we are assuming that the notion of "invasiveness" of a statute is independent of reasons one might adopt it. There are exceptions to this, of course. In particular, examples can be found in free speech cases (e.g., *United States v. O'Brien*, 391 U.S. 367 [1968]; *Brandenburg v. Ohio*, 395 U.S. 444 [1969]; *Spence v. Washington*, 418 U.S. 405 [1974]; and *Texas v. Johnson*, 491 U.S. 397 [1989]), in which the Court explicitly acknowledges that the infringement on speech *could* be a legislative purpose, albeit an impermissible one. A point of interest in this regard is that this possibility can be seen as a reason that the Court might apply strict scrutiny (particularly in the interest of ferreting out illicit motives) to such cases. We do not explore this possibility further here.

the reversion outcome (i.e., the policy following from reversal of the statute, denoted by r) is ranked strictly higher by the compelling interest of the statute, denoted by p:

$$\forall a \in N(s), \ s \ p \ a \text{ or } r \ p \ a. \tag{8.2}$$

Thus, we can formally represent strict scrutiny as follows:

$$\text{``}s\text{ passes strict scrutiny''} \Leftrightarrow \exists p \in P^* \text{ with } \begin{cases} s \ p \ r \text{ and} \\ \forall a \in N(s), \ s \ p \ a \text{ or } r \ p \ a. \end{cases} \tag{8.3}$$

Note that the condition expressed in (8.2) is related to, but not nested with, our notion of stability. The condition is weaker than stability because it does not refer to any alternative that is not more narrowly drawn than s. Thus, a statute might pass strict scrutiny even if there exists some alternative policy, t, that is not more narrowly drawn than s but is superior to both the statute s and to the policy represented by the reversal of the statute r (i.e., $t \ p \ s$ and $t \ p \ r$). To see that strict scrutiny as defined in (8.2) is stronger than stability, note that stability considers the entire decision sequence and requires only that, for each more narrowly drawn alternative $a \in N(s)$, there be *some* policy in the decision sequence leading to s that is superior to a. Strict scrutiny, on the other hand, requires that each more narrowly drawn alternative be dominated either by the statute itself or the policy that results from overturning the statute.

Each of these differences is important. The weakness of strict scrutiny with respect to our notion of legitimacy illustrates that strict scrutiny review is not intended to carry the compelling state interest (p) to its "logical end." Viewed another way, the application of strict scrutiny review generally does not result in a judicial mandate to the legislature of the form "well, if you're going to do this, then you need to take the next step and do *this*." In other words, strict scrutiny involves a limited kind of stability validation, focusing only on a subset of unchosen policies. From a practical standpoint, this might be the most that courts can be expected to verify: the set of all possible unchosen policies is simply too extensive. A true review of stability would potentially require an impossibly detailed description of the decision sequence or underlying principle. Furthermore, for such review to be meaningful, it would undoubtedly require the reviewing court to view even more skeptically the legislature's claims about the underlying principle or purpose of the statute. In the end, for example, the legislature might claim that an unchosen alternative was neither enacted nor actively considered precisely because it did not have the support of a majority of the legislators. How is a court supposed to treat such a claim? Even if the court accepts the statement, *should* the underlying principle always be conditioned on the support of a decisive coalition within the legislature? How could the court *not* accept the claim that a proposal would not have received enough votes as sufficient to establish stability without the court substituting its judgment for the collective judgment of the people's elected representatives? How can the court accept such an argument without effectively overturning the notion of protected or preferred rights?

The additional strength of strict scrutiny review relative to our notion of legitimacy is based on the fact that strict scrutiny does *not* rely on considered but unchosen alternatives (i.e., the decision sequence). Thus, there are legitimate policy choices that would not survive strict scrutiny. In fact, there may be *no* policy that would survive strict scrutiny (this is a point of our discussion, in Section 6.3, of refinements of our notion of legitimacy). However, as opposed to our notion of legitimacy, the potential emptiness of this set (the set of "strict scutiny survivors") should not be seen as problematic. This is because strict scrutiny review is not applied to the prevailing status quo policy. Only positive action by the legislature (i.e., policy change) is subject to such review. Theoretically, strict scrutiny review privileges the reversion policy – what would follow from reversal of the statute under review. This conception illuminates Gerald Gunther's famous description of strict scrutiny as "'strict' in theory and fatal in fact."[49]

It is arguably appropriate that strict scutiny review be more demanding than what one might term "mere" legitimacy. This scrutiny is intended to be brought to bear on a statute that is inherently claiming a "greater" legitimacy than one or more preferred rights. In a sense, all statutes should ideally satisfy our notion of legitimacy. Statutes that infringe on preferred rights – particularly explicitly protected rights such as speech – are necessarily claiming an underlying principle that is at least partially in conflict with the principle(s) upon which the state is founded (as least in a contractarian sense). Accordingly, courts *should* view such statutes with heightened skepticism.

8.5 LINKING JUDICIAL REVIEW AND LEGITIMACY

Having related our notion of legitimacy to two prominent doctrines of judicial review, it is appropriate to ask what role judicial review does or should play in maintaining the legitimacy of public policy in a democracy. Our theory has a distinctly procedural flavor – legitimacy is simply consistency with a broad notion of rationality. Verifying legitimacy requires knowledge of two principal components of the policy in question: the principle claimed to justify or rationalize the policy and the decision sequence that leads to the policy's selection. Each of these components is relevant in the empirical application of judicial review under both rational basis review and strict scrutiny. In addition to being structurally analogous to our notion of legitimacy insofar as these review procedures inquire about the correspondence between the

[49] Gunther (1972), p. 8.

goals and structure of legislative decision making, the tests imposed in each of these examples of judicial review at least partially mirror the requirements imposed by our Axioms 1 & 2. In this sense, it is arguable that judicial review might be associated with legitimate statutes because the judiciary at least partially verifies that contentious statutes were chosen through a legitimate process.

9

Structuring Discussion

A key implication of our notion of legitimacy is that legitimacy can require omitting one or more alternatives from the decision sequence.[1] In this chapter, we delve a little deeper into this somewhat perplexing implication. Specifically, we describe its relationship to specific procedural characteristics that can be broadly described as restrictions on *scope* – that is, standing rules precluding the consideration (or, perhaps, comparison) of one or more alternatives. Such restrictions are common to political and social institutions. In this chapter, we focus first on the U.S. House of Representatives and discuss a key way in which the scope of legislative business is structured in that institution: *germaneness*. We then turn to the related phenomena of *single-subject provisions*, a class of rule that limits the scope of statutes.

Before moving to detailed discussions of institutionalized restrictions on the scope of discussion, it is important to note that this chapter focuses exclusively on legislatures. This is by design: the other two chapters in which we discuss real-world institutions focus on the decisions of unelected government officials (judges and bureaucrats). As discussed in Chapter 4, the decisions of popularly elected officials are imbued with a higher level of innate legitimacy than those of unelected officials. Precisely because of this, institutional rules such those discussed in this chapter – rules that both constrain legislative autonomy and are consonant with our theory of legitimacy – are particularly interesting. Within the context of our theory, the germaneness requirement in the U.S. House of Representatives and the single-subject provisions governing many state legislatures are linked by a common thread: these institutional restrictions bolster both the transparency of the link between legislative action and the principle that justifies it and reinforce the internal consistency of legislative deliberations when considering, crafting, and enacting statutes. With that

---

[1] A precise instance of such a situation is provided and discussed in Chapter 5 (Example 2).

linkage in mind, we now turn to the germaneness requirement in the U.S. House of Representatives.

9.1 GERMANENESS IN THE HOUSE OF REPRESENTATIVES

This section focuses on the U.S. House of Representatives. In so doing, we frequently cite the *Constitution, Jefferson's Manual, and Rules of the House of Representatives of the United States, 112th Congress* simply as *Manual*.[2] This biennial publication of the House of Representatives is authored by the House Parliamentarian and includes broad and deep discussion of the history and interpretations of, and precedents undergirding, the various standing rules of the House. In many ways, this document is itself an instantiation of our theory of legitimacy. As described by the Parliamentarian, the origins, development, and usage of the rules are not only central to the processing of the nation's business; they also provide legitimacy to the choices made by the House of Representatives:

> In resolving questions of order, the Speaker and other presiding officers of the House adhere to the jurisprudential principle of *stare decisis* – a commitment to stand by earlier decisions. This fidelity to precedent promotes analytic consistency and procedural predictability and thereby fosters legitimacy in the parliamentary practice of the House. The commitment of the House to stand by its procedural decisions requires that we be rigorous about what constitutes precedent. In the parliamentary context, the term does not refer to a mere instance in which an event occurred or was suffered; rather, it refers to a decision or order actually disposing of a question of order. As we strive to apply pertinent precedent to each procedural question, the compilation of the parliamentary precedents of the House becomes as important as any other function of the Office of the Parliamentarian.
>
> The compilation of precedents depends implicitly on a transcript of the actual proceedings of the House. In this light, the people who form the leading edge of the process by which we compile the precedents of the House are the Official Reporters of Debate. The virtually verbatim transcript of floor proceedings that the reporters produce daily for publication in the Congressional Record is the indispensable raw material of the precedents-compilation process.[3]

In addition to the Parliamentarian's explicit reference to legitimacy as a justification for the tasks of his office, the quote is notable in its description of the material from which the legitimacy is formed: the verbatim records of the House's processing of its business, which is directly analogous to our notion of a decision sequence. With this point in mind, we now turn to a detailed consideration of a high profile restriction of scope that has been used in the House since the First Congress, known as *germaneness*.

---

[2] House Document No. 111-157.
[3] *Manual*, p. ix.

The House's Germaneness Rule

The standing rules of the House of Representatives require that an amendment be germane (i.e., related) to the bill to which it is offered. The modern version of the House's germaneness rule, essentially unchanged since 1822, is as follows:[4]

> No motion or proposition on a subject different from that under consideration shall be admitted under color of amendment.[5]

Historically, the germaneness requirement has been interpreted so as to imply real limits on the amendments that may be offered.[6] The rule provides significant constraints on what may be brought forward on the floor.[7] In fact, the House's notion of germaneness is more demanding than the colloquial notion of being related. For example, when considering a proposal to authorize certain activities, a proposal to have the bill also authorize the investigation of whether undertaking the activities was advisable is in general not germane.[8]

Tests for Germaneness

An amendment must pass a variety of tests to be construed as germane and receive consideration on the floor. We discuss the most significant and frequently encountered tests here. However, the following informal description of the rule summarizes the relationship between the germaneness restriction and the deliberative process:

> ... if the subject of a proposed amendment to a bill is not one that would reasonably be expected to be within the contemplation of those considering that bill, the amendment is probably not germane. Conversely, if consideration of the general subject matter of the amendment would naturally arise during consideration of the bill itself, it may be germane....[9]

Before continuing to the details of the various tests for germaneness, it is useful to reflect for a moment on the linkage this description draws between germaneness and the "natural" progression of the bill's consideration. In the context of our theory and specifically the implications of allowing too much

---

[4] It is interesting to note that the standing rules of the House of Representatives have included a germaneness requirement in each Congress since 1789. It is presumably the successor to a similar rule adopted in the Continental Congress in 1784, which read: "No new motion or proposition shall be admitted under colour of amendment, as a substitute for the question or proposition under debate, until it is postponed or disagreed to" (*Journals of the Continental Congress*, July 8, 1784, p. 574.)

[5] Clause 7 of Rule XVI, Rules of the House of Representatives, 112th Congress.

[6] For example, consider Tiefer (1989), pp. 420–448, Brown and Johnson (2003), Ch. 26.

[7] As a crude quantitative measure of this, the relevant chapter of the *Deschler-Brown* precedents concerning the germaneness rule (Ch. 28) is more than 1,850 pages long.

[8] Deschler-Brown Ch. 28 §5.29.

[9] Deschler-Brown Ch. 28 §1.

discussion as illustrated in Example 2, the germaneness rule represents an important instance of a "neutral" rule that helps the House maintain internal consistency of the decision sequence represented by its members' deliberations on the floor. In line with this, the rule has been repeatedly justified on the grounds that it engenders more careful deliberation within the House and, by extension, presumably promotes better collective decision making by the body as well. For example, on September 22, 1914, the Chair[10] ruled as follows:

> That an amendment be germane means that it must be akin to, or relevant to, the subject matter of the bill. It must be an amendment that would appropriately be considered in connection with the bill. The object of the rule requiring amendments to be germane – and such a rule has been adopted in practically every legislative body in the United States – is in the interest of orderly legislation. Its purpose is to prevent hasty and ill-considered legislation, to prevent propositions being presented for the consideration of the body which might not reasonably be anticipated and for which the body might not be properly prepared.[11]

The germaneness restriction has been explicitly described as refining majority preference within the House of Representatives.

> The germaneness rule implements the preference of the majority controlling the House, and the committee and leadership organs through which it acts, for keeping some issues off the floor – issues that belong to the minority party's agenda, or that would painfully divide the majority party. The germaneness rule implements that preference – not because it is interpreted in a partisan or biased way, but simply because, interpreted neutrally, it limits the subjects on the floor to those reported in bills.[12]

This description's reference to "painful division" of the majority party is an allusion to the possibility that a nongermane amendment might create a majority preference cycle that (necessarily) crosses partisan lines within the House. In the context of Example 2, if one conceives of the principle in that example as representing the majority preference relation over the three alternatives, any germaneness restriction that forbade proposals that divided a particular majority coalition would prohibit consideration of at least one of the three alternatives.[13]

As with any legislative rule, the proof is in the application: many rules are highly respected and even revered despite (or, perhaps, because of) their

---

[10] John J. Fitzgerald, of New York.

[11] VIII *Cannon* §2993.

[12] Tiefer (1989), p. 424.

[13] A restriction to "protect" a given majority coalition might prohibit consideration of two of the three alternatives, if the protected coalition was divided over two or more of the binary comparisons. This more extreme type of protection is arguably more illustrative of gatekeeping power through which the majority can block consideration of any proposal that would divide the coalition in a painful way (e.g., referral of proposals to a partisan-controlled committee system).

repeated violation. The germaneness restriction has undoubtedly been violated in practice. However, the rule has been applied for a sufficiently consistent and sustained period to generate a lengthy and detailed set of precedents for its application. Describing the application and interpretation of the rule in a reasonably succinct fashion, there are two main classes of tests that a proposed amendment must pass in order to be considered germane, which Tiefer describes as *subject-relatedness* and *formal generality*.[14] When applying these tests, the presumption is that an amendment is not germane, placing the burden of establishing the germaneness of the amendment on its proponents. Furthermore, it must pass each of the applicable tests we describe below.[15]

We now discuss each of these tests and how they relate to the claim that the germaneness restriction can promote the internal consistency of legislative activity on the floor of the U.S. House of Representatives.

Subject-Relatedness

Each of the tests in the first class considers how closely related are the amendment and the bill. As described by Tiefer, this class contains three basic tests, in no particular order of importance:

- subject matter,
- fundamental purpose, and
- committee jurisdiction.

Obviously, the test of subject matter depends crucially on the text of bill – oftentimes the title, section, or even paragraph at which the proposed amendment is directed – and that of the proposed amendment. Beyond obviously nongermane cases, the question of whether an amendment passes this test is, at least in practical terms, largely dependent on precedent and interpretation by the House Parliamentarian, his or her staff, and the Chair. Each of the three major sets of collected precedents (*Hinds*, *Cannon*, and *Deschler-Brown*) present and detail numerous and varied rulings about germaneness, and the interpretation and extension of these precedents is carried out in an analogical fashion.[16]

The test of fundamental purpose essentially involves comparing the method(s) called for in the bill with those proposed in the amendment. In applying this test, the Chair is expected to examine both the text of the bill and

---

[14] Tiefer (1989), pp. 427–438.
[15] *Manual*, §929.
[16] *Deschler-Brown* Ch. 28, §1, §4.109. It is worth noting that this test is formally independent of the later tests. For example, it does not tend to depend in a systematic way on either whether the amendment is broader in scope than the corresponding provision of the bill or whether the amendment would be within the jurisdiction of the committee(s) that considered and reported the bill (Tiefer, 1989, p. 429).

the language contained in the committee report(s) accompanying it.[17] Amendments that pass the subject matter test may still fail the fundamental purpose test. For example, neither an amendment focusing attention on one element of a larger class of subjects for specific scrutiny nor an amendment extending appropriations beyond the original bill's time horizon is germane.[18] While an amendment may propose an alternative but related method for achieving the corresponding goal(s) of the bill, the fundamental purpose test requires that any alteration of method be, in essence, foreseeable. Two examples of amendments ruled nongermane under this test include (1) for a bill extending unemployment benefits during an economic recession, an amendment calling for tax incentives and regulatory reform in an attempt to stimulate economic activity[19] and (2) an amendment calling for the censure of President Clinton when offered to an impeachment resolution.[20]

The structure of the fundamental purpose test highlights an important distinction – that between means and ends – that figures in other aspects of the procedures of both the House of Representatives and other legislative bodies, including the Senate. Specifically, the fundamental purpose test focuses attention not only on the end result but also the means by which it is obtained. Given that an amendment must pass each of the germaneness tests and, furthermore, that the Chair is directed to defer to an interpretation that would render an amendment nongermane when such an interpretation exists,[21] the fundamental purpose test protects a proposal from comparisons in terms of both means and ends.

The final subject matter-based test for germaneness of an amendment focuses on whether the amendment concerns a matter falling outside the reporting committee's jurisdiction. This matter is not an exclusive test for germaneness in any way and, given the fact that bills may be reported out with provisions that necessarily overlap committee jurisdictions, there are a number of exceptions to this test.[22] A important role of this test is the support it provides for the subject-based jurisdictional arrangement of the House's standing committees. In a sense, it is a "fallback" test that recognizes that some subjects have been deliberately divided by the membership of the House into subcategories.[23] There are numerous reasons why the House divides some subject

---

[17] *Deschler-Brown*, Ch. 28, §5.6.
[18] *Manual*, §933.
[19] Sept. 17, 1991, *CR* p. 23156.
[20] Dec. 19, 1998, *CR* p. 28107.
[21] *Manual*, §929.
[22] *Manual*, §934.
[23] The jurisdictions of the standing committees are described in detail in the House Rules (Clause 1 of Rule X). These rules are approved by a majority vote at the beginning of each Congress. It is important to note that this provision of the germaneness rule has an ancillary benefit of supporting the agenda setting power of the House leadership insofar as it provides a clear rationale for the Speaker to block attempts to circumvent the committee system by adding a bill

matter between different committees,[24] many of which are beyond the focus of this book. Nonetheless, this system also represents a restriction on scope, particularly to the degree that legislative business is confined (either by norm or formal procedure) to bills that fall within a single committee's jurisdiction.[25] As this restriction closely mirrors (and, indeed, is explicitly reflected in) the germaneness requirement, we leave this interesting and important aspect of the procedures of the House of Representatives to the side and focus on the germaneness requirement in more detail.

Formal Generality

The second class of tests of germaneness can be described as being composed of two somewhat related questions that focus on the relationship between the formal structures of the proposed amendment and the provision(s) of the bill at which it is aimed. The first of these tests considers whether the amendment proposes to broaden the provision(s) of the bill at which it is aimed.[26] This is most often invoked with respect to amendments that propose to widen the class of firms, individuals, or entities to which a provision would apply. For example, to a bill relating to corporations involved in interstate commerce, an amendment relating to all corporations was ruled nongermane.[27] Similarly, to a joint resolution proposing an amendment to the Constitution guaranteeing the right to vote for persons 18 years of age or older, an amendment requiring that all persons 18 years and older be treated as having reached the age of majority for all purposes under the law was ruled nongermane.[28]

A second test, in practice, provides particular protection to bills with single "propositions" of a limited nature. The most important example of this is the principle that an individual proposition may not be amended by another individual proposition even though the two belong to the same class. Two examples of amendments ruled nongermane on this principle include, to a provision providing for the extermination of the cotton-boll weevil, an amendment including the gypsy moth as well and, to a bill prohibiting cotton futures, an amendment to also prohibit wheat futures.[29]

---

referred to one committee to another committee's bill, referred to as "riders" in the U.S. Senate, where this practice is permitted (Tiefer, 1989, p. 434).

[24] For example, see Smith and Deering (1990); King (1994, 1997); and Baumgartner, Jones, and MacLeod (2000).

[25] Since the mid 1970s, the rules have allowed the Speaker of the House to use "multiple referrals" in which the Speaker may refer a bill simultaneously or sequentially to more than one committee.

[26] In both formal terms and the informal hierarchy of the variety of tests for germaneness, this test represents a "conditional" hurdle in the sense that it only applies to amendments that satisfy the subject-relatedness tests described earlier.

[27] V *Hinds*, §5842.

[28] *Manual* §937.

[29] *Manual* §936.

The importance of this principle is highlighted by the related but opposing precedent that an amendment adding an additional class may be germane to bills including multiple propositions in the same class. Under this principle, for example, an amendment for admission of another territory to the Union is not germane to a bill proposing the admission of one territory into the Union, a similar amendment (adding another territory to the Union) *is* germane to a bill admitting several territories into the Union.[30] Similarly, in terms of the fundamental purpose test described earlier, the proposal to include an additional method within a bill calling for the use of multiple methods for a general purpose may be germane. This test might be summarized as endowing a bill with germaneness protections in proportion to the degree that the bill's provisions are themselves germane to each other.

There are other, more narrowly applicable tests of germaneness,[31] but the two classes of tests provide an accurate portrait of the structure of the germaneness restriction and the degree to which it constrains floor consideration of a given bill in the House of Representatives. Accordingly, we now leave the House and turn to a restriction on legislation that, while not used in the House, is used quite broadly: "single-subject provisions" restricting the substantive breadth of legislation.

9.2 SINGLE-SUBJECT PROVISIONS

Many political institutions, including both legislatures and direct democracy procedures (initiatives and referenda), are governed to some degree by single-subject provisions.[32] Simply put, a single-subject provision requires that any enactment concern only one topic. We focus here on the use and application of such provisions in legislative institutions and simply note that there is a large literature on this type of restriction in direct democracy institutions.[33] A typical example of such a rule in the legislative context is provided by the Missouri State Constitution, which provides that

> No bill shall contain more than one subject which shall be clearly expressed in its title, except bills [dealing with certain bond issues] and general appropriation bills, which may embrace the various subjects and accounts for which moneys are appropriated.[34]

---

[30] *Manual* §936, 938; *Deschler-Brown* Ch. 28 §9.

[31] For example, there are specific sets of precedents dealing with appropriation bills, special rules, amendments in the nature of substitute, committee amendments, instructions in motions to recommit, and Senate amendments.

[32] For example, in the United States, more than 40 states have some version of it in their constitutions (Gilbert, 2006).

[33] For example, Lowenstein (1982, 2002), Magleby (1994), Kastorf (2005), Cooter and Gilbert (2010), and Matsusaka and Hasen (2010). The seminal treatment of single-subject provisions and related rules is provided by Ruud (1957).

[34] Missouri State Constitution (as of November 2012), Article III, §23.

In addition to the single-subject provision ("no bill shall contain more than one subject"), the Missouri provision is typical in two ways. First, the provision contains a *clear title provision* (the subject "shall be clearly expressed in its title"). Second, the provision also includes an exception for appropriations bills. Here, we focus on the single-subject provision and some of the rationales for restricting legislative choice in this way and compare these rationales with the impact of such a provision on legitimacy as defined in this book.

The usual arguments in favor of single-subject provisions focus on three related aspects of the legislative process: mitigating logrolling or vote trading, enhancing accountability and transparency, and veto bargaining between the legislature and governors.[35] For our purposes, the first two are the most relevant and we accordingly focus on these in this section.[36] Both of these arguments are related to the goals of our internal consistency requirement (Axiom 1), although the two rationales are implicitly appealing to a different instrumental mechanism in pursuit of collective welfare, as we now discuss.

Mitigating Logrolling

To the degree that single-subject provisions tend to reduce logrolling, it can be argued that such restrictions bolster the welfare effects of majority (or supermajority) requirements for the passage of legislation.[37] Such arguments typically begin with the presumption that logrolling is properly considered distasteful because it allows otherwise inchoate coalitions of legislators to bind themselves together in pursuit of their own, presumably narrowly construed, interests at the expense of the collective welfare of the citizenry as a whole.

We do not agree that logrolling should be imbued with such a pejorative connotation. In particular, while there are certainly many situations in which logrolling might be the requisite vehicle for nefarious attempts to enact policies with parochially focused benefits for a bare majority of legislators, it is also possible to construct robust examples of situations in which logrolling is not

---

[35] These factors are also discussed, although from a somewhat different perspective, by Gilbert (2006).

[36] Of course, this is not to imply that the impact of single-subject provisions on inter branch (legislative-executive) policymaking is not interesting or important. However, the ways in which this dynamic is relevant for legitimacy are subsumed by the electoral accountability concerns. The interbranch rationale is particularly important on its own in cases in which one wants to distinguish between imposing single-subject restrictions on the legislative process versus imposing them on direct democracy processes.

[37] In considering such arguments, Gilbert (2006) distinguishes between logrolling and "riding": logrolling involves the legislature passing a bill composed of policies that each would fail to secure sufficient votes for passage on their own, while riding occurs when a policy is added to a bill consisting of a policy that does possess the requisite support. In a nutshell, logrolling is arguably bad, and riding is arguably efficient. This distinction is irrelevant for our purposes, as we do not privilege a legislature's majority requirement in terms of the proper definition of the principle by which legislative enactments must be justified.

only welfare enhancing but, *a fortiore*, Pareto efficient. Nevertheless, the fact that logrolling is perceived in this way suggests the challenges that such behavior presents for legislative legitimacy. At least one reading of this challenge is clearly consistent with our theory of legitimacy. Namely, logrolling is in large part predicated on the presence of cyclical majorities.[38] Thus, logrolling in the form of a multi-subject bill arguably represents an attempt to mask a cycle in the underlying principle or goals that legislative choice should be governed by. To see this, consider the following example of what one might call a "three-subject logroll."

Example 5 Let x, y, and z denote three separable policy *changes* that might be enacted separately or collectively in any combination. Thus, there are eight possible policy choices, the set of which is denoted by X and equal to

$$X = \{\emptyset, \{x\}, \{y\}, \{z\}, \{x, y\}, \{x, z\}, \{y, z\}, \{x, y, z\}\},$$

where $\emptyset$ represents the choice to not enact any of the three possible policy changes, and each of the other seven policy choices is equal to the enactment of each of the corresponding policy changes. To capture the basic notion of a logroll, presume that the legislature would not choose x, y, or z individually as opposed to doing nothing, $\emptyset$, so that we can begin our description of the principle governing choice in the legislature, denoted by p, as follows:[39]

$\emptyset \; p \; \{x\}$,
$\emptyset \; p \; \{y\}$, and
$\emptyset \; p \; \{z\}$.

Then, to capture the notion that a three-subject logroll is necessary to gain sufficient support to defeat "doing nothing," presume that the legislature would not choose $\{x, y\}$, $\{x, z\}$, or $\{y, z\}$ individually (again, as opposed to doing nothing), so that we can further specify the principle p as follows:

$\emptyset \; p \; \{x, y\}$,
$\emptyset \; p \; \{x, z\}$, and
$\emptyset \; p \; \{y, z\}$.

Finally, to represent the idea that the three-subject logroll, $\{x, y, z\}$, would be chosen over doing nothing but would unravel if the legislature could

---

[38] For example, Tullock (1981), Wittman (1989), Stratmann (1996, 2003), and Parisi (1998).

[39] It is important to note that we are thinking of the principle p as the "principle" that would be constructed through binary revealed choice by the legislature. That is, this is not necessarily the principle that "should" govern choice in the legislature. This is made most clear by the presumption below that the three-subject logroll policy, $\{x, y, z\}$, is ranked by p as superior to the status quo policy of no policy change, $\emptyset$.

consider removing any of its components,[40] we further refine the principle p as follows:

$$\{x\} \; p \; \{x,y\} \; p \; \{x,y,z\}, \quad \{y\} \; p \; \{x,y\},$$
$$\{x\} \; p \; \{x,z\} \; p \; \{x,y,z\}, \quad \{z\} \; p \; \{x,z\},$$
$$\{y\} \; p \; \{y,z\} \; p \; \{x,y,z\}, \quad \{z\} \; p \; \{y,z\}, \quad \text{and}$$
$$\{x,y,z\} \; p \; \emptyset.$$

Now, supposing that X is the set of feasible choices and p is the governing principle, it is clear that the *only* legitimate decision sequence that begins with $\emptyset$ is $(\emptyset, \{x,y,z\})$. However, if multi-subject bills are prohibited, then any stable decision sequence within

$$X' = \{\emptyset, \{x\}, \{y\}, \{z\}\}$$

returns the status quo of no policy change ($\emptyset$) as the final policy.　　　　△

TABLE 9.1. *Example Criteria for a Logroll: Primitives*

Criteria	Policy Change x	Policy Change y	Policy Change z
Criterion A	10	-3	-4
Criterion B	-5	8	-2
Criterion C	-1	-7	11

Example 5 first illustrates that the imposition of a single-subject provision might eliminate some previously legitimizable policy choices by simply ruling them out of order. But as noted earlier, the principle p as constructed in the example represents how choice *would* occur in the legislature rather than how legislative choice necessarily "should" operate. This distinction makes clear an ambiguity inherent in discussion of whether such provisions are good or bad for legislative legitimacy. In essence, such arguments boil down to whether the "logroll" represented by proposal of $\{x,y,z\}$ should be chosen over the status quo of doing nothing, $\emptyset$, when the constituent components are properly related or compared with each other as in the example. That is, *should* a proposal that could not be passed piece by piece nonetheless be enacted if it would be voluntarily passed by the legislature as a combination of all the components?

This question is inherently unanswerable without further specification. Indeed, this fact is itself made clear by a more traditional aggregation argument similar to those discussed in Part I of this book. Continuing with the primitives of Example 5, the principle p can be thought of as coming about from the aggregation of the three criteria, A, B, and C, presented in Table 9.1, where

---

[40] This is motivated by the notion that a multi-subject logroll cannot be credibly implemented through successive votes on each of their constituent components.

TABLE 9.2. *Example Criteria for a Logroll: Induced Evaluations*

(Ordinal) Rank	Criterion A	Criterion B	Criterion C
1	$\{x\}$	$\{y\}$	$\{z\}$
2	$\{x, y\}$	$\{y, z\}$	$\{x, z\}$
3	$\{x, z\}$	$\{x, y\}$	$\{y, z\}$
4	$\{x, y, z\}$	$\{x, y, z\}$	$\{x, y, z\}$
5	$\emptyset$	$\emptyset$	$\emptyset$
6	$\{y\}$	$\{z\}$	$\{x\}$
7	$\{z\}$	$\{x\}$	$\{y\}$
8	$\{y, z\}$	$\{x, z\}$	$\{x, y\}$

the scores are net and relative to not including the policy change in the final policy.[41]

While the point we make here is robust, the scores in Table 9.1 are nonetheless deliberately designed to illustrate a classic aggregation problem. In particular, note that our assumption that the criteria evaluate bundles of policy changes in an additive fashion implies that the criteria rank the policy bundles as in Table 9.2.

In the context of the single-subject provision, Table 9.2 displays the essentials of what is often referred to as the *discursive dilemma* (or *doctrinal paradox*).[42] In a nutshell, the discursive dilemma describes situations in which there is a logical structure between beliefs and conclusions such as "I believe it is going to rain today, so therefore I will wear a raincoat." The dilemma itself occurs when aggregating individuals' beliefs (via majority rule, for example) produces a "collective belief" that logically induces a conclusion different from that produced when individuals' conclusions are aggregated.

To see that Table 9.2 possesses this structure, consider the following logical structure. In considering a choice between $\{x\}$ and $\{x, y, z\}$, one asks the following series of two questions. First, should we remove y from $\{x, y, z\}$, creating $\{x, z\}$? Second, should we remove z from $\{x, z\}$, creating $\{x\}$? If the answer to both questions is "True," then logically, one should approve $\{x\}$ over $\{x, y, z\}$. If the answer to both questions is "False," then the conclusion must be that one should approve $\{x, y, z\}$ over $\{x\}$. Finally, if the answer to one question is true and the answer to the other is false, then the conclusion is indeterminate,

---

[41] That is, we are making the simple assumption that each legislator evaluates bundles of policy changes as equal to the sum of the legislator's evaluation for each included policy change. Thus, for example, any legislator's net gain from enacting $\{x, y\}$ is the sum of the criterion's scores for x and y.

[42] The literature on this topic is large and growing. For example, see Kornhauser and Sager (1986, 1993, 2004), Kornhauser (1992), Chapman (1998, 2002), Pettit (2001), List and Pettit (2002, 2005), and Dietrich and List (2007, 2008). For a review by one of the principal contributors to this literature, see List (2012).

TABLE 9.3. *Logrolling and the Discursive Dilemma*

	Remove y from $\{x, y, z\}$?	Remove z from $\{x, z\}$?	Approve $\{x\}$ over $\{x, y, z\}$?
Legislator A	True	True	True
Legislator B	False	True	False
Legislator C	True	False	False
Beliefs → Conclusion	True	True	True
Majority Conclusion			**FALSE**

as it depends on the strength of the individual's preferences. Now, using the induced ranking of policies by the criteria as reported in Table 9.2 to answer each of the three questions for each of the three criteria, one obtains a classic instance of the dilemma. This is displayed in Table 9.3.

Enhancing Transparency and Accountability

Another justification for single-subject provisions is that they augment the transparency of the legislative process and, concomitantly, bolster the collective ability of the electorate to hold members individually and collectively accountable for their legislative choices.

One version of the argument begins with the recognition that, by requiring that each piece of legislation encompass a single topic (and, for the sake of argument, requiring a recorded vote on each piece of legislation), each legislator seeking reelection must approach his or her constituents with a verifiable record of how he or she has individually sought to "make policy" while in office. While this argument is simple insofar as it presumes that the legislation that will be proposed and voted on in the presence of a single-subject provision is at least as socially efficient as that which would arise in the absence of the provision,[43] the putative impact of single-subject provisions on transparency is nonetheless clear. We refer to this version of the argument as the "retention version."

A second version of this argument focuses on both the legislators and their constituents and concerns the practical realities of understanding the content and potential impacts of proposed and enacted legislation. After all, a bill that encompasses multiple subjects will tend in general to be more complex and require more time to read and comprehend than a bill that encompasses only one of those subjects. As with the retention version of the argument

---

[43] This is only one important caveat to such arguments. An equally important, and even more hopeful, assumption is that indirect democracy institutions are capable of enforcing faithful agency by the elected representatives. This is particularly important in the context of state legislatures, several of which have some form of legislative term limits (15 as of 2012).

discussed earlier, this argument is also simplistic in some ways: there are good reasons to suspect that requiring a separate bill for each topic or subject would result in a much longer corpus of legislation than would be produced if bills encompassing multiple subjects were allowed. Similarly, it is certainly arguable that comprehending legislation is no easier if it is presented as multiple, granular acts than if the same laws were enacted in a manner consisting of fewer, and commensurately broader, acts. Nonetheless, this version of the argument – which we dub the "clarity version" – has a certain plausibility to it.

Their simplicity notwithstanding, both the retention version and clarity version of the transparency argument in favor of the single-subject provision are each closely related to our theory's requirement of internal consistency. Each of the versions of the argument is focused on the ability to relate any given policy choice (e.g., enacted statute) chosen by the legislature to a desired policy outcome or legislative goal. Broadly speaking, each of these arguments is justifying the provision as a means by which one can both more clearly discern the policy choice and compare this choice with the previously prevailing policy overturned by the statute in question.

Single-Subject Provisions and Legitimacy

The link between single-subject provisions and our theory of legitimacy is best seen by considering the legislative history of a bill's consideration as the decision sequence with which the statute is accompanied when evaluated by external actors such as voters or courts. Both the retention version and clarity version of the transparency argument are based on an implicit presumption that the question of what policy "ought to be chosen" is unambiguous (or, perhaps, less ambiguous) within a given subject area than when one is forced to compare policies dealing with multiple subjects. More specifically, it is clear that restricting attention to a single subject makes it more plausible that the various policies can and should be evaluated by a single criteria. Following the logic of Part I and presuming that criteria are themselves well ordered (transitive), single-subject provisions can then obviate some of the aggregation concerns that follow from Arrow's Theorem. Following this line of logic, single-subject provisions help ensure internal consistency of the decision sequence, similar to the role played by the germaneness requirement discussed in the previous section.

More generally, one could relate single-subject provisions to our theory in a spirit similar to that of rational basis review and strict scrutiny as discussed in Chapter 8. Specifically, single-subject provisions arguably require the legislature to have a single principle for the entire statute. This is less restrictive than requiring that there be a single criterion, of course, and the principle need not be transitive. Requiring a single principle in practice means that the statute should itself account for potential conflicts between its various components. Thus, if a statute seeking to further both food safety requirements and fuel efficiency was based on a single principle, the statute would necessarily resolve conflicts between these two goals. To the degree that a single-subject provision induces the legislature to more explicitly tie the various components of a statute to a common unifying legislative end or purpose – even if that end or purpose is broad – the provision fosters the legitimacy of legislative policymaking as conceptualized in this book.

10

Administrative Legitimacy

Measured by the size of their impacts on the everyday life of most citizens, the legislature, executive, and judicial branches garner a disproportionately large share of scholarly attention relative to that received by the "administrative branch," the corpus of government composed of hundreds of agencies, commissions, quasi-governmental authorities, and public corporations. These organs of the state are the center of both interpretation and enforcement of the federal government's policies. Leaving aside issues of whether they must necessarily be such, the practical reality is that all interaction between the government and its citizenry involves administrators, whereas a relatively small proportion of government actions are the direct consequence of any decision made by elected representatives or federal judges. While much of public administration is focused on seemingly mundane tasks, the administrative branch is unique in the frequency with which it interacts *directly* with the citizens.[1] Congruence between government actions and popular will is properly measured relative to administrators' decisions and the explanations offered for these decisions. Viewed from another angle, the congruence between policy outcomes as experienced by the citizens and the policy decisions of the three traditional branches of government depends on the actions and decisions of the administrative branch.

In line with the discussion from Chapter 4 and precisely because administrative, or "bureaucratic," policy decisions are both frequent and potentially important, the provision of reasons is central to the legitimacy of this form of

---

[1] Rohr (1986) engages this point directly as a basis for the legitimacy of the administrative state. His historicist account differs from ours in the sense that he is concerned with establishing that the administrative state is consistent with the Constitution and, more important, the purposes and goals of its framers.

governance.[2] In instrumental terms, administration is largely ineffective without significant deference (i.e., voluntary compliance) by the citizenry and, just as important, the pronouncements of Congress, the president, and the courts are by and large merely exhortative unless actualized through administrative implementation. In theoretical-cum-practical terms, the decisions of these constitutional branches result in legitimate policies only to the degree that they are implemented in a legitimate fashion by the administrative branch. Accordingly, the various arms of the bureaucracy are arguably responsible for the outcomes by which the other branches' decisions will be judged by the governed.

The growth of the federal government since the Civil War has proceeded in large part with the consent of the electorate. However, this consent has been conditional: federal policies that have not been seen as legitimate have been challenged and sometimes successfully so.[3] Of course, preferences and coalitions evolve, so this is in some sense not surprising. Instead, the long-run sustenance, justification of, and deference to the growth of federal power is what requires explanation.[4] Anything approximating a complete history of the growth of administrative authority in the United States, even only within the federal government, is beyond the scope of this book. Rather, we focus our attention on the judicial treatment of administrative policymaking. A central question in this regard is when should the decision of an unelected bureaucrat be accorded the same respect and deference as a statute duly passed by a popularly elected and sovereign legislature?

The explicit authorization of unelected administrators to render important policy decisions has been historically viewed with suspicion and often still is. We argue that the broad use of administrative policymaking is widely accepted as legitimate in modern American politics.[5] Furthermore, we argue that this popular acceptance is a product of the mechanisms through which statutory authority is delegated to, and then used by, administrative agencies. In line with the theory presented in this book, we argue that the legitimacy of administrative policymaking is procedural in nature: the legitimacy of an agency's policy decision depends on the structure of the processes by which the decision is ultimately made. This chapter is intended to illuminate the similarities between the emergent and judicially idealized portrait of properly applied delegated authority and our theoretical framework.

---

[2] Of course, the literature on the legitimacy dilemma facing bureaucratic agencies and administrative policymaking in general is huge. Some particularly relevant contributions include Stewart (1975), Freedman (1978), Frug (1984), Horwitz (1994), and Mashaw (2001).

[3] For example, consider the rolling back of the Federal Trade Commission's consumer protection authority in 1980 (Kovacic, 1988).

[4] Of course, we do not mean to imply that deference has been universal. The occurrence of the growth is, however, widely accepted as empirically accurate.

[5] To be clear, we obviously do not claim that all administrative decisions are viewed as legitimate. Instead, we are simply arguing that the use of an administrative agency to make important policy decisions is not viewed as illegitimate per se.

STRUCTURE OF THE CHAPTER. In the following pages, we discuss the historical evolution of judicial review of administrative actions up through the twentieth century. In addition to bearing some important and illustrative similarities to parts of the discussion of equal protection review in Chapter 8, this discussion illuminates the challenges presented by administrative policymaking. An indispensable component of modern governance, the importance of administrative decisions amplifies normative concerns about how administration is carried out. In particular, the history of judicial review reveals an intimate connection between legitimate administrative policymaking and the provision of explicit reasons or justifications for the decisions rendered. Our historical discussion highlights the judiciary's notice and endorsement of this connection when reviewing administrative policymaking both in the abstract (i.e., whether it is appropriate or permissible to grant administrators discretionary authority to make binding policy decisions) and in the particular (i.e., whether to uphold a specific discretionary decision when judicial redress is sought by an aggrieved party).

Our central focus in this chapter is the evolution of federal courts' jurisprudence toward an acceptance of administrative policymaking as a legitimate form of governance.[6] Central in this evolution was the essential question of whether delegated authority can be legitimately used at all. Accordingly, we first consider the evolution of the federal judiciary's construction, qualification, and application of the nondelegation doctrine. In so doing, we draw several analogies between the doctrine's evolution and the foundations of our theory: namely, the notions of principles and decision sequences are both useful in understanding how the Court has shaped and refined the doctrine over the past two centuries.

Following this, we take a closer look at how procedural and practical aspects of administrative policymaking are considered when courts review specific decisions. When courts review the practical and procedural details of a specific decision, often framed as dealing with matters of due process,[7] they acknowledge that the nondelegation concerns do not apply. Rather, such review is generally concerned with fidelity of both the process and substance of the decision with both the facts of the case and the relevant statutory and constitutional mandates to the agency. The modern structure and application of the principles of this type of review are easily described as administrative law. Our discussion

---

[6] As mentioned earlier, this focus is in line with the focus in Chapter 8 in many ways, but the central phenomena are different in both theoretical and practical terms. In particular, the question of delegation is in a sense purely one of process, whereas equal protection necessarily confronts both process and issues about the equality of outcomes. Relatedly, equal protection issues pertain even to statutes that involve no delegated authority and delegation of legislative authority can be an issue for statutes that raise no equal protection issues.

[7] Of course, due process is arguably a subset of larger concepts such as representation and equal protection. For our purposes, though, the *due process* term is sufficiently broad and usefully specific for the matters at hand.

of modern administrative law principles focuses on the linkages between our notion of legitimacy and the requirements imposed on administrative policy-making processes.

10.1 DELEGATION AND LEGITIMACY

A prominent feature of constitutional thought, the nondelegation doctrine is frequently summarized in two Latin phrases: *delegata potestas non potest delegari*[8] and *delegatus non potest delegare*.[9] The fact that either of these arcane, foreign phrases are cited as the basis for a broad constitutional doctrine is actually somewhat telling.[10] Regardless, the basic idea of the doctrine in the context of the United States federal government is simple: even if the power in question is legitimately exercised by Congress, that same power cannot be legitimately exercised by an agent or agency to whom Congress has seen fit to delegate it.[11]

While the doctrine is remarkably simple, the reasoning behind its application to the United States federal government is murky at best.[12] For example, there is no explicit mention of the doctrine in the U.S. Constitution and, indeed, there was explicit allowance for delegation of legislative powers in the Constitution's predecessor, the Articles of Confederation.[13] In general, arguments that the Constitution implicitly bars delegation of legislative powers rely on the separation of powers inherent in the Constitution's structure.[14] Accordingly, the traditional argument goes, a statute that allows an officer of the executive branch to define what "is or is not against the law" is constitutionally suspect.

The authority to write economic and social regulations is, for all intents and purposes, the power to write law. Thus, the nondelegation doctrine challenges the very foundation of modern public policy. Accordingly, the courts face a conundrum when attempting to adjudicate nondelegation arguments:

---

[8] "Delegated power cannot be delegated."

[9] "A delegate cannot delegate."

[10] This is even more true when one considers for a moment that the main source of the phrases' "authority," each of which just directly restates a simple version of the doctrine, is at least arguably the fact that they are stated in Latin.

[11] Note that the doctrine, as traditionally stated, is a universal maxim that does not reference any specific entity as the residual claimant to the power in question. Thus, it arguably applies equally to Congress, the president, the judiciary, and even administrative agencies themselves (sometimes referred to as subdelegation). However, the doctrine is and has been most frequently invoked with respect to Congressional powers under Article I of the United States Constitution. Accordingly, we will simplify exposition in this chapter by interpreting the doctrine as being so construed.

[12] See Szabo (2006) for an extended discussion of the intellectual origins of the doctrine.

[13] Articles of Confederation, Art. IX. Indeed, the delegation provision encompasses appropriations "for defraying the public expenses."

[14] Article I, Section 1 of the U.S. Constitution states that "All legislative Powers herein granted shall be vested in a Congress of the United States...," and Article II, Section 1 states that the "executive Power shall be vested in a President of the United States of America."

any meaningful enforcement of the doctrine – not to mention a strict interpretation of it – would neuter the policymaking power of the federal government, rendering it incapable of responding to the wishes of the nation's citizens. In light of the Constitution's origins as a response to the Articles of Confederation and a desire for a more responsive and effective national governmental structure, such a conclusion is simply untenable.[15] Or, as the Court described the dilemma in 1935, denying to Congress the power to delegate its powers would create "the anomaly of a legislative power which in many circumstances calling for its exertion would be but a futility."[16]

Nonetheless, the nondelegation doctrine is still (at least in theory) an accepted constitutional principle,[17] and, particularly with respect to early examples of Congressional delegations, nondelegation challenges were occasionally successful.[18] Since the New Deal, however, such challenges have been universally unsuccessful at least in per se terms. On this point, the Court has acknowledged that "the cases establish that by virtue of congressional delegation, legislative power can be exercised by . . . agencies."[19]

Reconciling Nondelegation with Legitimate Delegation

While still accepted as a doctrine of constitutional law, the nondelegation doctrine as currently applied by federal courts seems to be, at worst, a minor impediment to the delegation of the authority to write and implement policies that have essentially the same power as law. Our theory provides a framework within which one can understand this historical development. Specifically, courts have established an extended rationale through successive decisions about the proper situations and means by which Congress may delegate its lawmaking authority and this rationale then confers presumptive legitimacy on future similar delegations. Or, to put it another way, delegated policymaking authority is not illegitimate merely because it is exercised by a delegate

---

[15] Additionally, it is easily seen that attempts to enforce a strict interpretation of the doctrine may very well simply void the judiciary's de facto power of judicial review, which itself relies almost entirely on the deference of both the elected branches and the general citizenry.

[16] *Panama Refining Co. v. Ryan*, 293 U.S. 388, 421 (1935).

[17] For example, *Whitman v. American Trucking Associations, Inc.*, 531 U.S. 457 (2001); *Loving v. United States*, 517 U.S. 748 (1996); and *Mistretta v. United States*, 488 U.S. 361 (1989).

[18] The most famous and clear examples are the three New Deal cases: *Panama Refining v. Ryan*, 293 U.S. 388 (1935); *A.L.A. Schechter Poultry Corp. v. United States*, 295 U.S. 495 (1935); and *Carter v. Carter Coal*, 298 U.S. 238 (1936). More recently, however, justices have occasionally suggested that the doctrine should be applied more stringently in interpreting statutes (e.g., *Whitman v. American Trucking Associations, Inc.*, 531 U.S. 457, 487 [2001], Thomas, J., concurring in judgment. Furthermore, it is arguably more accurate to think of the nondelegation doctrine as operating primarily through the canons of statutory construction, whereby it can be instrumental in limiting Congressional authority while rarely, if ever, being described as the basis for outright invalidation of a duly enacted statute (e.g., Sunstein, 2000 and Driesen, 2002).

[19] *INS v. Chadha*, 462 U.S. 919, 985 (1983). More generally, see Schwartz (1991), pp. 41–61, and Alexander and Prakash (2007).

because such a presumption leads to policy outcomes that are inferior in terms of the goal that elected representatives should be (or at least be able to be) responsive to the wishes of the governed.

We now discuss the judicial evolution of the nondelegation doctrine in an episodic fashion. Frequently nodded to by the Court, explicit discussion and interpretation of the doctrine has been infrequent. This happenstance is both convenient for our purposes and easily explicable in light of the conundrum discussed earlier. First, it seems reasonable to presume that most, if not all, justices are loathe to overturn such a longstanding and broadly accepted constitutional doctrine. However, meaningful judicial enforcement of the doctrine is at best counterproductive and more than likely practically impossible. Accordingly, it is rare that the Court needs to address a case that forces the justices to make explicit a logic that can reconcile the doctrine's conflicting normative and practical implications.

The episodic structure of our presentation is motivated not only by the historical record. The Court's treatment of the doctrine has proceeded in a "lumpy" fashion: after all, the central question at hand is not whether delegation is permissible but rather *what kind of* delegations are permissible. The Court has accordingly and gradually accumulated what amounts to a qualitative "checklist" to apply when reviewing whether a specific statutory grant of discretionary authority violates the doctrine. Each of the Court's occasional additions to this checklist is mirrored by one or more aspects of our theory of legitimacy. Accordingly, structuring our discussion in a linear, chronological fashion has the additional virtue of clarifying the linkages between the modern interpretation of the doctrine and our theory.[20]

The Evolution of the Nondelegation Doctrine

While the nondelegation doctrine was first explicitly dealt with by the Supreme Court in 1813,[21] the Court's first detailed treatment of the doctrine was

---

[20] Note that one could consider the even stronger case that the historical evolution of the Court's understanding of the doctrine can itself be usefully interpreted or understood within our framework. We do not pursue this for a number of reasons. In addition to the traditional constraints on time, space, and scope, we think a dynamic analysis of the Court's decision making in the context of judicial review is worthy of and, indeed, requires its own special treatment. In particular, while we believe that judicial review serves as one legitimating device for statutes, executive actions, and administrative decisions, it requires an additional, somewhat daunting logical step to conclude that judicial review has been legitimated by the processes through which the Court conducts this review. Put another way, while we believe that legitimate judicial review ought to be consistent with our theory, it is certainly plausible that judicial review is most in need of legitimating when, say, the judiciary and Congress disagree over the principle(s) that are themselves permissible. As discussed in Section 7.1, we sidestep this important issue for a variety of reasons.

[21] *The Aurora v. United States*, 11 U.S. 382 (1813) (upholding a statute that was to have effect only upon the determination of certain facts by the president).

offered in 1825, in *Wayman v. Southard*.[22] Acknowledging the doctrine and the dilemma it poses, Chief Justice Marshall wrote that

> It will not be contended that Congress can delegate to the courts, or to any other tribunals, powers which are strictly and exclusively legislative. But Congress may certainly delegate to others, powers which the legislature may rightfully exercise itself.... The line has not been exactly drawn which separates those important subjects, which must be entirely regulated by the legislature itself, from those of less interest, in which a general provision may be made, and power given to those who are to act under such general provisions to fill up the details.[23]

The phrase "filling up the details" has become widely used as a description of clearly permissible delegation within the nondelegation doctrine. The language indicates the considerations that courts typically encounter when confronted by a nondelegation challenge. In essence, Marshall's central point is that the delegation of authority to make unimportant decisions is not ripe for judicial meddling, but the legislature must be checked from handing over its authority to make decisions about "important subjects." Of course, this refinement of the doctrine hardly accomplishes much in practical terms, as it offers no guidance about what types of decisions should be properly construed as representing mere "details."

Nonetheless, Marshall's statement clearly establishes a baseline presumption that administrative decisions and legislative prescriptions may be fruitfully distinguished from one another in a manner that need not run afoul of the nondelegation doctrine. Explicit in this construction is an acknowledgement that various delegations of authority may be nontrivially compared in terms of degree. This opens the possibility that the nondelegation doctrine might be reframed as *delegatus non potest delegare nimias potestas*.[24] In this way, Marshall's opinion set the stage for the Court to engage the question of how much power is too much – how does one distinguish between "important subjects" and "details"? The first consideration in this regard was whether Congress could delegate the authority to make factual determinations that would then trigger important policy decisions, as statutorily prescribed by Congress.

Adjudicating Facts: Policy from "Findings"

For the next 120 years, the Court consistently demonstrated a willingness to defer to what might be termed "conditional delegations" of discretionary authority in a variety of policy areas. Conditional delegations were generally of the form "if *you determine* that *A* has happened, do *B*. If *you determine*

---

[22] 23 U.S. 1 (1825).
[23] 23 U.S. 1, 42–43 (1825).
[24] "A delegate cannot delegate too much power."

otherwise, do *C*." Upon determination of what has happened (i.e., upon a *finding* regarding "the facts"), such delegations grant the administrator little to no discretion about what to do. The notion of an administrator's findings – statements regarding the statutorily relevant prevailing conditions – is a central concept in delegation jurisprudence. In theory, statutorily requiring that administrators make certain findings before setting a given policy represents a clear way to "tie their hands." However, practical realities and other considerations often preclude the implementation of an objective and verifiable mechanism for determining the facts. Accordingly, this determination is properly understood as the delegated discretionary authority. The simple reality of gray areas and the need for interpretation implies that almost any such statute comes naturally imbued with a positive degree of residual discretionary authority.

Exactly such a statute was before the Supreme Court in the late nineteenth century case of *Field v. Clark*.[25] Congress required the president to levy a statutorily fixed punitive tariff on various goods if the president should determine the exporting nation to be imposing "reciprocally unequal and unreasonable" duties on American products. The case focused on several issues, including whether this provision constituted an unconstitutional delegation of power. The Court ruled it did not. Specifically, the Court argued that the president's policy discretion was permissible because the statute was sufficiently specific in its description of the punitive tariffs to be levied and the conditions under which they should be levied:

> Nothing involving the expediency or the just operation of such legislation was left to the determination of the President. The words "he may deem," in the third section, of course, implied that the president would examine the commercial regulations of other countries producing and exporting sugar, molasses, coffee, tea, and hides and form a judgment as to whether they were reciprocally equal and reasonable, or the contrary, in their effect upon American products. But when he ascertained the fact that duties and exactions reciprocally unequal and unreasonable were imposed ... it became his duty to issue a proclamation declaring the suspension, ... which Congress had determined should occur. He had no discretion in the premises except in respect to the duration of the suspension so ordered. But that related only to the enforcement of the policy established by Congress.[26]

Quoting Judge Ranney of the Supreme Court of Ohio, the Court argued that the "true distinction ... is between the delegation of power to make the law, which necessarily involves a discretion as to what it shall be, and conferring authority or discretion as to its execution, to be exercised under and in pursuance of the law. The first cannot be done; to the latter no valid objection can be made."[27] Practical concerns necessitate a flexible understanding of the delegation doctrine, particularly insofar as the determination of facts. Whereas *Wayman*

---

[25] 143 U.S. 649 (1892).
[26] *Field v. Clark*, 143 U.S. 649, 693 (1892).
[27] *Field v. Clark*, 143 U.S. 649, 693–694 (1892), quoting 1 Ohio St. 88.

170 Administrative Legitimacy

v. Southard established a distinction between discretionary authority in terms of whether it deals with an "important subject," *Field v. Clark* established a pragmatic principle of conditional delegation: straightforward determination of facts – regardless of the policy impacts of the ultimate determination – does not constitute an impermissible delegation of authority. Specifically, the Court wrote,

> The legislature cannot delegate its power to make a law, but it can make a law to delegate a power to determine some fact or state of things upon which the law makes or intends to make its own action depend. To deny this would be to stop the wheels of government. There are many things upon which wise and useful legislation must depend which cannot be known to the lawmaking power, and must therefore be a subject of inquiry and determination outside of the halls of legislation.[28]

Adjudicating Facts and Providing Reasons

The reasoning used in *Field v. Clark* establishes a concrete foundation for the connection between a decision and the rationale or explanation leading to it. In a very succinct fashion, the Court established that a statute that directly tied specific policy choices to a factual determination that could be clearly stated, if not necessarily verified, provided a practical test for delegated authority. More specifically, this framework clarified that the Court would be more likely to rule a delegation of Congressional authority constitutional as long as that statute required that use of the authority be accompanied by an explicit statement of *why* the authority was being used in that way.

This is a significant theoretical step beyond the distinctions based on the importance of the subject matter established in *Wayman v. Southard*. *Field v. Clark* subsumes *Wayman v. Southard* in the sense that one can naturally infer that to the degree that Congress has agreed that, conditional upon a given finding of fact *A*, the policy should be *B*, the actual carrying out of factual determination and subsequent policy implementation are properly construed as mere "details" of governance – details that may be properly delegated by Congress to administrators. The real theoretical advance in *Field v. Clark* is in its implicit provision of a test for judicial review of administrative decisions. While the opinion does not touch on the question of whether a court should review the basis of the president's determination beyond that such a determination was indeed made, the deference to the statute is clearly tied to the idea that the administrative decisions are justified by the determination. Blatantly inconsistent determinations would presumably be subject to review. This is a consideration that became more important in subsequent decisions.[29]

---

[28] *Field v. Clark*, 143 U.S. 649, 693–694 (1892).
[29] For example, consider the issues at play in the *Chenery* decisions, discussed in more detail later (p. 178).

Nonetheless, the discretionary authority as justified and upheld by the Court in *Field v. Clark* is very minimal in scope. In particular, the argument for deference relies on a strong (although not absolute) claim that the administrator is making only factual, as opposed to policy, determinations. This narrow understanding of permissible delegation would soon be broadened in *J. W. Hampton, Jr. & Co. v. United States*,[30] to which we now turn.

Hampton and the "Intelligible Principle" Standard

Matters related to Congressional delegations of power significantly increased in frequency following the creation of the Interstate Commerce Commission (ICC) in 1887. The number of federal agencies doubled during the first 30 years of the twentieth century,[31] and the new agencies were increasingly endowed with regulatory powers applicable to the actions of private individuals and firms.[32] The Court's position with respect to nondelegation challenges was abundantly clear to contemporary observers both on and off the Court: enforcing the nondelegation doctrine would represent a sweeping challenge to Congressional authority. What ultimately emerged from these cases is referred to as the "intelligible principle" standard. In upholding a statute that allowed the president to set custom duties under certain conditions, the Court ruled that this delegation was permissible because the statute described how this power should be utilized with sufficient precision:

> If Congress shall lay down by legislative act an intelligible principle to which the person or body authorized . . . is directed to conform, such legislative action is not a forbidden delegation of legislative power.[33]

The intelligible principle standard, described and reaffirmed in *Mistretta v. United States*,[34] is admittedly ironic. At least as far as a nondelegation challenge is concerned, it seems very likely that the central issue being litigated about the use of discretionary authority might be described as revolving around how Congress intended the discretion to be used. Accordingly, the intelligible principle standard essentially amounts to a (low) threshold test for the disposition of nondelegation claims. In practical terms, nearly all statutes satisfy the standard, meaning that successful challenges to discretionary authority must typically find another basis.

The Emerging Judicial Requirement of Consistency

The Court's opinions in *Wayman v. Southard*, *Field v. Clark*, and *Hampton* each refer to the internal structure of the agency's policymaking. Most

[30] 276 U.S. 394 (1928).
[31] Shepherd (1996), p. 1561.
[32] For example, see Keller (1990).
[33] *J.W. Hampton, Jr. & Co. v. United States*, 276 U.S. 394, 409 (1928).
[34] 488 U.S. 361 (1989).

clear is the notion that permissible delegation be constrained by a governing rule: upholding delegated authority required that the Court be able to argue that the statute in question be relatively clear in its expression of Congressional intent: this intent could be conditional, and the intent to leave simple matters of administration to those who would implement the statute was considered permissible. However, the Court was clear in repeatedly stating that matters of importance must not be left to the determination of administrators. The structure of this type of review is similar to rational basis review, as discussed in Chapter 8. In particular, the early evolution of the nondelegation doctrine centered on the notion that not only should there be a principle guiding the use of discretionary authority but also that the principle was clear in the sense of imposing real constraints on the actions consistent with that principle.

Second, it is important to note that the nondelegation decisions up through *Hampton* essentially ignored issues related to our stability condition, Axiom 2. That is, the Court did not consider the implications of what agencies did *not* choose when exercising delegated authority in determining whether the discretionary actions were valid. This is consonant with the analysis in Chapter 9 – a pure understanding of delegated power is that, excepting constraints imposed by the delegating authority (i.e., Congress), such power passes otherwise *en toto* to the delegate. Assuming that the delegation is considered permissible, per se, the choices of the agent possessing this power are accordingly subject to review only in two ways: first, were the actions within the bounds of the power dictated by Congress and, second, would the decisions be permissible if chosen and enacted directly by Congress? As discussed in Chapter 9, stability is secondary in importance to internal consistency when evaluating the choices made directly by a presumptive legitimate authority. In line with this, courts have historically tended to sidestep the "what if" style of reasoning implicit in questioning whether or why some alternatives were excluded from consideration in the decision process.

Panama, Schechter, and Standardless Delegation

While the federal administrative apparatus had already greatly expanded in terms of both size and activity in the years following the creation of the Interstate Commerce Commission (ICC), this expansion quickly accelerated following the inauguration of President Franklin Roosevelt in 1933. As noted at the American Bar Association's 1933 annual meeting,

> last spring witnessed a more formidable legislative output of administrative machinery than has ever before found its way into the statutes at large in time of peace ... It is significant that practically every important measure relied primarily on administrative machinery to accomplish its purpose.[35]

---

[35] 1933 *American Bar Association Annual Report*, p. 197–98 (statement of committee Chairman Louis G. Caldwell), quoted in Shepherd (1996), p. 1570.

For various reasons – ranging from sincere constitutional concerns to strategic political calculations – the initial wave of New Deal legislation spawned a similar surge in the concern among politicians, jurists, and scholars alike about the delegation of Congressional powers. Particularly in light of the broad popular demand for government action in the depths of the Great Depression, these concerns about delegation were increasingly focused on the practical questions of how delegated power might be constrained and overseen by Congress, the courts, or both.

Somewhat ironically, while the broad popular demand for government action simultaneously provided a clear justification for turning a blind eye to the scholarly and normative appeal of the nondelegation doctrine, it also led to the doctrine's most visible appearances in Supreme Court decision making. In particular, the Court specifically and forcefully invoked the doctrine to first overturn part of the National Industrial Recovery Act (NIRA) in *Panama Refining Co. v. Ryan*[36] and then in quick order essentially invalidate the entire Act in *A.L.A. Schechter Poultry Corp. v. United States*.[37]

One of the cornerstone pieces of New Deal legislation, the NIRA delegated sweeping and essentially unconstrained economic regulatory authority to the president.[38] The majority opinion in each case makes clear that the NIRA represented an especially extreme delegation of authority that failed even the low "intelligible principle" threshold established seven years earlier in *Hampton*. Even a generous reading of the NIRA suggests that there is no principle constraining the president's discretionary regulatory authority. From a due process standpoint, the NIRA fails to establish any grounds under which a plaintiff might successfully seek judicial relief from regulations (somewhat hopefully referred to as "codes of fair competition") promulgated under the Act. In *Panama*, the Court explicitly mentions the importance of both standards and, as a corollary, the need for a statute to require the administrator (in this case the president) to make a "finding," in line with the earlier discussion of *Field v. Clark*:

> the question ... is obviously one of legislative policy. Accordingly, we look to the statute to see whether the Congress has declared a policy with respect to that subject; whether the Congress has set up a standard for the President's action; whether the Congress has required any finding by the president in the exercise of the authority to enact the prohibition.[39]

In *Schechter*, the Court reiterated and expanded its concerns about the fact that NIRA's grant of discretionary authority to the president was nearly

[36] 293 U.S. 388 (1935)
[37] 295 U.S. 495 (1935).
[38] More than a simple violation of the intelligible principle standard articulated in *Hampton*, the NIRA explicitly empowered the president to subdelegate this power to nongovernmental actors (specifically, industry trade associations). However, it should also be noted that the NIRA, passed in 1933, was broadly unpopular by 1935 (e.g., Best, 1991).
[39] *Panama Refining Co. v. Ryan*, 293 U.S. 388, 415 (1935).

unconditional. For example, in line with its arguments in *Panama* (which was more limited than *Schechter* in terms of the scopes of their respective reviews of the NIRA), the Court found the act to be almost totally bereft of meaningful "findings" requirements. The president was required to find that a group who proposed a code of fair competition "impose no inequitable restrictions on admission to membership," and be "truly representative."[40] In addition, the president was required to find that the code would neither promote "monopolies or monopolistic practices" nor discriminate against small businesses. Beyond that, however, the president was required only to find that the code "will tend to effectuate the policy of this title." As the Court described this requirement:

> While this is called a finding, it is really but a statement of an opinion as to the general effect upon the promotion of trade or industry of a scheme of laws. These are the only findings which Congress has made essential in order to put into operation a legislative code having the aims described in the "Declaration of Policy."[41]

In many ways, *Panama* and *Schechter* may be thought of as representing the Court's "last stand" against the emerging federal administrative state. From our perspective, these cases are particularly important in that they mark the beginning of an important period of discussion of federal administrative procedure. For example, in *Schechter*, the Court compared the administrative structure and procedures established in the NIRA with those of its closest cousin, the Federal Trade Commission Act.[42] The Court notes that the Federal Trade Commission (FTC), a quasi-judicial body, was created with provisions made for "formal complaint, for notice and hearing, for appropriate findings of fact supported by adequate evidence, and for judicial review to give assurance that the action of the Commission is taken within its statutory authority," and then points out that the NIRA "dispenses with" the FTC's "administrative procedure and with any administrative procedure of an analogous character."[43]

While one can argue whether the Court was correct to overturn the NIRA, the opinion in *Schechter* establishes formal administrative procedures as a clear threshold condition for constitutionally permissible delegation. Thus, while the mid-1930s can be thought of as the final chapter of the nondelegation doctrine, this period represents the starting point for the emergence of the modern administrative state. In addition to the attention paid by the Court to administrative procedure, scholars and politicians were also becoming increasingly focused on matters of administrative law.[44]

---

[40] In addition, the president was granted the authority to impose his own codes, so this requirement was at most ancillary to the true scope of the president's discretionary authority.

[41] *A.L.A. Schechter Poultry Corp. v. United States*, 295 U.S. 495, 538 (1935).

[42] 38 Stat. 717.

[43] *A.L.A. Schechter Poultry Corp. v. United States*, 295 U.S. 495, 533 (1935).

[44] More generally, the structure and substance of procedures used by the administrative agencies were also a the attention of both scholars and jurists (Shepherd, 1996, pp. 1561–1593).

10.2 AGENCY EXPLANATIONS AND AVOIDING NONDELEGATION

Following *Schechter*, various justices began to explicitly link the constitutionality of delegated authority to the degree to which the agency in question justifies or explains its decision making when exercising its discretion. This jurisprudence made more explicit the legitimating effect of accompanying a decision with both a statutory goal (or, in our terms, principle) and with a rationale (i.e., decision sequence) rationalizing it. Again, we do not purport to offer a theory of judicial intent. Rather, the judicial understanding of what constitutes permissible discretionary authority that emerges in the decades following World War II produces a practical construction for judicial review of administrative policymaking that is both consonant with our theory and provides an escape route for any jurist seeking to avoid directly addressing nondelegation issues. In this section, we briefly discuss four cases from the 1940s in which the Court used the provision of an explanation by the agency of how its decision comported with the goals of the authorizing statute as a means by which to reconcile grants of broad discretionary authority with the "intelligible principle" interpretation of the nondelegation doctrine as set forth in *Hampton*.[45]

Yakus v. United States

Soon after *Schechter*, the Supreme Court was faced again with a case involving a broad delegation of Congressional authority. In *Yakus v. United States*,[46] the Court considered the Emergency Price Control Act of 1942 (EPCA),[47] which gave the price administrator, the head of the Office of Price Administration, the authority to establish maximum prices that he deemed "generally fair and equitable and will effectuate the purposes" described in the statute. The statute established the prices prevailing in 1941 as the default maximum price level but granted the administrator discretion to choose different levels if he made a "statement of the considerations" for his choice.

Considering whether the sweeping authority delegated by Congress in the EPCA was impermissibly broad, the Court upheld the statute. Central to upholding the relatively unconstrained authority implied by the allowance for the administrator to deviate from the 1941 price level was fulfillment of the

---

[45] While a complete treatment of the historical evolution of administrative law and procedure during this time period is beyond the scope of our current discussion, it is nonetheless interesting to note that there was significant interest in these topics across all three branches. For example, President Roosevelt ordered several studies of administrative procedure during this time and vetoed the Walter-Logan bill. In addition to passing the Walter-Logan bill, Congress ultimately passed the Administrative Procedure Act of 1946 (APA), which established the foundations of modern bureaucratic policymaking in the United States and, in particular, described what has come to be known as "notice and comment" rulemaking.

[46] 321 U.S. 414 (1944).

[47] 56 Stat. 23.

provision requiring a statement of the administrator's considerations when so deviating:

> Findings that the Regulation was necessary, that the prices which it fixed were fair and equitable, and that it otherwise conformed to the standards prescribed by the Act, appear in the Statement of Considerations.[48]

The Court described the statement of considerations as playing a key role in sustaining the statute more generally. In particular, the provision of such an explanation enables "Congress, the courts and the public to ascertain whether the Administrator, in fixing the designated prices, has conformed to" the standards of the act.[49] Furthermore, and directly confronting *Schechter*, the Court distinguished the EPCA from the NIRA in terms of the precision of the standards included in each of the statutes, stating that the EPCA differed from the NIRA in that the latter

> ... proclaimed in the broadest terms its purpose "to rehabilitate industry and to conserve natural resources." It prescribed no method of attaining that end save by the establishment of codes of fair competition, the nature of whose permissible provisions was left undefined. It provided no standards to which those codes were to conform.... The Constitution, as a continuously operative charter of government, does not demand the impossible or the impracticable. It does not require that Congress find for itself every fact upon which it desires to base legislative action, or that it make for itself detailed determinations which it has declared to be prerequisite to the application of the legislative policy to particular facts and circumstances impossible for Congress itself properly to investigate. The essentials of the legislative function are the determination of the legislative policy and its formulation and promulgation as a defined and binding rule of conduct...[50]

For our purposes, it is unimportant whether, as Justice Roberts contended in his dissent, *Yakus* effectively overturned *Schechter*. Rather, the decision is notable for the degree to which the Court references the explicit provision of a reason as an essential component of constitutionally permissible discretionary authority.

Phelps Dodge Corp. v. NLRB

The core of Yakus – that administrative explanation of discretionary action bolsters the legitimacy of that action – is the foundation for ensuing concerns about the requisite structure and permissible bases of such explanations. Several cases during this time period illustrate the importance the Court assigned

[48] 321 U.S. 414, 422 (1944).
[49] 321 U.S. 414, 426 (1944).
[50] 321 U.S. 414, 424 (1944).

to the provision of explicit reasons. In *Phelps Dodge Corp. v. NLRB*,[51] the Court simultaneously upheld delegated authority and clarified the importance of accompanying the delegated authority's decisions with an explicit explanation:

> The administrative process will best be vindicated by clarity in its exercise. Since Congress has defined the authority of the Board and the procedure by which it must be asserted and has charged the federal courts with the duty of reviewing the Board's orders, it will avoid needless litigation and make for effective and expeditious enforcement of the Board's order to require the Board to disclose the basis of its order. We do not intend to enter the province that belongs to the Board, nor do we do so. All we ask of the Board is to give clear indication that it has exercised the discretion with which Congress has empowered it. This is to affirm most emphatically the authority of the Board.[52]

Of particular interest in the quoted passage is the link drawn between the "clarity" of the exercise of administrative process and the desirability of the administrator disclosing "the basis of its order." This construction is analogous to the pairing of a principle (as set forth in the statute) with the decision sequence leading to the NLRB's decision.

City of Yonkers v. United States

In *City of Yonkers v. United States*,[53] the Court overturned an ICC order authorizing the dismantling of a rail line because the commission failed to include in the findings upon which the order was based an explicit statement that it had the jurisdiction to do so. Of importance for our purposes is the Court's explicit avoidance of the issue of whether such a finding would be merited: the infirmity was plainly procedural in the Court's eyes. The ICC's position, explicitly rejected by the Court, was that the ICC's finding of jurisdiction could be easily inferred from the issuance of the order. The Court disagreed, in essence requiring something akin to the connectedness requirement of our internal consistency axiom, Axiom 1. Demonstrating the converse of the logic in *City of Yonkers* in a case decided in the same year, the Court adopted an explicitly (although not absolutely) deferential stance toward agency interpretation in *Skidmore v. Swift & Co.*[54] In particular, a unanimous Court adopted the position that agency "interpretations . . . while not controlling on the courts by reason of their authority, do constitute a body of experience and informed judgment to which courts and litigants may properly resort for guidance."[55] With this, the Court made clear that it would defer to reasonable attempts,

---

[51] 313 U.S. 177 (1941).
[52] 313 U.S. 177, 197 (1941), citations omitted.
[53] 320 U.S. 685 (1944).
[54] 323 U.S. 134 (1944).
[55] 323 U.S. 134, 140 (1944).

including explicit statement of agency interpretation, to satisfy the connected-ness requirement.

SEC v. Chenery Corp.

Finally, in an important case argued and decided during and following the debates leading to the passage of the Administrative Procedure Act,[56] the Court clarified

> ...a simple but fundamental rule of administrative law...a reviewing court, in dealing with a determination or judgment which an administrative agency alone is authorized to make, must judge the propriety of such action solely by the grounds invoked by the agency. If those grounds are inadequate or improper, the court is powerless to affirm the administrative action by substituting what it considers to be a more adequate or proper basis. To do so would propel the court into the domain which Congress has set aside exclusively for the admin-istrative agency.... If the administrative action is to be tested by the basis upon which it purports to rest, that basis must be set forth with such clarity as to be understandable. It will not do for a court to be compelled to guess at the theory underlying the agency's action; nor can a court be expected to chisel that which must be precise from what the agency has left vague and indecisive.[57]

The *Chenery* decisions established that courts should not defer to ex post or ad hoc reasoning when considering agency actions: an agency must defend its decisions with the explanation offered at the time of the decision.[58] Further-more, the rationality threshold for administrative agencies' explanations of their decisions requires more than a "conceivable basis" for the action taken: agencies receive strictly less deferential treatment when choosing policies than accorded to statutes under rational basis review.[59]

Reason Giving, Delegation, and Legitimacy

The four cases discussed in this chapter (*Phelps Dodge*, *Yakus*, *City of Yonkers*, and *Chenery*) individually and collectively establish a strong analogy between

---

[56] *SEC v. Chenery Corp.*, 332 U.S. 194 (1947). This famous case actually began, in a sense, much earlier. The Court had heard it first and offered much of the same reasoning in *SEC v. Chenery Corp.*, 318 U. S. 80 (1943), stating; "The grounds upon which an administrative order must be judged are those upon which the record discloses that its action was based" (318 U. S. 87).

[57] *SEC v. Chenery Corp.*, 332 U.S. 194, 196–197 (1947).

[58] See, for example, *Burlington Truck Lines, Inc. v. United States*, 371 U.S. 156, 168–169 (1962) (requiring that the agency "articulate [a] rational connection between the facts found and the choice made"); *Citizens to Preserve Overton Park v. Volpe*, 401 U.S. 402 (1971); *FPC v. Texaco, Inc.*, 417 U.S. 380 (1974); and *Motor Vehicle Manufacturers Association v. State Farm Mutual Automobile Insurance Co.*, 463 U. S. 29 (1983).

[59] *Motor Vehicle Manufacturers Association v. State Farm Mutual Automobile Insurance Co.*, 463 U. S. 29, 43, . 9 (1983). See Chapter 8 for a discussion of the relationship between rational basis review and our theory.

judicial requirements on administrative decision making and the foundation of our theory of legitimacy. Specifically, as the Court began to construct the foundations of modern judicial deference to administrative policymaking,[60] the provision of an explicit explanation or justification of administrative policies promulgated under delegated statutory authority quickly emerged as an enduring and prominent threshold requirement. The link between our theory and the judicial interpretation of agency reasoning as required for legitimate decision making is succinctly captured in the following statement:

> Not only must an agency's decreed result be within the scope of its lawful authority, but the process by which it reaches that result must be logical and rational. Courts enforce this principle with regularity when they set aside agency regulations which, though well within the agencies' scope of authority, are not supported by the reasons that the agencies adduce.[61]

If we take the ideal view of statutes as providing a principle that agencies must then use to construct and justify their policy choices, the current judicial construction of permissible administrative decision making is consonant with our theory's construction of legitimate policymaking. This conclusion is, however, properly accompanied by an important caveat. In particular, the notion of a principle (much less an intelligible one) is inherently contested. Few real-world statutes contain an unambiguously described principle. Furthermore, even to the degree one can discern an uncontroversial construction of such a principle, the question remains of whether the principle is sufficiently precise to obviate concerns about excessive delegation of authority to unelected bureaucrats. In the next section, we discuss judicial treatment of this issue. In particular, the question of how much and what kinds of details can be properly left for the agency to "fill in" has recently attracted renewed judicial attention.

10.3 CHOOSING PRINCIPLES: LIMITS ON AGENCY DISCRETION

As the reach and extent of the federal administrative state grew from the New Deal through the 1960s, worries among scholars, practitioners, and jurists about this development became correspondingly acute. At this point, nondelegation jurisprudence began to focus more attention on the details of how delegated authority was used – that is, on questions of procedures – when considering whether delegated authority was impermissibly broad. In particular, while the cases discussed in Section 10.2 remained good law in the

---

[60] It is important to note here that our focus is on outcomes and not intentions. While it is certainly arguable that the Justices on the post-*Schechter* Court recognized a need or had a desire to rationalize a reconcillation of the delegation doctrine and judicial deference without explicitly jettisoning the logic of *Panama* and *Schechter*, our point here is agnostic about motivations: the main point from our perspective is the degree to which these decisions did in fact presage future judicial understandings of administrative process.

[61] *Allentown Mack Sales & Service, Inc. v. NLRB*, 522 U.S. 359, 374 (1998).

sense that agency reasoning for discretionary decisions was understood to be necessary for legitimate administrative policymaking, the vague goals set by Congress for agencies in many statutes forced courts to eventually confront the question of what constituted a permissible reason. Every agency using quasi-legislative authority should be able to justify its decisions in terms of "what Congress wanted" each time the agency renders a policy decision. In other words, maintaining fidelity to the intelligible principle approach to reconciling the practical requirements of modern governance with the nondelegation doctrine requires that agency decision making be consistent with the principle enacted by Congress.[62]

Of course, statutes are rarely transparent descriptions of unambiguous principles, and the Court recognizes this insofar as its "jurisprudence has been driven by a practical understanding that, in our increasingly complex society, replete with ever-changing and more technical problems, Congress simply cannot do its job absent an ability to delegate power under broad general directives."[63] Reconciling this reality with the intelligible principle directive enunciated in *Hampton* became the focus of nondelegation jurisprudence beginning in the 1970s. One version of the central question is when is a "general directive" *too* broad? A more pointed version of the question is how much residual discretion can Congress delegate to an agency in making its broad directive specific?

This question is partially addressed by the notion of "self-limiting" administrative behavior, a principle frequently linked to the district court opinion in *Amalgamated Meat Cutters v. Connally*.[64] Upholding the constitutionality of the Economic Stabilization Act of 1970,[65] District Court Judge Leventhal took special note of "the requirement that any action taken by the Executive under the law...must be in accordance with further standards as developed by the Executive. This requirement, inherent in the Rule of Law and implicit in the Act, means that however broad the discretion of the Executive at the outset, the standards once developed limit the latitude of subsequent executive action."[66] Judge Leventhal argued that the notion that subsequent administrative policies are necessarily bound in a dynamic fashion to or by earlier decisions is based on "an on-going requirement of intelligible administrative policy that is corollary to and implementing of the legislature's ultimate standard and objective."[67] At the heart of the principle is the notion that it might be more useful to consider the bounds of delegated power as it is understood and applied by the delegate.

---

[62] Specifically, the Court stated in *Hampton* that to be constitutionally permissible, delegation required "an intelligible principle to which the person or body authorized to [act] is directed to conform" (276 U. S. 394, 409 [1928]).

[63] *Mistretta v. United States*, 488 U. S. 361, 372 (1989).

[64] 337 F. Supp. 737 (D.D.C. 1971).

[65] 84 Stat. 799.

[66] 337 F. Supp. 737, 759 (D.D.C. 1971).

[67] 337 F. Supp. 737, 759 (D.D.C. 1971).

Leventhal's opinion operationalizes this understanding in terms of the standards developed by the agency itself, which is shorthand for the procedures and criteria laid out by the agency for the governance of its future actions.

The notion of self-limiting administrative behavior represents a compromise of sorts between judicial restraint and the nondelegation doctrine. Implicitly at the foundation of the notion of self-limitation is a statute that, as written, does not contain a sufficient specific "directive" to which the agency's decision making must conform. As we mention again later, in this way, the notion of self-limitation is a canon of avoidance, offering a route by which a court might rationalize avoiding the constitutional issue of nondelegation itself. In so doing, it grounds the understanding of due process more firmly in the administrative process itself. Leaving aside theoretical concerns with this approach for the moment, a virtue of self-limitation is that it arguably focuses the reviewing court's attention on whether the agency has provided explicit standards by which its decisions should be judged.

Questioning Self-Limitation: *Benzene*

The necessity of such standards for legitimate administrative policymaking was the focal point of the *Benzene* case.[68] In this case, the Court overturned (in a plurality opinion) a regulation governing airborne concentrations of benzene. A central issue was the agency's stated basis for the mandated maximum exposure limit. This basis subsumed matters both factual and statutory in nature. In particular, the Secretary of Labor had asserted that no safe exposure level could be determined, so that the statute then required him to choose the lowest technologically feasible exposure limit that would not impair the viability of the regulated industries.

The Court overturned the agency's regulation because the agency's findings did not establish to the Court's satisfaction that the exposure limit was indeed "reasonably necessary or appropriate to provide safe or healthful employment," as required by the Occupational Safety and Health Act of 1970.[69] The Court did not object to the level, *per se*. Rather, to a plurality of the Court, the fatal objection dealt with the agency's reasoning that accompanied the standard.

Similarly interesting from the standpoint of our theory is Justice Rehnquist's concurring opinion in this case, which argued that the statute's language of "to the extent feasible"[70] constituted an impermissible delegation of authority. Specifically, Justice Rehnquist argued that the statute represented an abdication of Congressional responsibility as set forth by the intelligible principle doctrine: allowing the agency to interpret such vague language of terms,

---

[68] *Industrial Union Department, AFL-CIO v. American Petroleum Institute*, 448 U.S. 607 (1980).
[69] 84 Stat 1590, §3(8).
[70] 84 Stat 1590, §6(b)(5).

even in a "reasonable" fashion, would grant the Department of Labor too much discretion over policy choices properly made by Congress:

> In the case of a hazardous substance for which a "safe" level is either unknown or impractical, the language of §6(b)(5) gives the Secretary absolutely no indication where on the continuum of relative safety he should draw his line. Especially in light of the importance of the interests at stake, I have no doubt that the provision at issue, standing alone, would violate the doctrine against uncanalized delegations of legislative power.[71]

While Justice Rehnquist's argument might be framed as dicta regarding the abstract foundations of the nondelegation principle, he focused in addition on practical matters of both legislative history – from which one might argue that a governing principle could be found if not explicitly stated in the text – and judicial review of permissible delegation:

> Nor ... do the provisions at issue or their legislative history provide the Secretary with any guidance that might lead him to his somewhat tentative conclusion that he must eliminate exposure to benzene as far as technologically and economically possible. Finally, I would suggest that the standard of "feasibility" renders meaningful judicial review impossible.[72]

While reasonable people may disagree regarding Justice Rehnquist's conclusion that the "extent feasible" language of §6(b)(5) of the Clean Air Act violated the nondelegation doctrine, his reasoning about the operation and application of the nondelegation doctrine is squarely consonant with our theoretical framework (the notion that legitimate agency decisions require both an explicit governing principle and a line of reasoning justifying the obtained outcome in the sense of internal consistency). The challenge he posed for the Court in his opinion was essentially whether Congress had described any principle to which the Occupational Safety and Health Administration was to be held to account when setting maximum exposure levels for benzene.

In plain language, Justice Rehnquist argued that if the Court took the language and legislative history of the act at face value, the Court would be able to invalidate a choice of exposure level by the agency only if the agency itself failed to pick a principle with respect to which the agency's self-provided reasoning was itself incompatible. In other words, no principles were inconsistent with the statute's language. Judicial review of this sort would be essentially equivalent to rational basis review, as discussed in Chapter 8. Subjecting an agency to such minimal review is equivalent to imbuing agency decision making with the same presumptive authority as that possessed by a popularly elected and sovereign legislature. Accordingly, adopting such a stance would arguably represent an absolute internment of the nondelegation principle itself.

---

[71] 448 U.S. 675 (1980) (Rehnquist, J., concurring in judgment).
[72] 448 U.S. 686 (1980) (Rehnquist, J., concurring in judgment).

Limiting Self-Limitation: *American Trucking*

Justice Rehnquist's concurrence in *Benzene* notwithstanding, the principle of self-limiting administrative behavior was generally considered good law for three decades. In practical terms, one might describe this as a canon of avoidance that exhorts judges to examine how the statute is interpreted for evidence that the application of the discretionary authority is resonant with a single intelligible principle that might be permissibly handed to the agency by Congress, even if it in fact was not.[73] Such an approach was explicitly addressed by Justice Scalia in *Whitman v. American Trucking Associations, Inc.*[74] Justice Scalia's treatment of the principle of self-limiting administrative behavior was not favorable, noting that the Court had

> never suggested that an agency can cure an unlawful delegation of legislative power by adopting in its discretion a limiting construction of the statute.... The idea that an agency can cure an unconstitutionally standardless delegation of power by declining to exercise some of that power seems to us internally contradictory. The very choice of which portion of the power to exercise – that is to say, the prescription of the standard that Congress had omitted – would itself be an exercise of the forbidden legislative authority. Whether the statute delegates legislative power is a question for the courts, and an agency's voluntary self denial has no bearing upon the answer.[75]

What makes this brief and critical treatment of the notion of self-limiting administrative behavior particularly notable is that it is included in an opinion explicitly upholding the statute and noting that the Court has "almost never felt qualified to second-guess Congress regarding the permissible degree of policy judgment that can be left to those executing or applying the law."[76]

While on its face it appears to be an attempt to constrain and reorient judicial review of administrative behavior, Justice Scalia's rejection of the principle of self-limiting administrative behavior is in reality an affirmation of the practical value of the "intelligible principle" construction and application of the nondelegation doctrine. In this way, Justice Scalia's critique is arguably reinforcing the analogy between judicial review of administrative policymaking and our theoretical framework. To put this another way, Justice Scalia's argument

---

[73] For example, see Manning (2000).
[74] 531 U.S. 457 (2001).
[75] 531 U.S. 472–473 (2001). Justice Scalia's intent is beyond our scope here, of course, but it is worthwhile to note that his hand may have been forced by the District of Columbia Circuit's decision in this case. In particular, Justice Scalia notes that the lower court thought "that the EPA [Environmental Protection Agency] could perhaps avoid the unconstitutional delegation by adopting a restrictive construction of" the relevant provision of the act and, therefore, "instead of declaring the section unconstitutional," the court remanded the regulation to the EPA and ordered the EPA "to develop a construction of the act that satisfies [the nondelegation doctrine]." (175 F.3d 1027, 1033 (1999))
[76] 531 U.S. 474–475 (2001), quoting *Mistretta v. United States*, 488 U. S. 361, 416 (1989) (Scalia, J., dissenting).

reinforces the need for an *exogenous* principle as the yardstick by which an agency's rationale for its decision making can be judged. To demand less is in reality to demand nothing at all.

Deference and Subservience: *Chevron*

In summarizing the modern judicial understanding of both the limits of permissible delegation and the nature of legitimate administrative decision making, one would be remiss to omit the Court's famously strong stand in favor of administrative interpretation of Congressional intent in what is known as the *Chevron* decision.[77] This case and its particulars have been discussed at length elsewhere.[78] For our purposes, the relevant particulars of the case are as follows.

In *Chevron*, the Court considered an Environmental Protection Agency (EPA) rule regarding the operational definition of a "stationary source" of air pollution under the Clean Air Act. In the rule under consideration, the EPA formally incorporated what is known as the "bubble concept." Described simply, the bubble concept called for a broad definition of a stationary source of air pollution. Instead of requiring that any modification to a single emission point (e.g., an individual smokestack) result in an improvement of air quality from that individual emission point, the bubble concept called for the EPA to evaluate the effect of the modification on the impact of the plant as a whole on air quality instead. Evaluation of "the effect" of a modification serves as a primary basis in determining whether a permit is required to modify a stationary source of air pollution. Under the Carter Administration, the EPA had begun the process of adopting a partial implementation of the bubble concept; following President Reagan's inauguration in 1981, the EPA revised its position to a universal adoption of the bubble concept.

Two related questions lay at the heart of *Chevron*. First, was the adoption of the bubble concept consistent with the EPA's statutory mandate and, second, was the EPA's revision of its earlier position a permissible exercise of discretionary authority under the statute? The first of these questions was fairly easily dealt with under long-established reasoning. Because the operationalization of the definition of stationary source was explicitly left to the EPA by Congress, one would need to assert that such operationalization represented excessively broad authority, a conclusion that does not concord well with a long history of judicial deference to much broader grants of authority. The second, however, is more interesting, particularly in light of Rehnquist's concurrence in *Benzene*. In *Chevron*, the Court upheld an agency's discretion to revise its policy precisely

---

[77] *Chevron U.S.A. v. Natural Res. Def. Council*, 467 U.S. 837 (1984). Although the decision is clearly sweeping in appearance, it has been argued that the apparent strength of the decision exceeds the extent of its subsequent effects (Merrill, 1992). Nonetheless, *Chevron* is still controlling after 30 years.

[78] See, among many others, Cohen and Spitzer (1994).

because Congress had provided no specific guidance regarding these details. To the degree that this definition had important policy implications (which it did), accepting this reasoning and Rehnquist's arguments in *Benzene* would seem to necessitate a finding that the statute represented an unconstitutionally broad delegation of authority.

The Court adopted a position almost perfectly opposed to this conclusion. A key distinction between *Chevron* and *Benzene* is the proximity between the EPA's decision and the principle represented by the statute under which the EPA was exercising discretion. In *Benzene*, the EPA's policy explicitly represented a decision about how to aggregate two criteria – economic feasibility and public health – that are sufficiently important to require that a trade-off between the two should be determined by the elected representatives of Congress in order to be legitimate. On the other hand, the EPA's decision considered by the Court in *Chevron* was about implementation of a fixed principle. While the EPA was interpreting statutory language in both cases, the two cases differ greatly in terms of the type of language being interpreted. Indeed, in *Chevron*, some decision about the bubble concept was necessary in order to pursue the goals of the Clean Air Act: without a practical definition of a stationary source, the EPA would be incapable of regulating so as to promote ambient air quality. The Court's opinion not only clarifies the importance of residual interpretative authority in this case but also offers both a strong defense of leaving such authority in the hands of agencies and an architecture for judicial deference that is reminiscent of the linkage between our internal consistency axiom and rational basis review, as discussed in Chapter 8.

Interpreting Statutes and Implementing Aggregation

In line with our portrait of policymaking as inherently concerned with the aggregation of potentially conflicting goals, the Court noted that the relevant statute[79] did not directly address the proper operational definition of a stationary source but did "plainly disclose that ... Congress sought to accommodate the conflict between the economic interest in permitting capital improvements to continue and the environmental interest in improving air quality."[80] In asking the agency to assist Congress in accommodating this conflict, the Court reasoned, Congress must have intended to grant to the EPA sufficient discretion required to implement such an accommodation. In this case, the Court reasoned, the EPA's interpretation represented

> a reasonable accommodation of manifestly competing interests, and is entitled to deference: the regulatory scheme is technical and complex, the agency considered the matter in a detailed and reasoned fashion, and the decision involves reconciling conflicting policies. Congress intended to accommodate both interests, but did not

[79] The Clean Air Act Amendments of 1977 (91 Stat. 685).
[80] 467 U.S. 837, 851 (1984).

do so itself on the level of specificity presented by these cases. Perhaps that body consciously desired the Administrator to strike the balance at this level, thinking that those with great expertise and charged with responsibility for administering the provision would be in a better position to do so; perhaps it simply did not consider the question at this level; and perhaps Congress was unable to forge a coalition on either side of the question, and those on each side decided to take their chances with the scheme devised by the agency. For judicial purposes, it matters not which of these things occurred.[81]

Furthermore, the Court took this opportunity to not only uphold both the statute and the EPA's interpretation but also state a quite general principle of judicial deference to agency interpretations of statutory language. In an exemplary statement from the majority opinion (authored by Justice Stevens), the Court stated

> If Congress has explicitly left a gap for the agency to fill, there is an express delegation of authority to the agency to elucidate a specific provision of the statute by regulation. Such legislative regulations are given controlling weight unless they are arbitrary, capricious, or manifestly contrary to the statute. Sometimes the legislative delegation to an agency on a particular question is implicit rather than explicit. In such a case, a court may not substitute its own construction of a statutory provision for *a reasonable interpretation* made by the administrator of an agency.

> We have long recognized that considerable weight should be accorded to an executive department's construction of a statutory scheme it is entrusted to administer, and the principle of deference to administrative interpretations has been consistently followed by this Court whenever decision as to the meaning or reach of a statute has involved reconciling conflicting policies, and a full understanding of the force of the statutory policy in the given situation has depended upon more than ordinary knowledge respecting the matters subjected to agency regulations.[82]

The majority opinion in *Chevron* is notable for a number of reasons. First, the decision clearly suggested that the Court viewed its own discretion with respect to interpretation more narrowly than that properly accorded to administrative agencies (insofar as such authority was originally granted by Congress). In a nutshell, the Court describes its own task when reviewing agency decision making as ensuring consistency between the Congressionally mandated principle, the agency's ultimate decision, and the agency's reasoning behind the decision. That is, the Court circumscribes judicial discretion precisely because of the legitimating effect of "express" Congressional delegation. The resulting and concomitant discretion, duly exercised in accordance with the statute's intelligible principle, is properly retained by the agency and not the courts.

---

[81] 467 U.S. 837, 865 (1984), notes omitted.
[82] *Chevron U.S.A. v. Natural Res. Def. Council*, 467 U.S. 837, 843–844 (1984), emphasis added, notes omitted.

Second, the passage highlights only one explicit constraint on administrative discretion with respect to an agency's proper construction of its statutory scheme: "reason." A reasonable interpretation is to receive judicial deference. Of course, this command is weighty in several respects. To the degree that *Chevron* does not represent a repudiation of the nondelegation doctrine, Justice Stevens is implicitly presupposing that the statute in question contains a principle intelligible enough for a reasonable interpretation to represent a fettering of agency whimsy. Additionally, the notion of reasonableness implies that the agency's interpretation was arguably foreseeable when the statute was enacted. Finally, however, the notion allows that the resulting position leaves meaningful residual discretion that might be legitimately exercised by the agency. In the end, after all, the Court did not uphold the rule as *the* reasonable construction of the statute. As it has historically done, the Court not only asserted that the agency's decision represented a meaningful political choice; it also justified judicial deference to the decision by virtue of this fact:

> While agencies are not directly accountable to the people, the Chief Executive is, and it is entirely appropriate for this political branch of the Government to make such policy choices – resolving the competing interests which Congress itself either inadvertently did not resolve, or intentionally left to be resolved by the agency charged with the administration of the statute in light of everyday realities.[83]

This stance is important in terms of linking judicial review of administrative decision making with legitimacy. Justice Stevens explicitly references responsiveness as a justification for partially setting aside traditional nondelegation concerns when reviewing the actions of *unelected* administrators. In so doing, this opinion, as with the entire line of nondelegation precedents discussed earlier, highlights a classical aggregation problem confronted by unelected courts.

Third, and specifically in the context of the principle of self-limitation and Scalia's subsequent criticism of this notion, *Chevron* clarifies that the legitimacy of an administrative decision is properly judged relative to the statute(s) the agency is seeking to implement. Presuming that the delegated authority is constitutional – essentially, presuming that the statute(s) in question provide an intelligible principle to govern the agency – the question properly entertained by a reviewing court is whether the agency's decision and accompanying explanation are consistent with the statutorily enshrined principle. While agency reasoning must be consistent with itself to the degree that it is based on a reasonable interpretation of the statute, the agency's choice at any given time is distinctly inferior to that of Congress in the sense that the agency's prior reasoning should not be held as foreclosing the provision of alternate reasoning to justify some other, future decision. In other words, while "*Chevron* deference" is temporally most proximate to agency decision making, its strongest implication is arguably its call for judicial deference to the presumption that

---

[83] 467 U.S. 837, 865–866 (1984).

a permissible statutory ambiguity represents an express and lasting grant of residual discretionary authority to the agency in question. Again, the argument that an ambiguous statute can still contain an intelligible principle is at least implicitly based on the presumption that Congress was aware, and accepting, of the fact that the agency would be able to choose from various, potentially conflicting policy decisions for which similarly reasonable explanations consistent with the statute might be provided.

11

Conclusion

Our thesis in this book is simple: choice often requires making trade-offs between various goals. In other words, individuals and groups have various ends and purposes they seek to achieve. For example, from its inception, the founding of the modern federal government of the United States was predicated on the need and desire to aggregate multiple goals:

> We the people of the United States, in order to form a more perfect union, establish justice, insure domestic tranquility, provide for the common defense, promote the general welfare, and secure the blessings of liberty to ourselves and our posterity, do ordain and establish this Constitution for the United States of America.[1]

Of course, it is rare that (say) establishing justice and securing the blessings of liberty will be simultaneously and maximally furthered by the same course of action. Unless such a fortuity occurs, governance – choosing and implementing public policies – requires making trade-offs between these goals. Regardless of whether these trade-offs are explicit or implicit, we have argued that aggregating goals is a ubiquitous characteristic of governance.

Aggregation is the heart of social choice theory. In Part I of the book, we have presented and discussed several seminal results from social choice theory. These results have been misinterpreted by scholars in various ways. The most important misconception about these results, in our minds, is an implicit presumption that the central results of social choice – Arrow's Theorem and the Gibbard-Satterthwaite Theorem – apply only to methods of aggregating individual *preferences*. We have emphasized that the impossibility theorems apply to *any* aggregation method. That is, regardless of the nature of the criteria one is attempting to combine to form a coherent ranking of a set of

---

[1] Preamble, United States Constitution.

possible choices, one must make strong assumptions about the nature of the criteria to ensure that any nontrivial aggregation of those criteria will always yield an unambiguously "best" alternative.

Our interpretation of these results is at odds with those offered by earlier scholars in a second and related way. Once one extends the scope of application of social choice theory to all aggregation problems, the impossibility theorems' seemingly nihilistic implications for democracy immediately recede. These results do not speak to preference aggregation in any special way: their implications are as true and relevant for autocratic, oligarchic, and dictatorial governments as they are for democracies. In other words, while the impossibility theorems are highly relevant to the classic questions of representation, they do not require that the aggregated inputs be preferences or ballots. Accordingly, the theorems do not tell us that legitimate democratic governance is impossible; they simply tell us that pure aggregation alone may not be enough to identify a uniquely most legitimate policy choice.

By highlighting the fact that aggregation of criteria cannot be guaranteed to produce a unique decision, the impossibility theorems themselves provide the foundation of what we believe to be the most important defense of democratic institutions. When simply appealing to democratic aggregation is insufficient to identify a best choice, democratic institutions and procedures beyond elections are required to make choices. We believe this a defense of democratic legitimacy precisely because, in an important way, the vast majority of situations in which "politics" and "policy" interact in modern democracies occur *after* aggregation (e.g., an election) has occurred. The indirect representation achieved to varying degrees through elections is then further translated into actual policy choices only through a combination of administrative, executive, judicial, and legislative actions. All of these actions have an inherent "legitimacy deficit" to the degree that they are each, at best, indirectly representative of the expressed wishes of the governed. After all, most actors who render and implement real-world policies are unelected and, furthermore, often explicitly insulated from immediate direction or retribution by the electorate by provisions such as lifetime tenure or civil service protections.

11.1 LEGITIMACY AND THE INADEQUACY OF STRUCTURE

Scholars have argued from various angles that the possibility of democratic legitimacy is at least partially inoculated against the challenges they perceive to be presented by the impossibility results. In particular, Mackie and others have argued, democratic choice can be unambiguously representative of a well-defined popular will (and, hence, unambiguously legitimate) because individuals have shared interests and common viewpoints that structure their preferences relative to each other. Such structure, they argue, obviates the presumption that democratic aggregation need be able to deal with every hypothetical collection of individual tastes and preferences.

We have argued that this position is untenable for a variety of reasons. First, governance is about more than simple elections. To the degree that aggregation is a general phenomenon encompassing more than mere preferences or ballots, the argument that preferences are structured does not suffice to render the social choice results mere mathematical curiosities. We have argued that aggregation of criteria other than preferences is an important feature of political decision making. Our primary example of this, chosen because of its direct tie to the question of representation, is the drawing of legislative districts. The federal judiciary has been, and continues to be, heavily involved in discerning and defining the proper ways to draw districts. This jurisprudence is clearly recognizable as an aggregation problem – namely, a question of how to aggregate objective criteria such as population sizes, racial composition, contiguity, compactness, and divisions of existing political communities. To the degree that districts affect political choices, the political relevance of the impossibility theorems accordingly reemerges.

Along the same lines, the simple reality of administration and jurisprudence is that decisions about matters as disparate as which drugs to approve, what pollution technologies to require, and which citizens are owed various benefits and services by the state are similarly resolved only through aggregation of various factors and criteria. To make such decisions in any other way is inconsistent with the rule of law: in essence, the authority to regulate drugs, require deployment of costly pollution technologies, and award or withhold government benefits is properly held by the legislature, so that unelected administrators must in a sense "follow a formula" of some form if their decisions are to be imbued with the concomitant authority emanating from the legislature's legitimacy. Again, the impossibility theorems actually augment the importance and potential legitimacy of democratic decision making.

A second objection to this attempt to reconcile the impossibility theorem with the possibility of democratic legitimacy is that it assumes away the challenge of – and arguably the need for – democratic institutions and practices beyond direct plebiscites. After all, if individual preferences are the proper basis for legitimate democratic choice *and* these preferences can be unerringly gauged through straightforward voting, why should government officials have discretion at all? To what end, beyond simple economic efficiency arguments, do we maintain and defer to elected legislatures and executives? This question might appear silly. But it is an important challenge for claims that the impossibility theorems are practically irrelevant to democracy. In particular, to claim that the preferences of the governed provide a sufficiently structured foundation for the legitimacy of democratic governance forces a follow-up question of whether real-world democratic governments can actually claim legitimacy for their choices on this basis. One must ask whether, for any given policy choice, the choice of an indirectly representative set of institutions is sufficiently closely tied to the choice that would have been made by the governed – a choice that is presumed to be unambiguously discernible from the wishes of the governed – to claim something akin to true democratic legitimacy. It is worth considering how one might answer such a question.

To determine whether one believes that simple efficiency arguments – that use of indirect representation and unelected administrators with meaningful discretion is less costly than direct governance through plebiscite – are sufficient to justify inserting and supporting a potentially contaminating indirect representation link in the policymaking chain, one must acknowledge the possibility, and gauge the severity, of the slippage between the wishes of the governed and the decisions likely to be made by elected representatives. Upon assessing this, then, a democratic theorist must then ascertain the proper trade-off between the costly but pure and faithful representation offered by direct governance and the less costly but concomitantly imperfect representation provided through indirect institutions of elected agents imbued with policy discretion.

It is important to pause for a moment at this point. Several giant leaps of faith have been required to reach this juncture, each of which lightened the theoretical load – presume that the preferences of the governed admit a "popular will" that selects an unambiguous "best" policy and suppose that one can elicit this choice through some mechanism – and yet we arrive at the penultimate stage with two hands still full. In one hand, we hold both our theoretical measurement of the popular will and the decision that a given indirect form of democratic choice would return. In the second hand, we have some measure of the costliness of choosing policy directly – or, in other words, the efficiency of delegating political decision making to a set of governing agents. To progress beyond this and render an ultimate judgment of whether the representation imperfections imposed by indirect governance are justified by the efficiency gains they yield, *we return to an aggregation problem*. Specifically, how should one trade off faithful representation against the costliness of direct governance?

Another way of viewing this point is that the impossibility theorems speak to the question of how to design political institutions. In addition to being directly relevant when we design institutions intended to aggregate information and criteria other than preferences, the claim that preferences are structured does not on its own suggest the proper institution for aggregating preferences. For example, should one use plurality rule or majority rule? How should we decide which alternatives or candidates are eligible? Should legislatures be elected from single member districts or through proportional representation? Should multimember races be determined by Borda count, approval voting, or the single transferable vote? Who should get to vote? Should everyone have the same weight in determining every decision? How do we trade off individual rights versus collective welfare? In any of these cases, it is *empirically* implausible that there is always, or even frequently, a clearly "best" institutional design from the standpoint of the "will of the people." In other words, the classic instantiation of the impossibility theorems is the fact that different democratic political institutions produce different choices from the same set of underlying preferences. Institutions affect political decisions, and they are accordingly properly an object of democratic choice themselves.

As discussed in Chapter 2, this point has not gone unnoticed, of course.[2] Furthermore, Arrow's impossibility theorem has understandably attracted the most attention on this point. However, it is important to note that the Gibbard-Satterthwaite Theorem is more directly on point. In particular, the claims by Mackie, Dryzek, and List and others that individual preferences have some latent and common structure that yields an unambiguous choice are themselves insufficient to yield a proper mechanism by which to elicit this choice. While individuals differ in their motivations, mendacity, and sophistication, the heart of the Gibbard-Satterthwaite Theorem's conclusion – that there is no democratic means that ensures no group of individuals will find it in their interests (however construed) to misrepresent their true preferences in pursuit of a more preferred outcome – holds *even when individual preferences are single-peaked*.[3] This conclusion directly implies that attempting to democratically select a democratic aggregation rule or choice function will necessarily be susceptible to manipulation, which implies that no democratic way to "choose how to choose" can assure one of faithfully representing the true preferences of the governed. In a nutshell, even if the claim that individuals preferences are structured so as to admit a popular will is true, the impossibility theorems remain relevant, only in a different, more subtle, but no less fundamental manner.

11.2 LEGITIMACY AND MAKING SENSE OF AGGREGATION

The impossibility theorems not only suggest the need for further refinement – a need that we argue is implicitly countenanced in the details of several long-standing real-world political institutions – they also clearly indicate the reason for this need. Aggregation is problematic in the sense of failing to yield an unambiguously best choice precisely when the criteria being aggregated – the inputs to the aggregation problem – are inherently in conflict with each other in the sense of being cyclic. Loosely speaking, aggregation must result in a transitive ranking of alternatives in order to yield an unambiguous choice in all situations. To claim that a chosen policy was consistent with an aggregation of a set of underlying criteria implies that, for every other feasible choice, there is some way *consistent with the aggregation method* to explain why the final choice was chosen instead of that alternative.

We have provided one theory of how such an explanation can be rendered. Our representation of legitimate choice is as a decision accompanied by a justification for its choice in terms of the other alternatives that could have

---

[2] Particularly on point and highly influential is the elegant response offered by Riker (1980) to Shepsle (1979).

[3] This point is proved in Penn, Patty, and Gailmard (2011).

been chosen and the principle that guided the choice. When the principle that justifies the choice is itself transitive – so that it yields an unambiguously best choice or set of choices – the principle and final choice are legitimate if and only if that final choice is "best." In such settings, our theory does little beyond demanding that a choice be accompanied by the principle that guided its selection.

From an empirical standpoint, many principles that are used to guide, explain, and legitimate collective choices are themselves the product of aggregation. For example, both legislation and judicial precedent frequently describe what "ought" to be done in terms of trade-offs between – that is, aggregation of – different criteria. Accordingly, the social choice arguments discussed in Part I imply that our theory of legitimacy would be incomplete from both a theoretical and an empirical standpoint if we presumed that the principle was transitive.

Incorporating this point and taking it seriously required us to formulate our notion of legitimacy in a two-step fashion. Specifically, our theory of legitimacy requires that the decision sequence accompanying a final choice as its justification satisfy two axioms with respect to the underlying principle. These axioms, *internal consistency* and *stability*, represent two complementary components of being justified as the final choice. Internal consistency describes the property of the decision sequence itself being logical, and the stability axiom captures the requirement that the combination of the decision sequence and the underlying principle explain why alternatives not on the decision sequence were not chosen.

Internal consistency requires that the decision sequence offered as a justification for the choice be logical in two ways. First, the decision sequence must be connected through the principle: each step in the sequence must be consistent with the underlying principle. This requirement is intended to be as demanding as possible in terms of requiring that any justification be intimately tied to the underlying principle. Second, a key aspect of legitimacy is an explanation for why the later steps in the explanation in some sense "follow from" the earlier ones. Thus, a logical justification should not contain any cycles.

Stability is best understood by thinking of every alternative that is superior to the final choice under the principle as an "objection" to the choice. In this terminology, any internally consistent decision sequence contains no objection to the final choice, as it would otherwise necessarily either contain a cycle or not be connected, as described earlier. Thus, a decision sequence is stable if for every objection to the final choice, there is an objection to that objection, or a "counterobjection" for that objection, *contained in* the decision sequence. The combination of a principle and a decision sequence that is stable can be thought of as a defense of a final choice or an explanation of why the alternatives not included on the decision sequence were excluded.

Internal consistency and stability are complementary characteristics of legitimacy in the sense that their joint satisfaction is very demanding. They are logically independent of one another and trivially satisfied by maximally different decision sequences: the singular announcement of any policy on its own is tautologically internally consistent, and any decision sequence that contains every possible alternative is similarly obviously stable. Conversely, when the principle is cyclic – as the arguments in Part I imply it may very well be if the principle is the result of aggregation of multiple criteria – no policy on its own is stable, and no decision sequence that contains every alternative is internally consistent.

Thus, again referring to the general theoretical and empirical possibility of cyclic evaluations following from the aggregation of multiple criteria, our central results are that not only can internal consistency and stability be simultaneously satisfied for *any* principle, but these axioms are as much as one can demand from a legitimating decision sequence without imposing restrictions on the structure of admissible principles. Such restrictions are undesirable insofar as they are equivalent to the arguments by Mackie, Dryzek, and List and others regarding individual preferences and, accordingly, simultaneously limit the scope of democratic choice and fly in the face of observed heterogeneity of principles applied in real-world decision settings.

In addition to proving that our notion of legitimacy is always satisfied by some decision sequence, we also characterize these decision sequences. From a practical standpoint, the notion is discriminating: for most principles, there are some policies for which there is no legitimating decision sequence. In particular, the policies that can be legitimated under a principle are uncovered (undominated) with respect to that principle. From a normative or welfare standpoint, the set of uncovered alternatives under a given principle is very attractive. For example, if one uses individual preferences as the criteria and form the principle through majority rule, every element in the uncovered set is Pareto efficient: when comparing any legitimate policy with to another policy, there is at least one individual who strictly prefers to retain the legitimate policy.

Our theory of legitimacy is a response to claims that the impossibility theorems render democratic choice meaningless (or, perhaps, less meaningful) because of the possibility that various democratic institutions will return different alternatives in any given situation (i.e., for a given collection individuals or set of criteria). Our theory demonstrates not only that one might still refine the set of outcomes following aggregation but, more importantly, that such a refinement can be accomplished by requiring that each of the refined choices be accompanied by a justification that is logical and, as far as possible, analogous to the maximal element of an interpretation of the underlying principle as a well-defined and transitive "popular will."

In this way, the theory illuminates the importance of procedures in democratic choice: when the aggregation of multiple criteria is insufficient to produce an unambiguous best choice, more must be done. According to our theory, democratic institutions – particularly those that accompany their pronouncements with more or less transparent renditions of the reasoning for the choice – are useful precisely when and because they trace out a series of logical steps within the potentially messy governing principle that links the ultimate choice with that principle. More broadly, we think the theory captures a key aspect of deliberative institutions: the provision of reasons in the process leading up to and following promulgation of a final choice.

Of course, our theory of legitimacy does not – and is not intended to – capture every possible basis for democratic legitimacy.[4] There are many psychological foundations and orientations of democratic legitimacy, with the idea of electoral accountability arguably representing the primary alternative. We are perfectly content with the reality that our notion of legitimacy is accordingly somewhat narrow. More generally, we accept that our definition is inherently contestable. As we have discussed, we have set aside any consideration of what types of principles should be considered proper as a basis for legitimation within our framework. Similarly, we have generally ignored the more refined question of whether one might compare multiple principles as bases of legitimacy. Such questions are indeed interesting, and we personally believe such comparisons can be and are carried out when legitimacy is evaluated in the real world. We ignore them here because our goal was to show that a meaningful and discriminating notion of legitimacy can be satisfied for any principle. Given that our framework is abstract, this is the proper goal for a theory such as ours: further refinement of the notion would require more structure or context.

The reality that our notion of legitimacy is contestable is, we believe, a testament to the fundamental starting point of our project. Politics is about making sense of both the problems we confront and the decisions we reach in confronting them. While many real-world, day-to-day political choices are obvious and taken for granted, these are the decisions that "aggregation alone" provides sufficient guidance to render a legitimate choice. It is exactly when we see protracted debate that the underlying decision involves, in Berlin's words, the need to choose, to sacrifice some ultimate values to others. To us, "democracy" describes the class of pluralistic and classically liberal approaches to eliciting, aggregating, and ultimately making sense of such values when choosing policy.

---

[4] Of course, the general concept of legitimacy is even broader than democratic legitimacy. For obvious reasons, we simply note and set this issue aside.

Bibliography

Alexander, Lawrence and Saikrishna Prakash. 2007. "Delegation Really Running Riot." *Virginia Law Review* 93:1035–1079.

Altman, Micah. 1998. Districting Principles and Democratic Representation. PhD thesis, California Institute of Technology.

Amadae, Sonja M. 2003. *Rationalizing Capitalist Democracy: The Cold War Origins of Rational Choice Liberalism*. Chicago: University of Chicago Press.

Arrow, Kenneth J. 1951. *Social Choice and Individual Values*. New York, NY: John Wiley and Sons.

Arrow, Kenneth J. 1963. *Social Choice and Individual Values*. 2nd ed. New York, NY: John Wiley and Sons.

Austen-Smith, David and Jeffrey S. Banks. 1999. *Positive Political Theory I: Collective Preference*. Ann Arbor, MI: University of Michigan Press.

Banks, Jeffrey S. 1985. "Sophisticated Voting Outcomes and Agenda Control." *Social Choice and Welfare* 1(4):295–306.

Banks, Jeffrey S. and Georges A. Bordes. 1988. "Voting Games, Indifference, and Consistent Sequential Choice Rules." *Social Choice and Welfare* 5(1):31–44.

Barry, Brian and Russell Hardin. 1982. *Rational Man and Irrational Society?: An Introduction and Sourcebook*. Beverly Hills, CA: Sage Publications.

Baumgartner, Frank R., Bryan D. Jones, and Michael C. MacLeod. 2000. "The Evolution of Legislative Jurisdictions." *Journal of Politics* 62(2):321–349.

Beetham, David. 1991. *The Legitimation of Power*. New York, NY: Palgrave.

Bennett, Robert W. 1979. "'Mere' Rationality in Constitutional Law: Judicial Review and Democratic Theory." *California Law Review* 67(5):1049–1103.

Best, Gary D. 1991. *Pride, Prejudice, and Politics: Roosevelt Versus Recovery, 1933–1938*. New York, NY: Praeger Publishers.

Bianco, William T. and Itai Sened. 2005. "Uncovering Evidence of Conditional Party Government: Reassessing Majority Party Influence in Congress and State Legislatures." *American Political Science Review* 99(3):361–371.

Bianco, William T., Ivan Jeliazkov, and Itai Sened. 2004. "The Uncovered Set and the Limits of Legislative Action." *Political Analysis* 12:256–276.

Bianco, William T., Michael S. Lynch, Gary J. Miller, and Itai Sened. 2006. "'A Theory Waiting to Be Discovered and Used': A Reanalysis of Canonical Experiments on Majority-Rule Decision Making." *Journal of Politics* 68(4):838–851.

Bickel, Alexander Mordecai. 1986. *The Least Dangerous Branch: The Supreme Court at the Bar of Politics*. New Haven, CT: Yale University Press.

Black, Duncan. 1958. *The Theory of Committees and Elections*. Cambridge, UK: Cambridge University Press.

Blau, Julian H. 1971. "Arrow's Theorem with Weak Independence." *Economica* 38(152):413–420.

Block, Cheryl D. 1998. "Truth and Probability—Ironies in the Evolution of Social Choice Theory." *Washington University Law Review* 76(3):975–1037.

Bordes, Georges. 1983. "On the Possibility of Reasonable Consistent Majoritarian Choice: Some Positive Results." *Journal of Economic Theory* 31:122–132.

Brilmayer, Lea. 1980. "Interest Analysis and the Myth of Legislative Intent." *Michigan Law Review* 78(3):392–431.

Brown, William Holmes and Charles W. Johnson. 2003. *House Practice: A Guide to the Rules, Precedents, and Procedures of the House*. Washington, DC: U.S. Government Printing Office.

Cass, Ronald A., Colin S. Diver, and Jack M. Beermann. 2002. *Administrative Law: Cases and Materials*. New York, NY: Aspen Law & Business.

Chambers, Christopher P. and Alan D. Miller. 2008. "A Measure of Bizarreness." *Quarterly Journal of Political Science* 5(1):27–44.

Chapman, Bruce. 1998. "More Easily Done Than Said: Rules, Reasons and Rational Social Choice." *Oxford Journal of Legal Studies* 18(2):293–329.

Chapman, Bruce. 2002. "Rational Aggregation." *Politics, Philosophy & Economics* 1(3):337–354.

Chemerinsky, Erwin. 1989. "Foreword: The Vanishing Constitution." *Harvard Law Review* 103(1):43–104.

Cohen, Joshua. 1997. Deliberation and Democratic Legitimacy. In *Deliberative Democracy: Essays on Reason and Politics*. Cambridge, MA: The MIT Press, pp. 67–92.

Cohen, Linda R. and Matthew L. Spitzer. 1994. "Solving the Chevron Puzzle." *Law & Contemporary Problems* 57:65.

Coleman, Jules and John Ferejohn. 1986. "Democracy and Social Choice." *Ethics* 97(1):6–25.

Cooter, Robert D. and Michael D. Gilbert. 2010. "A Theory of Direct Democracy and the Single Subject Rule." *Columbia Law Review* 110(3):687–730.

Cushman, Robert E. 1941. *The Independent Regulatory Commissions*. New York, NY: Oxford University Press.

Deephouse, David L. 1996. "Does Isomorphism Legitimate?" *Academy of Management Journal* 39(4):1024–1039.

Deephouse, David L. and Mark Suchman. 2008. "Legitimacy in Organizational Institutionalism." In *The Sage Handbook of Organizational Institutionalism*, Royston Greenwood, Christine Oliver, Roy Suddaby, and Kerstin Sahlin, eds. Los Angeles, CA: Sage Publications, pp. 49–77.

Dietrich, Franz and Christian List. 2007. "Arrow's Theorem in Judgment Aggregation." *Social Choice and Welfare* 29(1):19–33.

Dietrich, Franz and Christian List. 2008. "A Liberal Paradox for Judgment Aggregation." *Social Choice and Welfare* 31(1):59–78.

DiMaggio, Paul J. and Walter W. Powell. 1983. "The Iron Cage Revisited: Institutional Isomorphism and Collective Rationality in Organizational Fields." *American Sociological Review* 48(2):147–160.

Driesen, David M. 2002. "Loose Canons: Statutory Construction and the New Nondelegation Doctrine." *University of Pittsburgh Law Review* 64:1–74.

Dryzek, John S. and Christian List. 2003. "Social Choice Theory and Deliberative Democracy: A Reconciliation." *British Journal of Political Science* 33(1):1–28.

Dutta, Bhaskar. 1988. "Covering Sets and a New Condorcet Choice Correspondence." *Journal of Economic Theory* 44:63–80.

Dutta, Bhaskar and Jean-Francois Laslier. 1999. "Comparison Functions and Choice Correspondences." *Social Choice and Welfare* 16(4):513–532.

Dutta, Bhaskar, Matthew O. Jackson, and Michel Le Breton. 2004. "Equilibrium Agenda Formation." *Social Choice and Welfare* 23:21–57.

Easterbrook, Frank H. 1994. "Text, History, and Structure in Statutory Interpretation." *Harvard Journal of Law & Public Policy* 17:61–70.

Eliaz, Kfir. 2004. "Social Aggregators." *Social Choice and Welfare* 22(2):317–330.

Elsbach, K.D. and G. Elofson. 2000. "How the packaging of decision explanations affects perceptions of trustworthiness." *Academy of Management Journal* 43(1):80–89.

Elsbach, Kimberly D. 1994. "Managing Organizational Legitimacy in the California Cattle Industry: The Construction and Effectiveness of Verbal Accounts." *Administrative Science Quarterly* 39(1):57–88.

Epstein, David. 1997. "Uncovering Some Subtleties of the Uncovered Set: Social Choice Theory and Distributive Politics." *Social Choice and Welfare* 15(1):81–93.

Fallon, Jr., Richard H. 2006. "Strict Judicial Scrutiny." *UCLA Law Review* 54:1267.

Farber, Daniel A. and Philip P. Frickey. 1988. "Legislative Intent and Public Choice." *Virginia Law Review* 74(2):423–469.

Farrar, Cynthia, James S. Fishkin, Donald P. Green, Christian List, Robert C. Luskin, and Elizabeth Levy Paluck. 2010. "Disaggregating Deliberation's Effects: An Experiment within a Deliberative Poll." *British Journal of Political Science* 40(2):333–347.

Farrell, Robert C. 1992. "Legislative Purpose and Equal Protection's Rationality Review." *Villanova Law Review* 37:1–66.

Farrell, Robert C. 1998. "Successful Rational Basis Claims in the Supreme Court from the 1971 Term Through *Romer v. Evans.*" *Indiana Law Review* 32:357–420.

Fearon, James D. 1998. "Deliberation as Discussion." In *Deliberative Democracy*, Jon Elster, ed. New York, NY: Cambridge University Press, pp. 44–68.

Feld, Scott L. and Bernard Grofman. 1988. "Majority Rule Outcomes and the Structure of Debate in One-Issue-At-a-Time Decision-Making." *Public Choice* 59(3):239–252.

Feld, Scott L., Bernard Grofman, Richard Hartly, Marc Kilgour, and Nicholas Miller. 1987. "The Uncovered Set in Spatial Voting Games." *Theory and Decision* 23(2):129–155.

Fishburn, Peter. 1977. "Condorcet Social Choice Functions." *SIAM Journal on Applied Mathematics* 33:469–489.

Fletcher, Joseph F. 1966. *Situation Ethics: The New Morality*. London, UK: Westminster Press.

Freedman, J.O. 1978. *Crisis and Legitimacy: The Administrative Process and American Government*. New York, NY: Cambridge University Press.

Friedman, B. 1998. "The History of the Countermajoritarian Difficult, Part One: The Road to Judicial Supremacy." *New York University Law Review* 73:333–2064.

Frug, G.E. 1984. "The Ideology of Bureaucracy in American Law." *Harvard Law Review*, pp. 1276–1388.

Gailmard, Sean, John W. Patty, and Elizabeth Maggie Penn. 2008. "Arrow's Theorem on Single-Peaked Domains." In *The Political Economy of Democracy*, Enriquetta Aragones, Humberto Llavador, and Norman Schofield, eds. Barcelona: UAB.

Galaskiewicz, Joseph. 1985. "Interorganizational relations." *Annual Review of Sociology* 11:281–304.

Galloway, Russell W. 1988. "Means-End Scrutiny in American Constitutional Law." *Loyola of Los Angeles Law Review* 21:449–496.

Geanakoplos, John. 2005. "Three Brief Proofs of Arrow's Impossibility Theorem." *Economic Theory* 26(1):211–215.

Gibbard, Allan. 1973. "Manipulation of Voting Schemes: A General Result." *Econometrica* 41(4):587–601.

Gibbard, Allan. 1974. "A Pareto-Consistent Libertarian Claim." *Journal of Economic Theory* 7(4):388–410.

Gilbert, Michael D. 2006. "Single Subject Rules and the Legislative Process." *University of Pittsburgh Law Review* 67(4):803–870.

Goodin, Robert E. 1986. "Laundering Preferences." In *Foundations of Social Choice Theory*, Jon Elster and Aanund Hylland, eds. Cambridge, UK: Cambridge University Press, pp. 75–102.

Green, Donald P. and Ian Shapiro. 1994. *Pathologies of Rational Choice Theory*. New Haven, CT: Yale University Press.

Grofman, Bernard and Scott L. Feld. 1988. "Rousseau's General Will: A Condorcetian Perspective." *American Political Science Review* 82(2):567–576.

Gunther, Gerald. 1972. "Foreword: In Search of Evolving Doctrine on a Changing Court: A Model for a Newer Equal Protection." *Harvard Law Review* 86:1–48.

Habermas, Jurgen. 1987. *The Theory of Communicative Action*. Boston, MA: Beacon Press.

Hershkoff, Helen. 1999. "Positive Rights and State Constitutions: The Limits of Federal Rationality Review." *Harvard Law Review* 112(6):1131–1196.

Horwitz, Morton J. 1994. *The Transformation of American Law, 1870–1960: The Crisis of Legal Orthodoxy*. New York, NY: Oxford University Press.

Jeong, Gyung-Ho. 2008. "Testing the Predictions of the Multidimensional Spatial Voting Model with Roll Call Data." *Political Analysis* 16(2):179–196.

Johnson, Cathryn. 2004. *Legitimacy Processes in Organizations*. Amsterdam: Elsevier.

Johnson, R.H. 2000. *Manifest Rationality: A Pragmatic Theory of Argument*. Lawrence Erlbaum.

Kalai, Ehud and David Schmeidler. 1977. "Aggregation Procedure for Cardinal Preferences: A Formulation and Proof of Samuelson's Impossibility Conjecture." *Econometrica* 45(6):1431–1438.

Kastorf, Kurt G. 2005. "Logrolling Gets Logrolled: Same Sex Marriage, Direct Democracy, and the Single Subject Rule." *Emory Law Journal* 54:5–33.

Keller, Morton. 1990. *Regulating A New Economy: Public Policy and Economic Change in America, 1900–1933*. Cambridge MA: Harvard University Press.

Kennedy, Duncan. 1980. "Toward an Historical Understanding of Legal Consciousness: The Case of Classical Legal Thought in America, 1850–1940." *Research in Law and Sociology* 3(1):3–24.

Kernisky, D.A. 1997. "Proactive Crisis Management and Ethical Discourse: Dow Chemical's Issues Management Bulletins 1979–1990." *Journal of Business Ethics* 16(8):843–853.

King, David C. 1994. "The Nature of Congressional Committee Jurisdictions." *American Political Science Review* 88(1):48–62.

King, David C. 1997. *Turf Wars: How Congressional Committees Claim Jurisdiction*. Chicago: University of Chicago Press.

Kornhauser, Lewis A. 1992. "Modeling Collegial Courts. II. Legal Doctrine." *Journal of Law, Economics, and Organization* 8:441–470.

Kornhauser, Lewis A. and Lawrence G. Sager. 1986. "Unpacking the Court." *The Yale Law Journal* 96(1):82–117.

Kornhauser, Lewis A. and Lawrence G. Sager. 1993. "The One and the Many: Adjudication in Collegial Courts." *California Law Review* 81(1):1–59.

Kornhauser, Lewis A. and Lawrence G. Sager. 2004. "The Many as One: Integrity and Group Choice in Paradoxical Cases." *Philosophy & public affairs* 32(3):249–276.

Kovacic, William E. 1988. "Congress and the Federal Trade Commission." *Antitrust LJ* 57:869–906.

Laslier, Jean-Francois. 1997. *Tournament Solutions and Majority Voting*. New York, NY: Springer-Verlag.

Levitt, Justin. 2010. *A Citizen's Guide to Redistricting*. New York, NY: Brennan Center for Justice at New York University School of Law.

List, Christian. 2012. "The Theory of Judgment Aggregation: An Introductory Review." *Synthese* 187(1):1–29.

List, Christian and Philip Pettit. 2002. "Aggregating Sets of Judgments: An Impossibility Result." *Economics and Philosophy* 18:89–110.

List, Christian and Philip Pettit. 2005. "On the Many As One: A Reply to Kornhauser and Sager." *Philosophy & Public Affairs* 33(4):377–390.

Lowenstein, Daniel H. 1982. "California Initiatives and the Single-Subject Rule." *UCLA Law Review* 30:936–975.

Lowenstein, Daniel H. 2002. "Initiatives and the New Single Subject Rule." *Election Law Journal* 1(1):35–48.

Mackie, Gerry. 2003. *Democracy Defended*. New York, NY: Cambridge University Press.

Mackie, Gerry. 2006. "The Reception of Social Choice Theory by Democratic Theory." San Diego, CA: University of California at San Diego.

Magleby, D.B. 1994. "Let the Voters Decide-An Assessment of the Initiative and Referendum Process." *University of Colorado Law Review* 66:13–46.

Manning, John F. 2000. "The Nondelegation Doctrine as a Canon of Avoidance." *The Supreme Court Review* 223–277.

Mansbridge, Jane J. 1983. *Beyond Adversary Democracy*. Chicago: University of Chicago Press.

Mashaw, Jerry L. 2001. "Small Things Like Reasons Are Put in a Jar: Reason and Legitimacy in the Administrative State." *Fordham Law Review* 70:17.

Matsusaka, John G. and Richard L. Hasen. 2010. "Aggressive Enforcement of the Single Subject Rule." *Election Law Journal* 9(4):399–419.

McCubbins, Mathew, Roger Noll, and Barry Weingast. 1987. "Administrative Procedures as Instruments of Political Control." *Journal of Law, Economics, and Organization* 3(2):243–277.

McCubbins, Mathew, Roger Noll, and Barry Weingast. 1989. "Structure and Process, Politics and Policy: Administrative Arrangements and the Political Control of Agencies." *Virginia Law Review* 75(2):431–489.

McCubbins, Mathew, Roger Noll, and Barry Weingast. 1994. "Legislative Intent: The Use of Positive Political Theory in Statutory Interpretation." *Journal of Law and Contemporary Problems* 57(1):3–37.

McGann, Anthony J. 2006. *The Logic of Democracy: Reconciling Equality, Deliberation, and Minority Protection*. Ann Arbor, MI: University of Michigan Press.

McKelvey, Richard D. 1986. "Covering, Dominance, and Institution-Free Properties of Social Choice." *American Journal of Political Science* 30:283–314.

Merrill, T.W. 1992. "Judicial Deference to Executive Precedent." *Yale Law Journal* 101(5):969–1041.

Meyer, John W. and Brian Rowan. 1977. "Institutionalized Organizations: Formal Structure as Myth and Ceremony." *American Journal of Sociology* 83(2):340–363.

Meyer, J.W. and W.R. Scott. 1983. "Centralization and the Legitimacy Problems of Local Government." In *Organizational Environments: Ritual and Rationality*, J.W. Meyer and W.R. Scott, eds. Sage: Beverly Hills, CA: Sage, pp. 199–215.

Miller, David. 1992. "Deliberative Democracy and Social Choice." *Political Studies* 40(5):54–67.

Miller, Nicholas R. 1977. "Graph-Theoretical Approaches to the Theory of Voting." *American Journal of Political Science* 21(4):769–803.

Miller, Nicholas R. 1980. "A New Solution Set for Tournaments and Majority Voting: Further Graph-Theoretical Approaches to the Theory of Voting." *American Journal of Political Science* 24(1):68–96.

Miller, Nicholas R. 1983. "Pluralism and Social Choice." *American Political Science Review* 77(3):734–747.

Miller, Nicholas R. 2007. "In Search of the Uncovered Set." *Political Analysis* 15(1):21–45.

Miller, Nicholas R., Bernard Grofman, and Scott L. Feld. 1990. "Cycle Avoiding Trajectories, Strategic Agendas, and the Duality of Memory and Foresight: An Informal Exposition." *Public Choice* 64:265–277.

Moulin, Herve. 1986. "Choosing from a Tournament." *Social Choice and Welfare* 3:272–291.

Muller, Eitan and Mark A. Satterthwaite. 1977. "The Equivalence of Strong Positive Association and Strategy-Proofness." *Journal of Economic Theory* 14(2):412–418.

Murakami, Yasusuke. 1968. *Logic and Social Choice*. London: Routledge & Kegan Ltd.

Nash, Jr., John F. 1950. "Equilibrium Points in *n*-Person Games." *Proceedings of the National Academy of Sciences USA* 36:48–49.

Niemi, Richard G., Bernard Grofman, Carl Carlucci, and Thomas Hofeller. 1990. "Measuring Compactness and the Role of a Compactness Standard in a Test for Partisan and Racial Gerrymandering." *Journal of Politics* 52(4):1155–1181.

Nonet, Philippe. 1980. "The Legitimation of Purposive Decisions." *California Law Review* 68(2):263–300.

Parisi, Francesco. 1998. "The Market for Votes: Coasian Bargaining in an Arrovian Setting." *George Mason Law Review* 6:745–766.

Parsons, Talcott. 1960. *Structure and Process in Modern Societies.* New York, NY: Joh Wiley.

Parsons, Talcott. 1956. "Suggestions for a Sociological Approach to the Theory of Organizations – I." *Administrative Science Quarterly* 1(1):63–85.

Penn, Elizabeth M. 2006a. "Alternate Definitions of the Uncovered Set, and Their Implications." *Social Choice and Welfare* 27(1):83–87.

Penn, Elizabeth M. 2006b. "The Banks Set in Infinite Spaces." *Social Choice and Welfare* 27(3):531–543.

Penn, Elizabeth Maggie, John W. Patty, and Sean Gailmard. 2011. "Manipulation and Single-Peakedness: A General Result." *American Journal of Political Science* 55(2):436–449.

Peris, Josep E. and Begoña Subiza. 1999. "Condorcet Choice Correspondences for Weak Tournaments." *Social Choice and Welfare* 16(2):217–231.

Pettit, Philip. 2001. "Deliberative Democracy and the Discursive Dilemma." *Philosophical Issues* 11(1):268–299.

Pfeffer, J. and G.R. Salancik. 1978. *The Design and Management of Externally Controlled Organizations.* New York, NY: Harper & Row.

Pildes, Richard H. and Elizabeth S. Anderson. 1990. "Slinging Arrows at Democracy: Social Choice Theory, Value Pluralism, and Democratic Politics." *Columumbia Law Review* 90(8):2121–2214.

Powell, Walter W. and Paul J. DiMaggio. 1991. *The New Institutionalism in Organizational Analysis.* Chicago, IL: University of Chicago Press.

Radcliff, Benjamin. 1993. "The Structure of Voter Preferences." *The Journal of Politics* 55(3):714–719.

Reny, Philip J. 2001. "Arrow's Theorem and the Gibbard-Satterthwaite Theorem: A Unified Approach." *Economics Letters* 70(1):99–105.

Riker, William. 1980. "Implications from the Disequilibrium of Majority Rule for the Study of Institutions." *American Political Science Review* 74(2):432–46.

Riker, William H. 1982. *Liberalism Against Populism.* San Francisco, CA: W.H. Freeman & Company.

Riker, William H. and Barry R. Weingast. 1988. "Constitutional Regulation of Legislative Choice: The Political Consequences of Judicial Deference to Legislatures." *Virginia Law Review* 74(2):373–401.

Rohr, J.A. 1986. *To Run A Constitution. The Legitimacy of the Administrative State.* Lawrence, KS: University Press of Kansas.

Ruud, Millard H. 1957. "No Law Shall Embrace More Than One Subject." *Minnesota Law Review* 42:389–458.

Saari, Donald. 2001. *Decisions and Elections.* Cambridge, UK: Cambridge University Press.

Satterthwaite, Mark A. 1975. "Strategy-Proofness and Arrow's Conditions: Existence and Correspondence Theorems for Voting Procedures and Social Welfare Functions." *Journal of Economic Theory* 10(2):187–217.

Schofield, Norman. 1999. "The Heart and the Uncovered Set. In *Mathematical Utility Theory*," Gerhard Herden, Norbert Knoche, Christian Seidl, and Walter Trockel, eds.

Vol. 8 of *Journal of Economics Zeitschrift für Nationalökonomie Supplementum.* Vienna: Springer, pp. 79–113.

Schofield, Norman. 2006. *Architects of Political Change: Constitutional Quandaries and Social Choice Theory.* New York, NY: Cambridge University Press.

Schwartz, Bernard. 1991. *Administrative Law.* 3 ed. Boston, MA: Little, Brown & Co.

Schwartz, Thomas. 1986. *The Logic of Collective Choice.* New York, NY: Columbia University Press.

Schwartz, Thomas. 1990. "Cyclic Tournaments and Cooperative Majority Voting: A Solution." *Social Choice and Welfare* 7(1):19–29.

Scott, W. Richard. 1995. *Institutions and Organizations: Ideas and Interests.* Los Angeles, CA: Sage Publications.

Sen, Amartya. 1970a. *Collective Choice and Social Welfare.* San Francisco: Holden-Day.

Sen, Amartya. 1970b. "The Impossibility of a Paretian Liberal." *Journal of Political Economy* 78(1):152–157.

Sen, Amartya. 2012. "The Reach of Social Choice Theory." *Social Choice and Welfare* 39(2–3):259–272.

Shepherd, George B. 1996. "Fierce Compromise: The Administrative Procedure Act Emerges from New Deal Politics." *Northwestern University Law Review* 90(4):1557–1683.

Shepsle, Kenneth A. 1979. "Institutional Arrangements and Equilibrium in Multidimensional Voting Models." *American Journal of Political Science* 23(1):27–59.

Shepsle, Kenneth A. 1992. "Congress Is a "They," Not an "It": Legislative Intent as Oxymoron." *International Review of Law and Economics* 12(2):239–256.

Shepsle, Kenneth A. and Barry R. Weingast. 1984. "Uncovered Sets and Sophisticated Voting Outcomes with Implications for Agenda Institutions." *American Journal of Political Science* 28(1):49–74.

Shepsle, Kenneth A. and Mark S. Bonchek. 1997. *Analyzing Politics.* New York, NY: Norton.

Smith, Steven S. and Christopher J. Deering. 1990. *Committees in Congress.* 2nd ed. Washington, DC: CQ Press.

Stewart, Richard B. 1975. "The Reformation of American Administrative Law." *Harvard Law Review* 88(8):1667–1813.

Stratmann, Thomas. 1996. "Instability of Collective Decisions? Testing for Cyclical Majorities." *Public Choice* 88(1):15–28.

Stratmann, Thomas. 2003. "Logrolling." *The Encyclopedia of Public Choice*, New York, NY: Springer, pp. 696–699.

Suchman, Mark C. 1995. "Managing Legitimacy: Strategic and Institutional Approaches." *Academy of Management Review* 20(3):571–610.

Sunstein, Cass R. 2000. "Nondelegation Canons." *The University of Chicago Law Review* 67(2):315–343.

Sunstein, Cass R. 2001. *Designing Democracy: What Constitutions Do.* New York, NY: Oxford University Press.

Szabo, Nicholas. 2006. "Origins of the Non-Delegation Doctrine." Working paper. Available at http://ssrn.com/abstract=1156482.

Tiefer, Charles. 1989. *Congressional Practice and Procedure.* Westport, CT: Greenwood Press.

Tost, Leigh Plunkett. 2011. "An Integrative Model of Legitimacy Judgments." *Academy of Management Review* 36(4):686–710.

Tsebelis, George. 2002. *Veto Players: How Political Institutions Work.* Princeton, NJ: Princeton University Press.

Tullock, Gordon. 1981. "Why So Much Stability?" *Public Choice* 37(2):189–202.

Tversky, Amos. 1972. "Elimination by Aspects: A Theory of Choice." *Psychological Review* 79:281–299.

Ubeda, L. 2003. "Neutrality in Arrow and Other Impossibility Theorems." *Economic Theory* 23(1):195.

von Neumann, John and Oskar Morgenstern. 1947. *Theory of Games and Economic Behavior.* 2nd ed. Princeton, NJ: Princeton University Press.

Wadhwani, Neelum J. 2005. "Rational Reviews, Irrational Results." *Texas Law Review* 84:801.

Walton, D.N. 1990. "What Is Reasoning? What Is an Argument?" *The Journal of Philosophy* 87(8):399–419.

Weber, Max. 1968. *Economy and Society.* Berkeley, CA: University of California Press.

Wilson, Robert. 1972. "Social Choice Theory Without the Pareto Principle." *Journal of Economic Theory* 5(3):478–486.

Wittman, Donald A. 1989. "Why Democracies Produce Efficient Results." *Journal of Political Economy* 97:1395–1424.

Young, H. Peyton. 1988. "Measuring the Compactness of Legislative Districts." *Legislative Studies Quarterly* 13(1):105–115.

Index

Accountability, 139, 159–160, 196
Agenda-setting, 44, 93, 124–126, 152
Aggregation rules, 17, 189–190, 193–194
Arrow, Kenneth, 13–15
    Arrow's Theorem, 13–24, 26
    Rejectionist critiques of Arrow, 28–33
    Metatheorem concerning, 56–57
    See also Dictator, Independence of Irrelevant
        Alternatives, Transitivity, Unrestricted
        Domain, and Pareto Efficiency
Austin v. Michigan Chamber of Commerce,
    89–90

Banks Set, 111–112
Black, Duncan, 13, 45
Blau, 48–54
Borda count, 17–18, 22, 30–31, 48, 192
Buckley v. Valeo, 89, 122

Cardinal preferences, 49, 54, 58–65
Choice functions, 17–18
Citizens United v. Federal Election
    Commission, 89–90
Commensurability, 32, 118–119
Condorcet, 12
    cycle, paradox of voting, 13–14, 17
Countermajoritarian
    Difficulty, 135
    Interpretation of Social Choice Theory,
        26–28
Covering. *See* Uncovered Set

Davis v. Bandemer, 3–5

Decision Sequence
    Coherence, 91–93, 100–103
    Consistency. *See also* Legitimacy, As
        Consistency
    Consistency, Internal, 105–108
    Consistency, Strong, 115
    Stability. *See also* Legitimacy, And Stability
    Stability, 105–108
    Stability, Strong, 115
    Monotonicity, 101
    Connectedness, 101–102
    As a Rationale, 126–127
Delegation, 163–166, 169–170
    and Adjudicating Facts, 168–171
    and Providing Reasons, 170–171
    "Intelligible Principle", 171, 173, 180–181,
        183, 187–188
    and agency self-limitation, 180–184
    and statutory interpretation, 185–188
Dictator, 65–67
Due Process, 132–133, 164, 173, 181

Eliaz. *See* Social aggregators
Equal protection, 9, 132, 140, 164
Equal Protection. *See also* Due Process

Germaneness, 9
    Rule and tests for in US House of
        Representatives, 149–154
Gerrymandering. *See* redistricting
Gibbard-Satterthwaite Theorem, 15, 16,
    19
Government Interest, 137, 142

History, 93–95

Independence of Irrelevant Alternatives (IIA),
   21–24, 33, 48–56, 59–64
Impossibility theorems, 6, 13, 15, 24–35,
   43–48, 57, 65, 67, 123, 189–193
   See also Arrow's Theorem
   Gibbard-Satterthwaite
Incommensurability. *See* Commensurability
Index
   Things not contained in. *See* Russell's
     Paradox
Institutions
   Formal vs. Informal, 78
   Design of, 192–193
   Legitimating role of, 190–196
Isomorphism, 80

Judicial review, 9
   Rational Basis, 133–135, 137–140
   Strict Scrutiny, 9, 140–145
   Judicial deference, 184–188

Legislation. *See* Legislatures
Legislatures, 136–137
Legitimacy
   Justifications and, 6, 123–124
   As Consistency, 73–74, 91–93, 95–96,
     194–195
   Organizational, 75, 79
   Social, 75
   Institutional. *See* Legitimacy, Organizational
   vs. Authority, 75
   Measurement of, 75
   And Deference, 76, 78, 123–124
   vs. Fairness, 76
   of Processes, 76, 78
   of Actions, 76
   Legal Bases of, 80–81
   Social Bases of, 81–82
   Moral Bases of, 82
   Agnosticism about Base of, 82–83, 196
   And Stability, 96–97, 194–195, 98–100,
     103–108, 118–119, 124–126, 138–139,
     143, 194–195
   Formal Definition of, 105–108
   and Rational Basis Review, 138–140
Logrolling, 155–159

Mackie, 14–15, 28–34, 39, 42, 44, 46, 48, 52,
   55, 58–59, 65, 118, 124, 190, 193, 195

Nash equilibrium, 10, 121
No dictator. *See* Dictator
Nondelegation Doctrine, 167–168. *See also*
   Delegation
Notice and comment rulemaking, 9,
   125

Pareto efficiency, 20–24, 64–66, 195
Preference domain, 19–20
   See also unrestricted domain
   See also Single-peakedness
Preference Structuration, 43
Principles
   Competing, 84–86
   As Binary Relations, 86–87
   Origins of, 87
   Comparing, 87–88
   As Rationales. *See* Decision Sequence, As a
     Rationale

Rational Basis. *See* Judicial Review
Record-keeping, 78
Redistricting, 3–5, 38–41, 54, 58, 60, 63–66,
   122
Reny, Philip, 16, 55
Riker, 7–8, 14–15, 26–35, 47, 65, 68–69, 94,
   109, 119–120, 124
Russell's Paradox. *See* Index, Things not
   contained in

Sensibility, 91, 98–100
Single-peakedness, 44–46
Social Aggregators, 57–58
State Interest. *See* Government Interest
Strategy-proof, 24–25, 48, 57–58

Transitivity, 20–23, 30, 57, 66–68
Transparency, 159–160
Two-Step Principle, 111, 114

Uncovered Set, 99, 110–111
Unilateral flip independence, 52–53, 64
Unrestricted domain, 19–20

Vieth v. Jubelirer, 3–5

Other Books in the Series (continued from page iii)

Gary W. Cox, *The Efficient Secret: The Cabinet and the Development of Political Parties in Victorian England*

Gary W. Cox, *Making Votes Count: Strategic Coordination in the World's Electoral System*

Gary W. Cox and Jonathan N. Katz, *Elbridge Gerry's Salamander: The Electoral Consequences of the Reapportionment Revolution*

Raymond M. Duch and Randolph T. Stevenson, *The Economic Vote: How Political and Economic Institutions Condition Election Results*

Jean Ensminger, *Making a Market: The Institutional Transformation of an African Society*

David Epstein and Sharyn O'Halloran, *Delegating Powers: A Transaction Cost Politics Approach to Policy Making under Separate Powers*

Kathryn Firmin-Sellers, *The Transformation of Property Rights in the Gold Coast: An Empirical Study Applying Rational Choice Theory*

Clark C. Gibson, *Politicians and Poachers: The Political Economy of Wildlife Policy in Africa*

Daniel W. Gingerich, *Political Institutions and Party-Directed Corruption in South America: Stealing for the Team*

Avner Greif, *Institutions and the Path to the Modern Economy: Lessons from Medieval Trade*

Stephen Haber, Armando Razo, and Noel Maurer, *The Politics of Property Rights: Political Instability, Credible Commitments, and Economic Growth in Mexico, 1876–1929*

Ron Harris, *Industrializing English Law: Entrepreneurship and Business Organization, 1720–1844*

Anna L. Harvey, *Votes Without Leverage: Women in American Electoral Politics, 1920–1970*

Murray Horn, *The Political Economy of Public Administration: Institutional Choice in the Public Sector*

John D. Huber, *Rationalizing Parliament: Legislative Institutions and Party Politics in France*

John E. Jackson, Jacek Klich, and Krystyna Poznanska, *The Political Economy of Poland's Transition: New Firms and Reform Governments*

Jack Knight, *Institutions and Social Conflict*

Michael Laver and Kenneth Shepsle, eds., *Cabinet Ministers and Parliamentary Government*

Michael Laver and Kenneth Shepsle, eds., *Making and Breaking Governments: Cabinets and Legislatures in Parliamentary Democracies*

Margaret Levi, *Consent, Dissent, and Patriotism*

Brian Levy and Pablo T. Spiller, eds., *Regulations, Institutions, and Commitment: Comparative Studies of Telecommunications*

Leif Lewin, *Ideology and Strategy: A Century of Swedish Politics* (English Edition)

Gary Libecap, *Contracting for Property Rights*

John Londregan, *Legislative Institutions and Ideology in Chile*

Arthur Lupia and Mathew D. McCubbins, *The Democratic Dilemma: Can Citizens Learn What They Need to Know?*

C. Mantzavinos, *Individuals, Institutions, and Markets*

Mathew D. McCubbins and Terry Sullivan, eds., *Congress: Structure and Policy*

Gary J. Miller, *Managerial Dilemmas: The Political Economy of Hierarchy*

Ilia Murtazashvili, *The Political Economy of the American Frontier*

Douglass C. North, *Institutions, Institutional Change, and Economic Performance*

Elinor Ostrom, *Governing the Commons: The Evolution of Institutions for Collective Action*

Sonal S. Pandya, *Trading Spaces: Foreign Direct Investment Regulation, 1970–2000*

Daniel N. Posner, *Institutions and Ethnic Politics in Africa*

J. Mark Ramseyer, *Odd Markets in Japanese History: Law and Economic Growth*

J. Mark Ramseyer and Frances Rosenbluth, *The Politics of Oligarchy: Institutional Choice in Imperial Japan*

Jean-Laurent Rosenthal, *The Fruits of Revolution: Property Rights, Litigation, and French Agriculture, 1700–1860*

Michael L. Ross, *Timber Booms and Institutional Breakdown in Southeast Asia*

Shanker Satyanath, *Globalization, Politics, and Financial Turmoil: Asia's Banking Crisis*

Alberto Simpser, *Why Governments and Parties Manipulate Elections: Theory, Practice, and Implications*

Norman Schofield, *Architects of Political Change: Constitutional Quandaries and Social Choice Theory*

Norman Schofield and Itai Sened, *Multiparty Democracy: Elections and Legislative Politics*

Alberto Simpser, *Why Governments and Parties Manipulate Elections: Theory, Practice, and Implications*

Alastair Smith, *Election Timing*

Pablo T. Spiller and Mariano Tommasi, *The Instituional Foundations of Public Policy in Argentina: A Transactions Cost Approach*

David Stasavage, *Public Debt and the Birth of the Democratic State: France and Great Britain, 1688–1789*

Charles Stewart III, *Budget Reform Politics: The Design of the Appropriations Process in the House of Representatives, 1865–1921*

George Tsebelis and Jeannette Money, *Bicameralism*

Georg Vanberg, *The Politics of Constitutional Review in Germany*

Nicolas van de Walle, *African Economies and the Politics of Permanent Crisis, 1979–1999*

Stefanie Walter, *Financial Crises and the Politics of Macroeconomic Adjustments*

John Waterbury, *Exposed to Innumerable Delusions: Public Enterprise and State Power in Egypt, India, Mexico, and Turkey*

David L. Weimer, ed., *The Political Economy of Property Rights: Institutional Change and Credibility in the Reform of Centrally Planned Economies*